Hands-On Artificial Intelligence for Beginners

An introduction to AI concepts, algorithms, and their implementation

Patrick D. Smith

BIRMINGHAM - MUMBAI

Hands-On Artificial Intelligence for Beginners

Commissioning Editor: Veena Naik
Acquisition Editor: Namrata Patil
Content Development Editor: Snehal Kolte
Technical Editor: Chintan Thakkar, Dinesh Chaudhary
Copy Editor: Safis Editing
Project Coordinator: Manthan Patel
Proofreader: Safis Editing
Indexer: Priyanaka Dhadke
Graphics: Jisha Chirayil
Production Coordinator: Aparna Bhagat

First published: October 2018

Production reference: 1301018

Published by Packt Publishing Ltd.
Livery Place
35 Livery Street
Birmingham
B3 2PB, UK.

ISBN 978-1-78899-106-3

www.packtpub.com

`mapt.io`

Mapt is an online digital library that gives you full access to over 5,000 books and videos, as well as industry leading tools to help you plan your personal development and advance your career. For more information, please visit our website.

Why subscribe?

- Spend less time learning and more time coding with practical eBooks and Videos from over 4,000 industry professionals

- Improve your learning with Skill Plans built especially for you

- Get a free eBook or video every month

- Mapt is fully searchable

- Copy and paste, print, and bookmark content

Packt.com

Did you know that Packt offers eBook versions of every book published, with PDF and ePub files available? You can upgrade to the eBook version at `www.packt.com` and as a print book customer, you are entitled to a discount on the eBook copy. Get in touch with us at `customercare@packtpub.com` for more details.

At `www.packt.com`, you can also read a collection of free technical articles, sign up for a range of free newsletters, and receive exclusive discounts and offers on Packt books and eBooks.

Contributors

About the author

Patrick D. Smith is the Data Science Lead for Excella in Arlington, Virginia, where he founded the data science and machine learning team. Prior to Excella, Patrick was the lead instructor for the data science program at General Assembly in Washington, DC, as well as a data scientist with Booz Allen Hamilton's Strategic Innovations Group.

He holds a bachelor's degree from The George Washington University in International Economics, and is currently a part-time masters student in software engineering at Harvard University.

My journey into technology never would have been possible without my father, Curtis Griswold Smith, who was director of I.T. for one of the the world's first pioneering computer companies, Digital Equipment Corporation. It was he who introduced me to computing at three years old, and where my love of all technology stems from.

About the reviewer

David Dindi received a M.Sc. and a B.Sc. in chemical engineering with a focus on artificial intelligence from Stanford University. While at Stanford, David developed deep learning frameworks for predicting patient-specific adverse reactions to drugs at the Stanford Center for Biomedical Informatics. He currently advises a number of early stage start-ups in Silicon Valley and in New York.

Packt is searching for authors like you

If you're interested in becoming an author for Packt, please visit `authors.packtpub.com` and apply today. We have worked with thousands of developers and tech professionals, just like you, to help them share their insight with the global tech community. You can make a general application, apply for a specific hot topic that we are recruiting an author for, or submit your own idea.

Table of Contents

Preface

Virtual assistants such as Alexa and Siri process our requests, Google's cars have started to read addresses, and Amazon's prices and Netflix's recommended videos are decided by AI. AI is one of the most exciting technologies, and is becoming increasingly significant in the modern world.

Hands-On Artificial Intelligence for Beginners will teach you what AI is and how to design and build intelligent applications. This book will teach you to harness packages such as TensorFlow to create powerful AI systems. You will begin by reviewing the recent changes in AI and learning how **artificial neural networks** (**ANNs**) have enabled more intelligent AI. You'll explore feedforward, recurrent, convolutional, and generative neural networks (FFNNs, RNNs, CNNs, and GNNs), as well as reinforcement learning methods. In the concluding chapters, you'll learn how to implement these methods for a variety of tasks, such as generating text for chatbots, directing self-driving cars, and playing board and video games.

By the end of this book, you will be able to understand exactly what you need to consider when optimizing ANNs and how to deploy and maintain AI applications.

Who this book is for

This book is designed for beginners in AI, aspiring AI developers, and machine learning enthusiasts with an interest in leveraging various algorithms to build powerful AI applications.

What this book covers

Chapter 1, *The History of AI*, begins by discussing the mathematical basis of AI and how certain theorems evolved. Then, we'll look at the research done in the 1980s and 90s to improve ANNs, we'll look at the AI winter, and we'll finish off with how we arrived at where we are today.

Chapter 2, *Machine Learning Basics*, introduces the fundamentals of machine learning and AI. Here, we will cover essential probability theory, linear algebra, and other elements that will lay the groundwork for the future chapters.

Chapter 3, *Platforms and Other Essentials*, introduces the deep learning libraries of Keras and TensorFlow and moves onto an introduction of basic AWS terminology and concepts that are useful for deploying your networks in production. We'll also introduce CPUs and GPUs, as well as other forms of compute architecture that you should be familiar with when building deep learning solutions.

Chapter 4, *Your First Artificial Neural Networks*, explains how to build our first artificial neural network. Then, we will learn ability of the core elements of ANNs and construct a simple single layer network both in Keras and TensorFlow so that you understand how the two languages work. With this simple network, we will do a basic classification task, such as the MNIST OCR task.

Chapter 5, *Convolutional Neural Networks*, introduces the convolutional neural network and explains its inner workings. We'll touch upon the basic building blocks of convolutions, pooling layers, and other elements. Lastly, we'll construct a Convolutional Neural Network for image tagging.

Chapter 6, *Recurrent Neural Networks*, introduces one of the workhorses of deep learning and AI—the recurrent neural network. We'll first introduce the conceptual underpinnings of recurrent neural networks, with a specific focus on utilizing them for natural language processing tasks. We'll show how one can generate text utilizing you of these networks and see how they can be utilized for predictive financial models.

Chapter 7, *Generative Models*, covers generative models primarily through the lens of GANs, and we'll look at how we can accomplish each of the above tasks with GANs.

Chapter 8, *Reinforcement Learning*, introduces additional forms of neural networks. First, we'll take a look at autoencoders, which are unsupervised learning algorithms that help us recreate inputs when we don't have access to input data. Afterwards, we'll touch upon other forms of networks, such as the emerging geodesic neural networks.

Chapter 9, *Deep Learning for Intelligent Assistant*, focuses on utilizing our knowledge of various forms of neural networks from the previous section to make an intelligent assistant, along the lines of Amazon's Alexa or Apple's Siri. We'll learn about and utilize word embeddings, recurrent neural networks, and decoders.

Chapter 10, *Deep Learning for Game Playing*, explains how to construct game-playing algorithms with reinforcement learning. We'll look at several different forms of games, from simple Atari-style games to more advanced board games. We'll touch upon the methods that Google Brain utilized to build AlphaGo.

Chapter 11, *Deep Learning for Finance*, shows how to create an advanced market prediction system in TensorFlow utilizing RNNs.

Chapter 12, *Deep Learning for Robotics*, uses deep learning to teach a robot to move objects. We will first train the neural network in simulated environments and then move on to real mechanical parts with images acquired from a camera.

Chapter 13, *Scale, Deploy and Maintain AI Application*, introduces methods for creating and scaling training pipelines and deployment architectures for AI systems.

To get the most out of this book

The codes in the chapter can be directly executed using Jupyter and Python. The code files for the book are present in the GitHub link provided in the following sections.

Download the example code files

You can download the example code files for this book from your account at www.packt.com. If you purchased this book elsewhere, you can visit www.packt.com/support and register to have the files emailed directly to you.

You can download the code files by following these steps:

1. Log in or register at www.packt.com.
2. Select the **SUPPORT** tab.
3. Click on **Code Downloads & Errata**.
4. Enter the name of the book in the **Search** box and follow the onscreen instructions.

Once the file is downloaded, please make sure that you unzip or extract the folder using the latest version of:

- WinRAR/7-Zip for Windows
- Zipeg/iZip/UnRarX for Mac
- 7-Zip/PeaZip for Linux

The code bundle for the book is also hosted on GitHub at https://github.com/PacktPublishing/Hands-On-Artificial-Intelligence-for-Beginners. In case there's an update to the code, it will be updated on the existing GitHub repository.

We also have other code bundles from our rich catalog of books and videos available at https://github.com/PacktPublishing/. Check them out!

Conventions used

There are a number of text conventions used throughout this book.

CodeInText: Indicates code words in text, database table names, folder names, filenames, file extensions, pathnames, dummy URLs, user input, and Twitter handles. Here is an example: "The tf.add function adds a layer to our network."

A block of code is set as follows:

```
import tensorflow as tf
from tensorflow.examples.tutorials.mnist import input_data
mnist = input_data.read_data_sets("/tmp/data/", one_hot=True)
```

Any command-line input or output is written as follows:

```
tf.train.AdamOptimizer(learning_rate=learning_rate).minimize(loss_func)
```

Bold: Indicates a new term, an important word, or words that you see onscreen. For example, words in menus or dialog boxes appear in the text like this. Here is an example: "Select **System info** from the **Administration** panel."

 Warnings or important notes appear like this.

 Tips and tricks appear like this.

Get in touch

Feedback from our readers is always welcome.

General feedback: If you have questions about any aspect of this book, mention the book title in the subject of your message and email us at customercare@packtpub.com.

Errata: Although we have taken every care to ensure the accuracy of our content, mistakes do happen. If you have found a mistake in this book, we would be grateful if you would report this to us. Please visit www.packt.com/submit-errata, selecting your book, clicking on the Errata Submission Form link, and entering the details.

Piracy: If you come across any illegal copies of our works in any form on the Internet, we would be grateful if you would provide us with the location address or website name. Please contact us at copyright@packt.com with a link to the material.

If you are interested in becoming an author: If there is a topic that you have expertise in and you are interested in either writing or contributing to a book, please visit authors.packtpub.com.

Reviews

Please leave a review. Once you have read and used this book, why not leave a review on the site that you purchased it from? Potential readers can then see and use your unbiased opinion to make purchase decisions, we at Packt can understand what you think about our products, and our authors can see your feedback on their book. Thank you!

For more information about Packt, please visit packt.com.

The History of AI 1

The term **Artificial Intelligence** (**AI**) carries a great deal of weight. AI has benefited from over 70 years of research and development. The history of AI is varied and winding, but one ground truth remains – tireless researchers have worked through funding growths and lapses, promise and doubt, to push us toward achieving ever more realistic AI.

Before we begin, let's weed through the buzzwords and marketing and establish what AI really is. For the purposes of this book, we will rely on this definition:

AI is a system or algorithm that allows computers to perform tasks without explicitly being programmed to do so.

AI is an interdisciplinary field. While we'll focus largely on utilizing deep learning in this book, the field also encompasses elements of robotics and IoT, and has a strong overlap (if it hasn't consumed it yet) with generalized natural language processing research. It's also intrinsically linked with fields such as **Human-Computer Interaction** (**HCI**) as it becomes increasingly important to integrate AI with our lives and the modern world around us.

AI goes through waves, and is bound to go through another (perhaps smaller) wave in the future. Each time, we push the limits of AI with the computational power that is available to us, and research and development stops. This day and age may be different, as we benefit from the confluence of increasingly large and efficient data stores, rapid fast and cheap computing power, and the funding of some of the most profitable companies in the world. To understand how we ended up here, let's start at the beginning.

In this chapter, we will cover the following topics:

- The beginnings of AI – 1950–1974
- Rebirth – 1980–1987
- The modern era takes hold – 1997–2005
- Deep learning and the future – 2012–Present

The beginnings of AI –1950–1974

Since some of the earliest mathematicians and thinkers, AI has been a long sought after concept. The ancient Greeks developed myths of the *automata,* a form of robot that would complete tasks for the Gods that they considered menial, and throughout early history thinkers pondered what it meant to human, and if the notion of human intelligence could be replicated. While it's impossible to pinpoint an exact beginning for AI as a field of research, its development parallels the early advances of computer science. One could argue that computer science as a field developed out of this early desire to create self-thinking machines.

During the second world war, British mathematician and code breaker Alan Turing developed some of the first computers, conceived with the vision of AI in mind. Turing wanted to create a machine that would mimic human comprehension, utilizing all available information to reason and make decisions. In 1950, he published *Computing Machinery and Intelligence,* which introduced what we now call the **Turing test of AI**. The Turing test, which is a benchmark by which to measure the aptitude of a machine to mimic human interaction, states that to pass the test, the machine must be able to sufficiently fool a discerning judge as to if it is a human or not. This might sound simple, but think about how many complex items would have to be conquered to reach this point. The machine would be able to comprehend, store information on, and respond to natural language, all the while remembering knowledge and responding to situations with what we deem common sense.

Turing could not move far beyond his initial developments; in his day, utilizing a computer for research cost almost $200,000 per month and computers could not store commands. His research and devotion to the field, however, has earned him accolades. Today, he is widely considered the father of AI and the academic study of computer science.

It was in the summer of 1956, however, that the field was truly born. Just a few months before, researchers at the RAND Corporation developed the Logic Theorist – considered the world's first AI program – which proved 38 theorems of the *Principia Mathematica*. Spurred on by this development and others, John McCarthy, Marvin Minsky, Nathaniel Rochester, and Claude Shannon hosted the now famous *Dartmouth Summer Research Project* on AI, coining the term *Artificial Intelligence* itself and providing the groundwork for the field. With funding from the Rockefeller Foundation, these four friends brought together some of the most preeminent researchers in AI over the course of the summer to brainstorm and effectively attempt to provide a roadmap for the field. They came from the institutions and companies that were on the leading edge of the computing revolution at the time; Harvard, Dartmouth, MIT, IBM, Bell Labs, and the RAND Corporation. Their topics of discussion were fairly forward-thinking for the time – they could have easily been those of an AI conference today—**Artificial Neural Networks (ANN)**, **natural language processing (NLP)**, theories of computation, and general computing frameworks. The Summer Research Project was seminal in creating the field of AI as we know it today, and many of its discussion topics spurred the growth of AI research and development through the 1950s and 1960s.

After 1956, innovation kept up a rapid pace. Years later, in 1958, a researcher at the Cornell Aeronautical Laboratory named Frank Rosenblatt invented one of the founding algorithms of AI, the **Perceptron**. The following diagram shows the Perceptron algorithm:

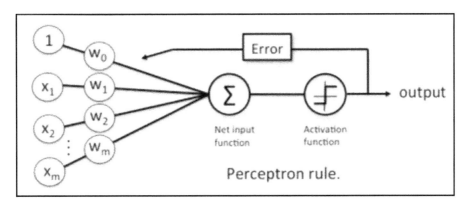

The Perceptron algorithm

Perceptrons are simple, single-layer networks that work as linear classifiers. They consist of four main architectural aspects which are mentioned as follows:

- **The input layer**: The initial layer for reading in data
- **Weight and biases vectors**: Weights help learn appropriate values during training for the connections between neurons, while biases help shift the activation function to fit the desired output
- **A summation function**: A simple summation of the input
- **An activation function**: A simple mapping of the summed weighted input to the output

As you can see, these networks use basic mathematics to perform basic mathematical operations. They failed to live up to the hype, however, and significantly contributed to the first AI winter because of the vast disappointment they created.

Another important development of this early era of research was adaline. As you can see, adaline attempted to improve upon the perceptron by utilizing continuous predicted values to learn the coefficients, unlike the perceptron, which utilizes class labels. The following diagram shows the adaline algorithm:

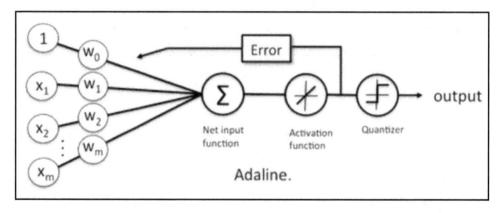

Adaline.

These golden years also brought us early advances such as the student program that solved high school algebra programs and the ELIZA Chatbot. By 1963, the advances in the field convinced the newly formed **Advanced Research Projects Agency (DARPA)** to begin funding AI research at MIT.

By the late 1960s, funding in the US and the UK began to dry up. In 1969, a book named *Perceptrons* by MIT's Marvin Minsky and Seymour Papert (`https://archive.org/details/Perceptrons`) proved that these networks could only mathematically compute extremely basic functions. In fact, they went so far as to suggest that Rosenblatt had greatly exaggerated his findings and the importance of the perceptron. Perceptrons were of limited functionality to the field, effectively halting research in network structures.

With both governments releasing reports that significantly criticized the usefulness of AI, the field was shuttled into what has become known as the AI winter. AI research continued throughout the late 1960s and 1970s, mostly under different terminology. The terms **machine learning**, **knowledge-based system**, and **pattern recognition** all come from this period, when researchers had to think up creative names for their work in order to receive funding. Around this time, however, a student at the University of Cambridge named Geoffrey Hinton began exploring ANNs and how we could utilize them to mimic the brain's memory functions. We'll talk a lot more about Hinton in the following sections and throughout this book, as he has become one of the most important figures in AI today.

Rebirth –1980–1987

The 1980s saw the birth of deep learning, the brain of AI that has become the focus of most modern AI research. With the revival of neural network research by John Hopfield and David Rumelhart, and several funding initiatives in Japan, the United States, and the United Kingdom, AI research was back on track.

In the early 1980s, while the United States was still toiling from the effects of the AI Winter, Japan was funding the fifth generation computer system project to advance AI research. In the US, DARPA once again ramped up funding for AI research, with business regaining interest in AI applications. IBM's T.J. Watson Research Center published a statistical approach to language translation (`https://aclanthology.info/pdf/J/J90/J90-2002.pdf`), which replaced traditional rule-based NLP models with probabilistic models, the shepherding in the modern era of NLP.

Hinton, the student from the University of Cambridge who persisted in his research, would make a name for himself by coining the term **deep learning**. He joined forces with Rumelhart to become one of the first researchers to introduce the backpropagation algorithm for training ANNs, which is the backbone of all of modern deep learning. Hinton, like many others before him, was limited by computational power, and it would take another 26 years before the weight of his discovery was really felt.

By the late 1980s, the personal computing revolution and missed expectations threatened the field. Commercial development all but came to a halt, as mainframe computer manufacturers stopped producing hardware that could handle AI-oriented languages, and AI-oriented mainframe manufacturers went bankrupt. It had seemed as if all had come to a standstill.

The modern era takes hold – 1997-2005

AI further entered the public discourse in 1997 when IBM's Deep Blue system beat world champion chess grandmaster Garry Kasparov. Within a year, a former student of Geoffrey Hinton's, Yann LeCun, developed the Convolutional Neural Network at Bell Labs, which was enabled by the backpropagation algorithm and years of research into computer vision tasks. Hochreiter and Schmidhuber invented the first memory unit, the **long short-term memory unit** (**LSTM**), which is still used today for sequence modeling.

ANNs still had a way to go. Computing and storage limitations prevented these networks from scaling, and other methods such as **support vector machines** (**SVMs**) were developed as alternatives.

Deep learning and the future – 2012-Present

AI has made further strides in the past several years than in the 60-odd years since its birth. Its popularity has further been fueled by the increasingly public nature of its benefits – self-driving cars, personal assistants, and its ever-ubiquitous use in social media and advertising. For most of its history, AI was a field with little interaction with the average populace, but now it's come to the forefront of international discourse.

Today's age of AI has been the result of three trends:

- The increasing amount of data and computing power available to AI researchers and practitioners
- Ongoing research by Geoffrey Hinton and his lab at the University of Toronto into deep neural networks
- Increasingly public applications of AI that have driven adoption and further acceptance into mainstream technology culture

Today, companies, governments, and other organizations have benefited from the big data revolution of the mid 2000s, which has brought us a plethora of data stores. At last, AI applications have the requisite data to train. Computational power is cheap and only getting cheaper.

On the research front, in 2012, Hinton and two of his students were finally able to show that deep neural networks were able to outperform all other methods in image recognition in the large-scale visual recognition challenge. The modern era of AI was born.

Interestingly enough, Hinton's team's work on computer vision also introduced the idea of utilizing **Graphics Processing Units** (**GPUs**) to train deep networks. It also introduced dropout and ReLu, which have become cornerstones of deep learning. We'll discuss these in the coming chapters. Today, Hinton is the most cited AI researcher on the planet. He is a lead data scientist at Google Brain and has been tied to many major developments in AI in the modern era.

AI was further thrown into the public sphere when, in 2011, IBM Watson defeated the world Jeopardy champions, and in 2016 Google's AlphaGo defeated the world grand champion at one of the most challenging games known to man: Go.

Today, we are closer than ever to having machines that can pass the Turing test. Networks are able to generate ever more realistic sounding imitations of speeches, images, and writing. Reinforcement learning methods and Ian Goodfellow's GANs have made incredible strides. Recently, there has been emerging research that is working to demystify the inner workings of deep neural networks. As the field progresses, however, we should all be mindful of overpromising. For most of its history, companies have often overpromised regarding what AI can do, and in turn, we've seen a consistent disappointment in its abilities. Focusing the abilities of AI on only certain applications, and continuing to view research in the field from a biological perspective, will only hurt its advancement going forward. In this book, however, we'll see that today's practical applications are directed and realistic, and that the field is making more strides toward true AI than ever before.

Summary

Since its beginnings in the 1940s and 1950s, AI has made great bounds. Many of the technologies and ideas that we are utilizing today are directly based on these early discoveries. Over the course of the latter half of the 20th century, pioneers such as Geoffrey Hinton have pushed AI forward through peaks and busts. Today, we are on track to achieve sustained AI development for the foreseeable future.

The development of AI technology has been closely aligned with the development of new hardware and increasingly large data sources. As we'll see throughout this book, great AI applications are built with data constraints and hardware optimization in mind. The next chapter will introduce you to the fundamentals of machine learning and AI. We will also cover probability theory, linear algebra, and other elements that will lay the groundwork for the future chapters.

2
Machine Learning Basics

Artificial Intelligence (**AI**) is rooted in mathematics and statistics. When creating an **Artificial Neural Network** (**ANN**), we're conducting mathematical operations on data represented in linear space; it is, by nature, applied mathematics and statistics. Machine learning algorithms are nothing but function approximations; they try and find a mapping between an input and a correct corresponding output. We use algebraic methods to create algorithms that learn these mappings.

Almost all machine learning can be expressed in a fairly straight-forward formula; bringing together a dataset and model, along with a loss function and optimization technique that are applicable to the dataset and model. This section is intended as a review of the basic mathematical tools and techniques that are essential to understanding *what's under the hood* in AI.

In this chapter, we'll review linear algebra and probability, and then move on to the construction of basic and fundamental machine learning algorithms and systems, before touching upon optimization techniques that can be used for all of your methods going forward. While we will utilize mathematical notation and expressions in this chapter and the following chapters, we will focus on translating each of these concepts into Python code. In general, Python is easier to read and comprehend than mathematical expressions, and allows readers to get off the ground quicker.

We will be covering the following topics in this chapter:

- Applied math basics
- Probability theory
- Constructing basic machine learning algorithms

Technical requirements

In this chapter, we will be working in Python 3 with the scikit-learn scientific computing package. You can install the package, you can run `pip install sklearn` in your terminal or command line.

Applied math basics

When we talk about mathematics as related to deep learning and AI, we're often talking about linear algebra. Linear algebra is a branch of continuous mathematics that involves the study of vector space and operations performed in vector space. If you remember back to grade-school algebra, algebra in general deals with unknown variables. With linear algebra, we're extending this study into linear systems that have an arbitrary number of dimensions, which is what makes this a form of continuous mathematics.

AI relies on the basic building block of the tensor. Within AI, these mathematical objects store information throughout ANNs that allow them to operate; they are data structures that are utilized throughout AI. As we will see, a tensor has a **rank**, which essentially tells us about the **indices** of the data (how many rows and columns the data has).

While many problems in deep learning are not formally linear problems, the basic building blocks of matrices and tensors are the primary data structures for solving, optimizing, and approximating within an ANN.

Want to see how linear algebra can help us from a programmatic standpoint? Take a look at the following code block:

```
import numpy as np
## Element-wise multiplication without utilizing linear algebra techniques

x = [1,2,3]
y = [4,5,6]

product = []
for i in range(len(x)):
    product.append(x[i]*y[i])

## Element-wise multiplication utilizing linear algebra techniques

x = np.array([1,2,3])
y = np.array([4,5,6])
x * y
```

We can eliminate strenuous loops by simply utilizing NumPy's built-in linear algebra functions. When you think of AI, and the thousands upon thousands of operations that have to be computed at the runtime of an application, the building blocks of linear algebra can also help us out programmatically. In the following sections, we'll be reviewing these fundamental concepts in both mathematical notation and Python.

 Each of the following examples will use the Python package NumPy; `import numpy as np`

The building blocks – scalars, vectors, matrices, and tensors

In the following section, we'll introduce the fundamental types of linear algebra objects that are used throughout AI applications; **scalars**, **vectors**, **matrices**, and **tensors**.

Scalars

Scalars are nothing but singular, **real numbers** that can take the form of an integer or floating point. In Python, we create a scalar by simply assigning it:

```
my_scalar = 5
my_scalar = 5.098
```

Vectors

Vectors are one-dimensional arrays of integers. Geometrically, they store the direction and magnitude of change from a point. We'll see how this works in machine learning algorithms when we discuss **principal component analysis** (**PCA**) in the next few pages. Vectors in Python are created as `numpy array` objects:

```
my_vector = np.array([5,6])
```

Vectors can be written in several ways:

$$v = \begin{bmatrix} 5 \\ 6 \end{bmatrix} = \begin{pmatrix} 5 \\ 6 \end{pmatrix} = [5, 6]$$

Matrices

Matrices are two-dimensional lists of numbers that contain rows and columns. Typically, rows in a matrix are denoted by *i*, while columns are denoted by *j*.

Matrices are represented as:

$$m = \begin{bmatrix} 5 & 6 \\ 6 & 9 \end{bmatrix} = \begin{pmatrix} 5 & 8 \\ 6 & 9 \end{pmatrix}$$

We can easily create matrices in Python as NumPy arrays, much like we can with vectors:

```
matrix = np.array([[5,6], [6,9]])
```

The only different is that we are adding an additional vector to the array to create the matrix.

Tensors

While you may have heard of vectors and matrices before, the name **tensor** may be new. A tensor is a generalized matrix, and they have different sizes, or ranks, which measure their dimensions.

Tensors are three (or more)-dimensional lists; you can think of them as a sort of multi-dimensional object of numbers, such as a cube. Tensors have a unique transitive property and form; if a tensor transforms another entity, it too must transform. Any rank 2 tensor can be represented as a matrix, but not all matrices are automatically rank 2 tensors. A tensor must have this transitive property. As we'll see, this will come into play with neural networks in the next chapter. We can create tensors in Python such as the following:

```
tensor = [[[1,2,3,4]],[[2,5,6,3]],[[7,6,3,4]]]
```

Within the context of AI, tensors can represent things such as word embeddings or weights in a neural network. We'll talk about these more as we encounter at them in upcoming chapters.

Matrix math

The basic operations of an ANN are based on matrix math. In this section, we'll be reviewing the basic operations that you need to know to understand the mechanics of ANNs.

Scalar operations

Scalar operations involve a vector (or matrix) and a scalar. To perform an operation with a scalar on a matrix, simply apply to the scalar to every item in the matrix:

$$\begin{bmatrix} 1 & 2 \\ 1 & 2 \end{bmatrix} + 2 = \begin{bmatrix} 3 & 4 \\ 3 & 4 \end{bmatrix}$$

In Python, we would simply do the following:

```
vector = np.array([[1,2], [1,2]])
new_vector = vector + 2
```

Element–wise operations

In element-wise operations, position matters. Values that correspond positionally are combined to create a new value.

To add to and/or subtract matrices or vectors:

$$\begin{bmatrix} a & b \\ c & d \end{bmatrix} + \begin{bmatrix} e & f \\ g & h \end{bmatrix} = \begin{bmatrix} ae & bf \\ cg & dh \end{bmatrix}$$

$$\begin{bmatrix} a & b \\ c & d \end{bmatrix} - \begin{bmatrix} e & f \\ g & h \end{bmatrix} = \begin{bmatrix} a-e & b-f \\ c-g & d-h \end{bmatrix}$$

And in Python:

```
vector_one = np.array([[1,2],[3,4]])
vector_two = np.array([[5,6],[7,8]])
    a + b
    ## You should see:
        array([[ 6,  8],[10,  12]])
        array([[ 6,  8],[10,  12]])
    a - b
    ## You should see:
        array([[-4, -4], [-4, -4]])
```

There are two forms of multiplication that we may perform with vectors: the **Dot product**, and the **Hadamard product**.

The dot product is a special case of multiplication, and is rooted in larger theories of geometry that are used across the physical and computational sciences. It is a special case of a more general mathematical principle known as an **inner product**. When utilizing the dot product of two vectors, the output is a scalar:

$$\begin{bmatrix} a \\ b \end{bmatrix} \cdot \begin{bmatrix} c \\ d \end{bmatrix} = ac + bd$$

Dot products are a workhorse in machine learning. Think about a basic operation: let's say we're doing a simple classification problem where we want to know if an image contains a cat or a dog. If we did this with a neural network, it would look as follows:

$$y = f(w \cdot x + b)$$

Here, y is our classification cat or dog. We determine y by utilizing a network represented by f, where the input is x, while w and b represent a weight and bias factor (don't worry, we'll explain this in more detail in the coming chapter!). Our x and w are both matrices, and we need to output a scalar y, which represents either cat or dog. We can only do this by taking the dot product of w and x.

Relating back to our example, if this function were presented with an unknown image, taking the dot product will tell us how similar in direction the new vector is to the cat vector (a) or dog vector (b) by the measure of the angle (θ) between them:

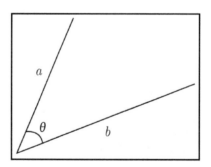

If the vector is closer to the direction of the cat vector (a), we'll classify the image as containing a cat. If it's closer to the dog vector (b), we'll classify it as containing a dog. In deep learning, a more complex version of this scenario is performed over and over; it's the core of how ANNs work.

In Python, we can take the dot product of two vectors by using a built-in function from numpy, np.dot():

```
## Dot Product
vector_one = np.array([1,2,3])
vector_two = np.array([2,3,4])
np.dot(vector_one,vector_two) ## This should give us 20
```

The Hadamard product, on the other hand, outputs a vector:

$$\begin{bmatrix} a \\ b \end{bmatrix} \circ \begin{bmatrix} c \\ d \end{bmatrix} = \begin{bmatrix} a \cdot c \\ b \cdot d \end{bmatrix}$$

The Hadamard product is element-wise, meaning that the individual numbers in the new matrix are the scalar multiples of the numbers from the previous matrices. Looking back to Python, we can easily perform this operation in Python with a simple * operator:

```
vector_one = np.array([1,2,3])
vector_two = np.array([2,3,4])
vector_one * vector_two
## You should see:
array([ 2,  6, 12])
```

Now that we've scratched the surface of basic matrix operations, let's take a look at how probability theory can aid us in the artificial intelligence field.

Basic statistics and probability theory

Probability, the mathematical method for modeling uncertain scenarios, underpins the algorithms that make AI intelligent, helping to tell us how our systems should reason. So, what is probability? We'll define it as follows:

> *Probability is a frequency expressed as a fraction of the sample size, n [1].*

Simply said, probability is the mathematical study of uncertainty. In this section, we'll cover the basics of probability space and probability distributions, as well as helpful tools for solving simple problems.

The probability space and general theory

When probability is discussed, it's often referred to in terms of the probability of a certain **event** happening. Is it going to rain? Will the price of apples go up or down? In the context of machine learning, probabilities tell us the likelihood of events such as a comment being classified as positive vs. negative, or whether a fraudulent transaction will happen on a credit card. We measure probability by defining what we refer to as the **probability space**. A probability space is a measure of *how* and *why* of the probabilities of certain events. Probability spaces are defined by three characteristics:

1. The sample space, which tells us the possible outcomes or a situation
2. A defined set of events; such as two fraudulent credit card transactions
3. The measure of probability of each of these events

While probability spaces are a subject worthy of studying in their own right, for our own understanding, we'll stick to this basic definition.

In probability theory, the idea of **independence** is essential. Independence is a state where a random variable does not change based on the value of another random variable. This is an important assumption in deep learning, as non–independent features can often intertwine and affect the predictive power of our models.

In statistical terms, a collection of data about an event is a **sample,** which is drawn from a theoretical superset of data called a **population** that represents everything that is known about a grouping or event. For instance, if we were poll people on the street about whether they believe in Political View A or Political View B, we would be generating a **random sample** from the population, which would be entire population of the city, state, or country where we are polling.

Now let's say we wanted to use this sample to predict the likelihood of a person having one of the two political views, but we mostly polled people who were at an event supporting Political View A. In this case, we may have a **biased sample**. When sampling, it is important to take a random sample to decrease bias, otherwise any statistical analysis or modeling that we do with sample will be biased as well.

Probability distributions

You've probably seen a chart such as the following one; it's showing us the values that appear in a dataset, and how many times those values appear. This is called a **distribution** of a variable. In this particular case, we're displaying the distribution with the help of a **histogram**, which shows the **frequency** of the variables:

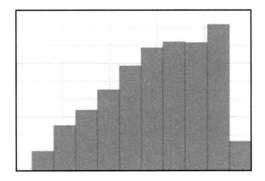

In this section, we're interested in a particular type of distribution, called a **probability distribution**. When we talk about probability distributions, we're talking about the likelihood of a random variable taking on a certain value, and we create one by dividing the frequencies in the preceding histogram by the total number of samples in the distribution, in a process called **normalization**. There are two primary forms of probability distributions: **probability mass functions** for discrete variables, and **probability density functions** for continuous variables, as well as; **cumulative distribution functions**, which apply to any random variables, also exist.

Probability mass functions

Probability mass functions (**PMFs**) are discrete distributions. The random variables of the distribution can take on a finite number of values:

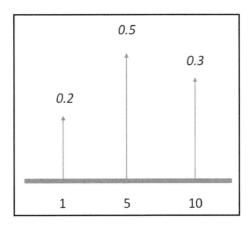

PMFs look a bit different from our typical view of a distribution, and that is because of their finite nature.

Probability density functions

Probability density functions (**PDFs**) are continuous distributions; values from the distribution can take on infinitely many values. For example, take the image as follows:

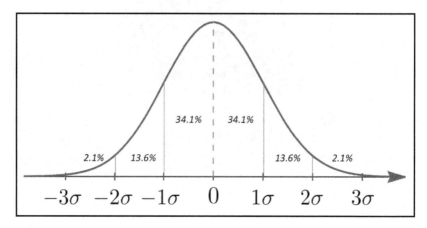

You've probably seen something like this before; it's a probability density function of a **standard normal**, or **Gaussian distribution**.

Conditional and joint probability

Conditional probability is the probability that *x* happens, given that *y* happens. It's one of the key tools for reasoning about uncertainty in probability theory. Let's say we are talking about your winning the lottery, given that it's a sunny day. Maybe you're feeling lucky! How would we write that in a probability statement? It would be the probability of your lottery win, *A*, given the probability of it being sunny, *B*, so *P(A|B)*.

Joint probability is the probability of two things happening simultaneously: what is the probability of you winning the lottery *and* it being a sunny day?

Chain rule for joint probability

Joint probability is important in the AI space; it's what underlies the mechanics of **generative models**, which are able to replicate voice, pictures, and other unstructured information. These models learn the joint probability distribution of a phenomenon. They generate all possible values for a given object or event. A chain rule is a technique by which to evaluate the join probability of two variables. Formally, it is written as follows:

$$Pr(A, B, C) = (A|B, C)Pr(B|C)Pr(C).$$

Bayes' rule for conditional probability

Bayes' rule is another essential tenet of probability theory in the machine learning sphere. It allows us to calculate the conditional probability of an event happening by inverting the conditions of the events. Bayes' rule is formally written as:

$$P(A \mid B) = \frac{P(B \mid A)P(A)}{P(B)}$$

Let's use Bayes' rule to look at a simple conditional probability problem. In the following table, we see the likelihood of a patient contacting a disease:

	Disease (1%)	No Disease (99%)
Test Positive	80%	9.6%
Test Negative	20%	90.4%

How do we interpret this table? The x axis tells us the percentage of the population who have the disease; if you have it, you are firmly in the Disease column. Based on that condition, the y axis is the likelihood of you testing positive or negative, based on whether you actually have the disease or not.

Now, let's say that we have a positive test result; what is the chance that we actually have the disease? We can use Bayes' formula to figure solve:

$$P(Disease|PosTest) = \frac{P(PosTest|Disease)P(Disease)}{P(FalsePositive)}$$

Our answer comes out to 7.8%, the actual probability of having the disease given a positive test:

In the following code, we can see how Bayes' formula can model these conditional events based on likelihood. In machine learning and AI in general, this comes in handy when modeling situations or perhaps classifying objects. Conditional probability problems also play into discriminative models, which we will discuss in our section on **Generative adversarial networks**.

```
.p_diseasePos = 0.8 ## Chance of having the disease given a positive result
p_diseaseNeg = 0.2 ## Chance of having the disease given a negative result
p_noPos = 0.096
p_noNeg = 0.904
p_FalsePos = (.80 * .01) + (.096 * .99)
p_disease_given_pos = (.80 * .01) / p_FalsePos
print(p_disease_given_pos)
```

Remember : when conducting multiplication, the type of operation matters. We can use the Hadamard product to multiply two equally-sized vectors or matrices where the output will be another equally-sized vector or matrix. We use the dot product in situations where we need a single number as an output. The dot product is essential in machine learning and deep learning; with neural networks, inputs are passed to each layer as a matrix or vector, and these are then multiplied with another matrix of weights, which forms the core of basic network operations.

Probability distributions and the computations based on them rely on Bayesian thinking in the machine learning realm. As we'll see in later chapters, some of the most innovative networks in AI directly rely on these distributions and the core concepts of Baye's theorem. Recall that there are two primary forms of probability distribution: PMFs for discrete variables, and probability density functions PDFs for continuous variables; CDF, which apply to any random variables, also exist.

Baye's rule, in fact, has inspired an entire branch of statistics known as **Bayesian statistics**. Thus far, we have discussed frequent statistics, which measure probability based on an observed space of repeatable events. Bayesian probability, on the other hand, measures degrees of belief; how likely is an event to happen based on the information that is currently available? This will become important as we delve into ANNs in the following chapters.

Constructing basic machine learning algorithms

 As mentioned in the last chapter, machine learning is a term that was developed as a reaction to the first AI winter. Today, we generally consider machine learning to be the overarching subject area for deep learning and ANNs in general.

Most machine learning solutions can be broken down into either a **classification** problem or a **regression** problem. A classification problem is when the output variables are categorical, such as fraud or not fraud. A regression problem is when the output is continuous, such as dollars or site visits. Problems with numerical output can be categorical, but are typically transformed to have a categorical output such as first class and second class.

Within machine learning, we have **supervised algorithms** and **unsupervised algorithms**. In this section, we will introduce these types of algorithms and explore two examples of each.

Supervised learning algorithms

Supervised algorithms rely on human knowledge to complete their tasks. Let's say we have a dataset related to loan repayment that contains several demographic indicators, as well as whether a loan was paid back or not:

Income	Age	Marital Status	Location	Savings	Paid
$90,000	28	Married	Austin, Texas	$50,000	y

The Paid column, which tells us if a loan was paid back or not, is called the **target** - it's what we would like to predict. The data that contains information about the applicants background is known as the **features** of the datasets. In supervised learning, algorithms learn to predict the target based on the features, or in other words, what indicators give a high probability that an applicant will pay back a loan or not? Mathematically, this process looks as follows:

$$y = f(x) + \epsilon$$

Here, we are saying that our label y *is a function of* the input features x, plus some amount of error ϵ that it caused naturally by the dataset. We know that a certain set of features will likely produce a certain outcome. In supervised learning, we set up an algorithm to *learn* what function will produce the correct mapping of a set of features to an outcome.

To illustrate how supervised learning works, we are going to utilize a famous example toy dataset in the machine learning field, the Iris Dataset. It shows four features: Sepal Length, Sepal Width, Petal Length, and Petal Width. In this dataset, our target variable (sometimes called a **label**) is *Name.* The dataset is available in the GitHub repository that corresponds with this chapter:

```
import pandas as pd
data = pd.read_csv("iris.csv")
data.head()
```

The preceding code generates the following output:

	SepalLength	SepalWidth	PetalLength	PetalWidth	Name
0	5.1	3.5	1.4	0.2	Iris-setosa
1	4.9	3.0	1.4	0.2	Iris-setosa
2	4.7	3.2	1.3	0.2	Iris-setosa
3	4.6	3.1	1.5	0.2	Iris-setosa
4	5.0	3.6	1.4	0.2	Iris-setosa

Now that we have our data ready to go, let's jump into some supervised learning!

Random forests

Random forests are one of the most commonly utilized supervised learning algorithms. While they can be used for both classification and regression tasks, we're going to focus on the former. Random forests are an example of an **ensemble method**, which works by aggregating the outputs of multiple models in order to construct a stronger performing model. Sometimes, you'll hear this being referred to as a grouping of **weak learners** to create a **strong learner**.

Setting up a random forest classifier in Python is quite simple with the help of scikit-learn. First, we import the modules and set up our data. We do not have to perform any data cleaning here, as the Iris dataset comes pre-cleaned.

Before training machine learning algorithms, we need to split our data into **training and testing sets**. When we train algorithms to learn, we want them to learn how to predict on unseen data, not just memorize the patterns of existing data. To do this, we split our dataset into different sets, typically using 75% of the data for training and 25% for testing. The `train_test_split` function from sklearn will help us create a training and testing set for our model automatically:

```
from sklearn.model_selection import train_test_split

features = data.iloc[:,0:4]
labels = data.iloc[:,4]
x_train, x_test, y_train, y_test = train_test_split(features, labels,
test_size = 0.25, random_state = 50)
```

Random forests work from the basic structure of the **decision tree**, and are trained utilizing the **bagging method** (bootstrap aggregating). Bagging randomly samples subsets of the training data with replacement, which helps reduce **variance** in the model that can arise from fitting too closely to a particular dataset. Each of these subsets are then used to train a decision tree, whose outputs are then aggregated for a final prediction.

Random forests take the basic bagging technique further by introducing random feature selection into the mix. The key to random forests is, in fact, this randomness. By applying the bagging method to the entire feature space, the algorithm reduces the variance of its individual trees. As a result, however, these algorithms create high bias. Overall error is determined by how close the correlation between two trees is, as well as the error rate of the individual trees.

In Python, to create a random forest, we first initiate the random forest. Then we define the `n_estimators` parameter, which tells us how many trees we want in our forest; and lastly, we fit the model:

```
from sklearn.ensemble import RandomForestClassifier

rf_classifier = RandomForestClassifier(n_estimators=1000)
rf_classifier.fit(x_train, y_train)
```

Upon fitting the forest, the algorithm is applied to the data. Let's take a look at what's going on behind the scenes:

1. The algorithm randomly samples the dataset for the defined number of trees. In this case, we defined 1000 trees.
2. For each tree, the algorithm randomly selects features and tests the prediction power of those features by using a metric.
3. This process iteratively continues until the trees are fully grown.
4. The predictions of all of the trees are aggregated into a final prediction.

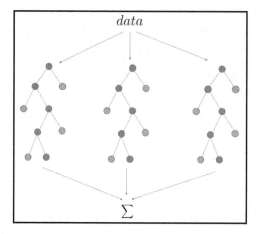

For classification tasks, trees and forests grow and divide in this algorithm based on one of two metrics, **gini impurity** or **information gain**.

- **Gini Impurity**: A metric that measures the probability of obtaining two different outputs from a classification; the more impure a leaf is, the less likely it is that one classification has a higher probability over the other. Gini impurity can create bias towards certain variables.
- **Information Gain**: Also called **entropy**, is a measure of randomness and uncertainty . It is slightly slower to compute compared to Gini Impurity.

If we look at the mathematical formulas for both of these, you can see where they differ:

$$Gini = 1 - \sum_{j=1}^{c} p_j^2$$

$$Entropy = -\sum_{j=1}^{c} p_j \log p_j$$

In the majority of cases, your choice of gini impurity versus entropy will not affect the performance of the model. For regression trees, the algorithms seeks to minimize the **variance**.

For more information on random forests, or to see more code examples, reference the code examples and exercises at the end of this chapter for other common supervised algorithms. Besides the commonly found logistic regression and random forest models that we've discussed, other supervised learning algorithms are:

- Linear regression
- Naive Bayes
- Support vector machines (SVMs)

Unsupervised learning algorithms

Unsupervised learning algorithms learn the properties of data on their own without explicit human intervention or labeling. Typically within the AI field, unsupervised learning technique learn the probability distribution that generated a dataset. These algorithms, such as **autoencoders** (we will visit these later in the book), are useful for a variety of tasks where we simply don't know important information about our data that would allow us to use traditional supervised techniques.

 PCA is an unsupervised method for feature extraction. It combines input variables in such a way that we can drop those variables that provide the least amount of information to us. Afterwards, we are left with new variables that are independent of each other, making them easy to utilize in a basic linear model.

AI applications are fundamentally hampered by the **curse of dimensionality**. This phenomenon, which occurs when the number of **dimensions** in your data is high, makes it incredibly difficult for learning algorithms to perform well. PCA can help alleviate this problem for us. PCA is one of the primary examples of what we call **dimensionality reduction**, which helps us take high-feature spaces (lots of data attributes) and transform them into lower-feature spaces (only the important features).

Dimensionality reduction can be conducted in two primary ways: **feature elimination** and **feature extraction**. Whereas feature elimination may involve the arbitrary cutting of features from the dataset, feature extraction (PCA is a form of) this gives us a more intuitive way to reduce our dimensionality. So, how does it work? In a nutshell:

- We create a matrix (correlation or covariance) that describes how all of our data relates to each other
- We decompose this matrix into separate components, called the **eigenvalues** and the **eigenvectors**, which describe the direction and magnitude of our data
- We then transform or project our original data onto these components

Let's break this down in Python manually to illustrate the process. We'll use the same Iris dataset that we used for the supervised learning illustration. First, we'll create the correlation matrix:

```
features = (features - features.mean()) / features.std()

corr_matrix = np.corrcoef(data.values.T)
corr_matrix.corr()
```

The output should look as follows:

	SepalLength	SepalWidth	PetalLength	PetalWidth
SepalLength	1.000000	-0.109369	0.871754	0.817954
SepalWidth	-0.109369	1.000000	-0.420516	-0.356544
PetalLength	0.871754	-0.420516	1.000000	0.962757
PetalWidth	0.817954	-0.356544	0.962757	1.000000

Our correlation matrix contains information on how every element of the matrix relates to each other element. This record of association is essential in providing the algorithm with information. Lots of variability typically indicates a signal, whereas a lack of variability indicates noise. The more variability that is present in a particular direction, the more there is to detect. Next, we'll create our `eigen_values` and `eigen_vectors`:

```
eigen_values, eigen_vectors = np.linalg.eig(corr_matrix)
```

The output should look as follows:

```
[2.91081808 0.92122093 0.14735328 0.02060771]
[[ 0.52237162 -0.37231836 -0.72101681  0.26199559]
 [-0.26335492 -0.92555649  0.24203288 -0.12413481]
 [ 0.58125401 -0.02109478  0.14089226 -0.80115427]
 [ 0.56561105 -0.06541577  0.6338014   0.52354627]]
```

Eigenvectors and Eigenvalues come in pairs ; each eigenvectors are directions in of data, and eigenvalues tell us how much variance exists within that direction. In PCA, we want to understand which inputs account for the most variance in the data (that is: how much do they explain the data). By calculating eigenvectors and their corresponding eigenvalues, we can begin to understand what is most important in our dataset.

We now want to sort the pairs of eigenvectors/eigenvalues from highest to lowest.

```
eigenpairs = [[eigen_values[i], eigen_vectors[:,i]] for i in
range(len(eigen_vectors))]

eigenpairs.sort(reverse=True)
```

Lastly, we need to project these pairs into a *lower dimensional space*. This is dimensionality reduction aspect of PCA:

```
projection = np.hstack((eigenpairs[0][1].reshape(eig_vectors.shape[1],1),
eigenpairs[1][1].reshape(eig_vectors.shape[1],1)))
```

We'll then conduct this transformation on the original data:

```
transform = features.dot(projection)
```

We can then plot the components against each other:

```
fig = plt.figure(figsize=(8,8))

ax = fig.gca()
ax = sns.regplot(transform.iloc[:,0], transform.iloc[:,1],fit_reg=False,
scatter_kws={'s':70}, ax=ax)

ax.set_xlabel('principal component 1', fontsize=10)
ax.set_ylabel('principal component 2', fontsize=10)


for tick in ax.xaxis.get_major_ticks():
    tick.label.set_fontsize(12)
for tick in ax.yaxis.get_major_ticks():
```

```
    tick.label.set_fontsize(12)
ax.set_title('Pricipal Component 1 vs Principal Component 2\n',
fontsize=15)

plt.show()
```

You should see the plot as follows:

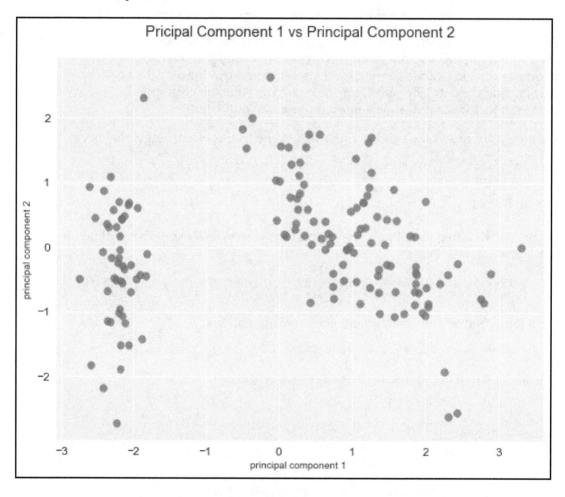

So when should we use PCA? Use PCA when the following are true:

- Do you have high dimensionality (too many variables) and want a logical way to reduce them?
- Do you need to ensure that your variables are independent of each other?

One of the downsides of PCA, however, is that it makes the underlying data more opaque, thus hurting it's interpretability. Besides PCA and the k–means clustering model that we precedingly described, other commonly seen non-deep learning unsupervised learning algorithms are:

- K-means clustering
- Hierarchical clustering
- Mixture models

Basic tuning

So you've built a model, now what? Can you call it a day? Chances are, you'll have some optimization to do on your model. A key part of the machine learning process is the optimization of our algorithms and methods. In this section, we'll be covering the basic concepts of optimization, and will be continuing our learning of tuning methods throughout the following chapters.

Sometimes, when our models do not perform well with new data it can be related to them **overfitting** or **underfitting**. Let's cover some methods that we can use to prevent this from happening. First off, let's look at the random forest classifier that we trained earlier. In your notebook, call the `predict` method on it and pass the `x_test` data in to receive some predictions:

```
predicted = rf_classifier.predict(x_test)
```

From this, we can create evaluate the performance of our classifier through something known as a **confusion matrix**, which maps out misclassifications for us. Pandas makes this easy for us with the `crosstab` command:

```
pd.crosstab(y_test, predicted, rownames=['Actual'], colnames=['Predicted'])
```

You should see the output as follows:

Predicted Actual	Iris-setosa	Iris-versicolor	Iris-virginica
Iris-setosa	11	0	0
Iris-versicolor	0	14	1
Iris-virginica	0	1	11

As you can see, our model performed fairly well on this dataset (it is a simple one after all!). What happens, however, if our model didn't perform well? Let's take a look at what could happen.

Overfitting and underfitting

Overfitting is a phenomenon that happens when an algorithm learns it's training data *too well* to the point where it cannot accurately predict on new data. Models that overfit learn the small, intricate details of their training set and don't generalize well. For analogy, think about it as if you were learning a new language. Instead of learning the general form of the language, say Spanish, you've learned to perfect a local version of it from a remote part of South America, including all of the local slang. If you went to Spain and tried to speak that version of Spanish, you would probably get some puzzled looks from the locals! Underfitting would be exact opposite of this; you didn't study enough Spanish, and so you do not have enough knowledge to communicate effectively. From a modeling standpoint, an underfit model is not complex enough to generalize to new data.

Overfitting and underfitting are tried to a machine learning phenomenon known as the **bias/variance** tradeoff:

- **Bias** is the error that your model learns as it tries to approximately predict things. Understanding that models are simplified versions of reality, bias in a model is the error that develops from trying to create this simplified version.
- **Variance** is the degree to which your error changes based on variations in the input data. It measures your model's sensitivity to the intricacies of the input data.

The way to mitigate bias is to increase the complexity of a model, although this will increase variance and will lead to overfitting. To mitigate variance on the other hand, we could make our model to generalize well by reducing complexing, although this would lead to higher bias. As you can see, we cannot have a both low bias and low variance at the same time! A good model will be balanced between it's bias and variance. There are two ways to combat overfitting; cross-validation and regularization. We will touch upon cross-validation methods now, and come back to regularization in Chapter 4, *Your First Artificial Neural Network* when we begin to build our first ANNs.

K-fold cross-validation

You've already seen a form of cross-validation before; holding out a portion of our data is the simplest form of cross- validation that we can have. While this is generally a good practice, it can sometimes leave important features out of the training set that can create poor performance when it comes time to test. To remedy this, we can take standard cross validation a step further with a technique called **k-fold cross validation**.

In k-fold cross validation, our dataset is evenly divided in *k* event parts, chosen by the user. As a rule of thumb, generally you should stick to k = 5 or k = 10 for best performance. The model is then trained and tested *k* times over. During each training episode, one *k* segment of the data held out as a testing set and the other segments used as training. You can think of this like shuffling a deck of cards - each time we are taking one card out for testing, and leaving the rest for training. The total accuracy of the model and it's error is then the combination of all of the train/test episode that were conducted.

There are some models, such as Logistic Regression and Support vector machines, which benefit from k-fold cross validation. Neural network models, such as the ones that we will be discussing in the coming chapter, also benefit from k-fold cross validation methods. Random Forest models like we described precedingly, on the other hand, do not require k-fold cross-validation. K-fold is used as a tuning and optimization method for balancing feature importances, and Random Forests already contain a measure of feature importance.

Hyperparameter optimization

Aside from protecting against overfitting, we can optimize models by searching for the best combination of **model hyperparameters**. Hyperparameters are configuration variables that tell the model what methods to use, as opposed to **model parameters** which are learned during training - we'll learn more about these in upcoming chapter. They are programmatically added to a model, and are present in all modeling packages in Python. In the random forest model that we built precedingly, for instance, n_estimators is a hyperparameter that tells the model how many trees to build. The process of searching for the combination of hyperparameters that leads to the best model performance is called **hyperparameter tuning**.

In Python, we can tune hyperparameter with an exhaustive search over their potential values, called a **Grid Search**. Let's use our random forest model to see how we can do this in Python by import `GrisSearchCV`:

```
from sklearn.model_selection import GridSearchCV

parameters = {
  'n_estimators': [100, 500, 1000],
  'max_features': [2, 3, 4],
  'max_depth': [90, 100, 110, 120],
  'min_samples_split': [6, 10, 14],
  'min_samples_leaf': [2, 4, 6],
}
```

In this case, we are going to pass the Grid Search a few different hyperparameters to check; you can read about what they do in the documentation for the classifier (`http://scikit-learn.org/stable/modules/generated/sklearn.ensemble.RandomForestClassifier.html`).

To create the search, we simply have to initialize it:

```
search = GridSearchCV(estimator = rf_classifier, param_grid = parameters,
cv = 3)
```

We can then apply it to the data:

```
search.fit(x_train, y_train)
search.best_params_
```

If we then want to check the performance of the best combination of parameters, we can easily do that in sklearn by evaluating it on the test data:

```
best = search.best_estimator_
accuracy = evaluate(best, x_test, y_test)
```

Hyperparameter tuning searches can be applied to the neural network models that we'll be utilizing in the coming chapters.

Summary

Machine learning, and by extension, deep learning, relies on the building blocks of linear algebra and statistics at its core. Vectors, matrices, and tensors provide the means by which we represent input data and parameters in machine learning algorithms, and the computations between these are the core operations of these algorithms. Likewise, distributions and probabilities help us model data and events in machine learning.

We also covered two classes of algorithms that will inform how we think about ANNs in further chapters: supervised learning methods and unsupervised learning methods. With supervised learning, we provide the algorithm with a set of features and labels, and it learns how to appropriately map certain feature combinations to labels. In unsupervised learning, the algorithm isn't provided with any labels at all, and it must infer relationships and information from the data. Lastly, we learned about basic ways to tune our models to help us improve their accuracy.

Now that we have a core understanding of some of the underlying mechanisms that allow us to create extraordinary AI systems, let's learn about the platforms and tools that we will create these systems with.

Platforms and Other Essentials

3

In this chapter, we'll discuss important libraries and frameworks that one needs to get started in **Artificial Intelligence** (**AI**). We'll cover the basic functions of the three most popular deep learning frameworks—TensorFlow, PyTorch, and Keras—show you how to get up and running in each of these frameworks, as we will be utilizing them in the following chapters. We'll touch upon computing for AI, and discuss how GPUs and other advanced memory units can improve it. Lastly, we'll discuss the fundamentals of two popular cloud computing frameworks for deep learning: AWS and Google Cloud.

The following topics will be covered in this chapter:

- Essential libraries for deep learning in Python: TensorFlow, PyTorch, and Keras
- CPUs, GPUs, and compute frameworks that are used for AI
- The fundamentals of AWS and Google Cloud

Technical requirements

We will be working with TensorFlow, PyTorch, and Keras in Python 3. It is recommended that you have an NVIDIA GPU on your computer. The following models are recommended:

- GTX 1080 Ti
- GTX 1070
- GTX 1060

If you do not have an NVIDIA GPU, please follow the prompts in the *Cloud Computing* section to utilize a GPU instance on AWS.

You must also have an AWS and Google Cloud account; both are free, and you can sign up at their respective websites.

TensorFlow, PyTorch, and Keras

In this section, we'll introduce three of the most popular deep learning frameworks: TensorFlow, PyTorch, and Keras. While we'll look at the basic functionality of each of the packages, we'll learn about specific deep learning functions for each of the frameworks in later chapters as part of our hands-on approach to learning AI.

TensorFlow

TensorFlow is the most popular, and most contributed to, deep learning library. Originally developed by Google Brain for use on Google's own AI products, it was open sourced in 2015 and has since become the standard for deep learning. TensorFlow underlies all of Google's own deep learning based products such as Google Translate and the Google Cloud Platform's machine learning APIs. Google has setup TensorFlow specifically to be parallelized, and as such it performs really well in distributed environments.

TensorFlow provides APIs for Python, C++, Java, and others; however, in this book we are going to stick to utilizing Python. TensorFlow can be installed from PyPy with the simple: `pip install tensorflow`.

Basic building blocks

As you may have guessed from the name, TensorFlow relies on the algebraic concept of tensors that we learned about in the previous chapter. Everything, from input data to parameters, is stored in a tensor in TensorFlow. As such, TensorFlow has its own functions for many of the basic operations normally handled by NumPy.

When writing tensors in TensorFlow, we're really writing everything in an array structure. Remember how an array can be a rank 1 tensor? That is exactly what we are passing in the preceding example. If we wanted to pass a rank 3 tensor, we'd simply write `x = tf.constant([1,2,3,4],[5,6,7,8],[9,10,11,12])`. You'll notice that we defined constants in the following code; these are just one of three types of data structure we can use in TensorFlow:

- **Constants**: Defined values that cannot change
- **Placeholders**: Objects that will be assigned a value during a TensorFlow **session**
- **Variables**: Like constants, only the values can change

Alright, back to the code. If we had run the following code block, we would have been left with a **TensorFlow object**, which looks something like tensor (`"Mul:0"`, `shape=(4,)`, `dtype=int32`).

```
## Import Tensorflow at tf for simplicity
import tensorflow as tf

## Define two constants
const1 = tf.constant([4])
const2 = tf.constant([5])

## Multiply the constants
product = tf.multiply(const1, const2)
```

Why? because TensorFlow runs on the concept of **sessions**. The underlying code of TensorFlow is written in C++, and a session allows a high-level TensorFlow package to communicate with the low-level C++ runtime.

 Before we run a TensorFlow session, we need to tell it to initialize all of the variables we declared, and then run the initialization## In Tensorflow, we must first initialize a session object

```
## Variable Initializer
init = initialize_all_variables()

## Initialize the session
sess = tf.Session()
sess.run(init)

## Run the session
print(sess.run(product))

## Close the session
sess.close()
```

One last important concept in TensorFlow is that of **scopes**. Scopes help us control various operational blocks within our model:

```
with tf.name_scope("my_scope"):
        ## Define two constants
        const1 = tf.constant([4])
        const2 = tf.constant([5])

        ## Multiply the constants
        product = tf.multiply(const1, const2)
```

That's it! We've successfully performed out first operation in TensorFlow. We'll also be learning more about the in-depth operations of TensorFlow in the next chapter on building **Artificial Neural Networks (ANNs)**.

The TensorFlow graph

One of the more important and powerful features of TensorFlow is its graph. When you define one of the three types of TensorFlow data structures previously described, you automatically add a **node** and an **edge** to your graph. Nodes represent operations and edges represent tensors, so if we were to do basic multiplication such as the preceding example, `const1` and `const2` would represent edges in the graph, `tf.multiply` would represent a node, and `product` would represent an outgoing edge from that node. TensorFlow's graph is **static**, which means we cannot change it at runtime.

Remember, an ANN performs hundreds of computations; computing and interpreting at each step would be extremely compute-intensive. The TensorFlow graph helps solve this problem by creating a graph of all tensors and operations in your network and executing them in your runtime session that we previously described. Adjacent operations are compiled together in the graph for faster computation. On top of that, the graph structure allows us to easily distribute computational tasks across multiple CPUs or GPUs, and the TensorFlow session object automatically manages access to these multiple resources, whether local or in the cloud. This is where TensorFlow gets it flow; data and operations flow through the graph at runtime.

You can either manually define graphs in TensorFlow, or use it's default graph. When we declared the variables precedingly, we declared them in the default graph that TensorFlow sets up for us when we import it. You can access that default graph with:

```
default_graph = tf.get_default_graph()
```

If we're creating multiple models or processes in the same file however, it's necessary to create multiple graphs. For that, TensorFlow allows us to simply declare a new one:

```
my_graph = tf.Graph()

with new_graph.as_default():
        x = tf.constant(2)
        y = tf.constant(2)
```

If you are manually defining multiple graphs, you'll also want to remember to pass those graphs when running a TensorFlow session:

```
sess = tf.Session(graph=my_graph)
```

PyTorch

PyTorch is a newer, but growing deep learning library that is based on the Torch framework used for Facebook's deep learning algorithms. Unlike TensorFlow, PyTorch is not a wrapper that compiles to an underlying language, but is written to mimic native Python. If you have had any experience with Python programming, PyTorch will feel extremely familiar to you.

PyTorch can be easily installed with:

```
conda install pytorch torchvision -c pytorch
```

Currently, PyTorch does not have a Windows distribution, which may make it out of reach for some users.

Basic building blocks

Such as TensorFlow, PyTorch represents data in tensor form. Torch tensors are defined as standard data types, such as `torch.FloatTensor()`, `torch.charTensor()`, and `torch.intTensor()`. As mentioned, operations in PyTorch are highly Pythonic. To repeat the exact same multiplication operation that we performed in preceding TensorFlow:

```
import torch
x = torch.IntTensor([4])
y = torch.IntTensor([5])
product = x * y
```

As a result of it native Python feel, PyTorch allows for easy interaction between standard numpy arrays and PyTorch tensors. It's easy to switch back and forth between the two:

```
import torch
import numpy as np

## Create a numpy array
numpy_array = np.random.randn(20,20)

##Convert the numpy array to a pytorch tensor
pytorch_tensor = torch.from_numpy(numpy_array)

## Convert it back to Numpy
numpy_again = pytorch_tensor.numpy()
```

PyTorch tensors can easily be indexed and sliced in a Pythonic way as well. For instance, let's say that we want to access a particular value of a tensor in PyTorch; we can easily do that with NumPy-like indexing:

```
tensor = torch.FloatTensor([[1, 2, 3], [4, 5, 6], [7, 8, 9]])

## print the third element of the 2nd row of the tensor
print(tensor[1][2])
```

Likewise, we can easily manipulate the contents of the tensor in a NumPy-like manner:

```
## replace the second value of the first tensor
tensor[0][1] = 1
print(tensor)
```

Like TensorFlow, PyTorch runs on the concept of variables, which are values that are intended to change and be updated during training processes. To create a variable in PyTorch, we wrap a tensor with the `Variable` function:

```
from torch.autograd import Variable
tensor_two = torch.tensor([[1, 2, 3], [4, 5, 6], [7, 8, 9]])
variable = Variable(tensor_two)
```

If you'd like to gain access to the tensor that's inside of the variable wrapper, you can call `.data` on the variable:

```
variable.data

## Returns:
tensor([[1, 2, 3],
        [4, 5, 6],
        [7, 8, 9]])
```

While PyTorch is relatively new and still developing, its Python-like structure is leading to fast adoption rates in the community.

The PyTorch graph

PyTorch seems more Pythonic because of its **dynamic graph compute structure**. Since Python is an interpreted language, meaning that operations are executed at runtime, PyTorch's graphing feature seeks to replicate this by allowing us to alter variables in the graph at runtime. In simpler words, PyTorch's graphs are created at the time you actually execute the code, not defined statically beforehand like in TensorFlow. Architecturally, this means that you can actually change your network architecture during training, which means PyTorch can accommodate a lot more cutting edge, dynamic architectures.

Keras

Keras is the most high-level deep learning library available, and is often where people begin on their AI journey. While we will focus on applications with TensorFlow in this book, it is important to introduce Keras because of its ubiquity and ease of use.

Written by François Chollet at Google, Keras is a wrapper that can run on top of TensorFlow or other libraries such as Apache, MXNet, or Theano. Like the other libraries, it is available through PyPy by running `pip install keras` in your terminal or command line. Functionally, it's very similar to the way the scikit-learn works, and hence is a popular library for those who wish to get their hands dirty with deep learning as quickly as possible.

Like PyTorch, Keras was designed to be pythonic; everything utilizes native Python functions. It was also designed to be modular and minimal so that code is easily portable and reusable. To run Keras, you must already have TensorFlow installed, as it will act as it's back-end operator.

Basic building blocks

As Keras is designed as a model-level library, it does not contain methods for doing basic operations as PyTorch of base TensorFlow does. Instead, it utilizes TensorFlow as a backend. As such, its basic operations are the same as basic TensorFlow operations:

```
import keras.backend as K
x = K.constant(5)
y = K.constant(6)
product = x * y
```

Keras also uses the same graph structure as Tensorflow. We'll learn more about Keras model building methods in the next chapter on *Your First Artificial Neural Networks*.

Wrapping up

So, what is the best library to use? As you can see in the following screenshot, one benchmark places PyTorch firmly in the lead when compared with other deep learning libraries when running an ANN:

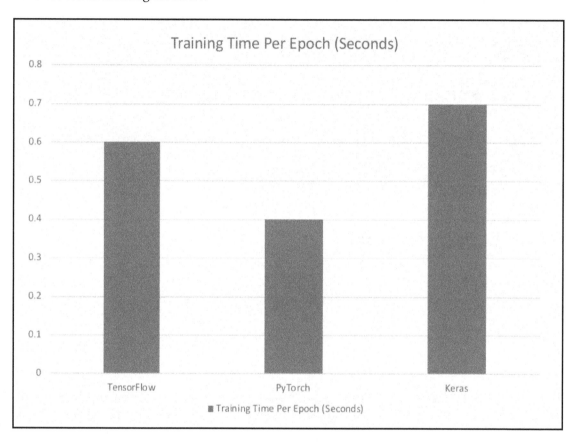

Ultimately, your choice of library mostly comes down to personal preference; however, in general:

- **Keras**: Best for beginners or those looking to do *quick and dirty* work on ANNs
- **TensorFlow**: Widely used, there are great code bases and tutorials available online and it is widely integrated into cloud machine images and all types of computing frameworks
- **PyTorch**: Provides exceptional speed and ease of use, but is largely still underdeveloped, with fewer resources available

Cloud computing essentials

Often, on-premise GPU clusters are not always available or practical. More often than not, many businesses are migrating their AI applications to the cloud, utilizing popular cloud provider services such as **Amazon Web Services** (**AWS**) or the **Google Cloud Platform** (**GCP**). When we talk about the cloud, we are really talking about database and compute resources, offered as a service. Cloud solution providers such as AWS and GCP have data centers across the world that store data and run computing jobs for people remotely. When your data is in the cloud, or when you are running a program in the cloud, you are really running or storing in one of these data centers. In cloud terminology, we call these data centers or cluster of data centers **regions**.

Cloud services are divided into three different offering structures:

- **Infrastructure as a Service** (**IaaS**): Raw computing and network resources that you can use to build infrastructure, just as you would locally
- **Platform as a Service** (**PaaS**): Managed services that obfuscate away infrastructure components
- **Software as a Service** (**SaaS**): Fully managed solutions, such as online email

In this section, we'll cover both IaaS solutions, as well as PaaS solutions. While cloud providers do offer SaaS solutions for AI, they are a bit too high level for our needs. In this section, we'll discuss the basic tools that you'll need to utilize the compute power of the cloud. Towards the end of this chapter, we'll discuss cloud computing in more detail in the *Maintaining AI applications* section.

AWS basics

AWS is the most popular cloud computing provider on the market. In this section, we'll explore the basics for getting set up in the cloud, including creating and connecting to EC2 instances (Amazon's main cloud computing framework), as well as how to set up virtual machines in the cloud.

We'll also touch upon how to utilize Amazon's bulk storage component, S3. While AWS offers several machine learning services, we're going to focus solely on the basic need to utilize AWS cloud computing architectures to power your AI systems.

EC2 and virtual machines

The building block for AWS systems is the **Elastic Cloud Compute** (**EC2**) instance; it is a virtual server that allows you to run applications in the cloud. In this chapter, EC2 will be the basis for our cloud computing work. For developers and data scientists, Amazon has a suite of virtual machines called **Amazon Machine Images** (**AMI**) that come preloaded with everything you need to get up and running with deep learning in the cloud. For our purposes, Amazon has both an Ubuntu AMI as well as an Amazon Linux distribution AMI, which are preloaded with Python 3 and TensorFlow, PyTorch, and Keras.

To get started with utilizing EC2 for deep learning, we'll just have to follow a few steps:

1. Log in to your Amazon Web Services Account.
2. Search for EC2 in the Search bar and select the service to open a new console.
3. Choose the **Launch Instance** button and search for the AWS deep learning AMI in the AWS Marketplace. You can select either the Ubuntu version or Amazon Linux.
4. Select a GPU instance to run your image on. We suggest either a G2 or P2 instance. Choose Next on each page until you reach Configure Security Group. Under Source, choose My IP to allow access using only your IP address.
5. Click **Launch Instance.**
6. Create a new Private Key and store this somewhere locally; this will help you connect to your instance later on.

Now, you should have your AMI set up and ready to utilize. If you already have an EC2 instance up and running 0n your AWS account, select the instance and right-click on **Image**, **Create Image** under the dropdown for that instance:

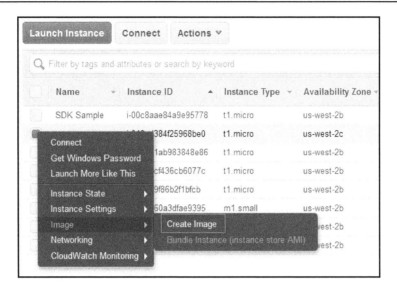

Follow the prompts and select **Create Image**. Afterwards, you can find that AMI by selecting **EC2 -> AMIs** under the main Explorer toolbar. If you still can't see your AMI, you can find more detailed instructions on AWS website `https://docs.aws.amazon.com/ toolkit-for-visual-studio/latest/user-guide/tkv-create-ami-from-instance.html`.

To utilize your new virtual machine, first launch the instance on AWS. Here `ssh` is initialized by utilizing the following command (make sure you are in the same directory as the `pem` key file you just downloaded):

```
cd /Users/your_username/Downloads/
ssh -L localhost:8888:localhost:8888 -i <your .pem file name> ubuntu@<Your
instance DNS>
```

Once you've connected with your terminal or command line, you can utilize the interface just as you would the command line on your local computer.

S3 Storage

Amazon Simple Storage Service (**Amazon S3**), is AWS's bulk cloud storage solution. S3 is designed to be simple, cheap, and efficient - it works just like a local directory on your computer would. These storage locations are known as **Buckets**, and can store up to 5 Terabytes of data.

To setup an S3, log onto your AWS console, find the S3 service, and click **Create bucket**

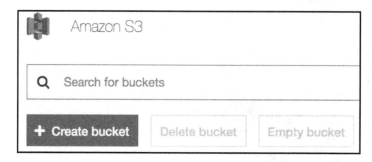

You can set permissions for who can and cannot access the data in an S3 bucket, should you need to restrict access.

AWS Sagemaker

SageMaker is Amazon's fully managed cloud machine learning offering. As a **Platform as a Service** (**PaaS**) product, SageMaker is one of the simplest ways in which you can deploy a machine learning model. Unlike it's competitors, Amazon SageMaker only runs Python 2.7. SageMaker has two options for handling machine learning services in the cloud:

1. Creating and training your model in a hosted Jupyter notebook
2. Training from a dockerized version of the model

We'll be diving into how to train and deploy models with SageMaker in the coming sections.

Google Cloud Platform basics

While AWS is the major player in the cloud marketplace and has been for some time now, over the past few years the **Google Cloud Platform** (**GCP**) has been gaining popularity, especially in the field of machine learning. You can sign up for GCP for free by navigating to `https://cloud.google.com/free/`, and entering the console. Keep in mind that you do need a Google user account, such as a gmail account, to sign up for Google services. While many small tasks can be completed within the platform's free tier, GCP offers a $300.00 credit to new users to get started.

All services in GCP run under the umbrella of a project. Projects are tools for organizing computing tools, users and access rights, as well as billing. After signing up for a GCP account, you can easily create a **New Project** from projects tab at the top of the console toolbar.

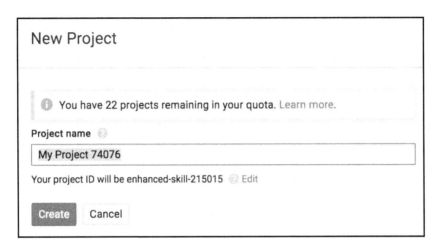

Once a project is created, you can manage it's users, usage, and billing from the central GCP console.

From here, we can start walking through GCP's service offering.

GCP cloud storage

Cloud storage is a simple, bucket-structured storage option that is similar to AWS S3. Like AWS, GCP cloud storage holds up to 5 Terabytes of data. As opposed to competitors such as AWS, or even Microsoft Azure, GCP's cloud storage has upload and download speeds for large files that are about three times faster than it's competitors. Cloud storage also has some of the fastest **throughput** on the market. Throughput, a cloud concept that measures how much data is processed at a given time - in simpler words, how fast can data be processed. When creating certain applications that rely on streaming data, this can be critical. Cloud storage also has the option to create buckets that span across service regions, which helps with fault tolerance and availability of your data.

To setup a Cloud storage bucket, log-on to the GCP console, search for storage, and click **CREATE BUCKET**:

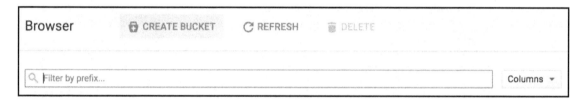

In addition to their standard compute and storage services, the GCP has another tool, ML engine, which provides seamless training and deployment operations for machine learning models.

GCP Cloud ML Engine

Google Cloud Platform's Cloud ML Engine is Google's equivalent to AWS SageMaker. As a managed PaaS, Cloud ML handles the training and deployment processes for machine learning algorithms. If you're thinking - what about a basic compute service like EC2 on AWS? GCP has that as well. Compute Engine is GCP's answer to Amazon EC2; it provides basic, scalable cloud compute services. While we could use Compute Engine to setup AI platforms, GCP has made it extremely simple for us to build with Cloud ML Engine and as such, we will note be covering the basic Compute Engine.

Let's dive into the details. Cloud ML engine allows you to:

- Train scikit-learn and TensorFlow models both locally for testing and in the cloud
- Create retrainable machine learning models that are stored in the cloud
- Easily deploy trained models to production

Cloud ML jobs are setup through the terminal. We'll work on running these training jobs in the coming chapters as we start to work with various ANN models.

CPUs, GPUs, and other compute frameworks

Progress in AI has always been tied to our compute abilities. In this section, we will discuss CPUs and GPUs for powering AI applications, and how to set up your system to work with accelerated GPU processing.

The main computational hardware in your computer is known as the **central processing unit** (**CPUs**); CPUs are designed for general computing workloads. While your local CPU can be used to train a deep learning model, you might find your computer hanging up on the training process for hours. When training AI applications on hardware, it's smarter to use the CPU's cousin, the **Graphics Processing Unit** (**GPU**). GPUs are designed to process in parallel, just as an ANN process in parallel. As we learned in the last chapter, AI applications require many linear algebra operations, the exact same type of operations that are required for video games. GPUs, originally designed for the gaming industry, provide us with thousands of cores to process these operations as well as parallelize them. In this manner, they lend themselves naturally to constructing deep learning algorithms.

When selecting a GPU to utilize in deep learning applications, we're looking at three main characteristics:

- **Processing power**: How fast the GPU can compute; defined as *cores* x *speed*
- **Memory**: The ability of the GPU to handle various sizes of data
- **RAM**: The amount of data you can have on your GPU at any given time

In this section, we'll be focusing on utilizing the most popular GPU brand for deep learning, **NVIDIA**, whose CUDA toolkit makes out-of-the-box deep learning an easy task. As the major competitor to NVIDIA, Radeon AMD GPUs utilize a toolkit called **OpenCL**, which does not have direct compatibility with most deep learning libraries out of the box. While AMD GPUs provide great hardware at a reasonable price, it is best to go with an NVIDIA product to make getting up to speed easy.

Should you have another GPU on your computer or no GPU at all, it is recommended that you utilize a GPU instance on AWS to follow the steps.

Installing GPU libraries and drivers

Now, let's get our computers set up for building AI applications. If you wish to do this task on your local computer, it's advised that you have either Windows or a Linux distribution installed. Unfortunately, most macOS are not built to accommodate GPUs, and therefore we will not be touching on macOS in this section. If you do not have an NVIDIA GPU on your computer, please perform the following steps. If you do have an NVIDIA GPU, you may choose to follow along with the AWS-based section, or skip to the following section.

If you're not sure whether you have an NVIDIA GPU, you can check for its existence with the following terminal command:

```
lspci -nnk | grep -i nvidia
```

With Linux (Ubuntu)

Linux and AI go together such as natural complements. When you talk to Google Assistant on your Android phone, talk to Cortana on your Windows device, or wonder how Watson won a round at Jeopardy on TV, it's all based on Linux.

When we talk about Linux in this chapter, we'll be talking about a particular distribution called **Ubuntu**, one of the most popular distributions of the Linux operating system. It's recommended that you stick with an older, more stable version of Ubuntu (Version 14.04), as although it will do wonders for your AI applications; it's certainly not as stable as your standard Windows OS.

If you'd like to use Ubuntu on your local machine, check out Ubuntu's tutorials for installing on a Windows machine (https://tutorials.ubuntu.com/tutorial/tutorial-ubuntu-on-windows#0). If you don't have a PC or you'd like to set up a virtual instance, AWS has a great tutorial (https://aws.amazon.com/getting-started/tutorials/launch-a-virtual-machine/) to walk you through the steps:

1. To get started with deep learning for GPUs on Ubuntu, we first have to install the GPU's driver. In this example, we're going to utilize wget and chmod to retrieve and set up read/write access:

```
wget
http://us.download.nvidia.com/XFree86/Linuxx86_64/367.44/NVIDIA-Lin
ux-x86_64-367.44.run

sudo chmod +x NVIDIA-Linux-x86_64-367.35.run
./NVIDIA-Linux-x86_64-367.35.run --silent
```

2. Once the installation finishes, you can check if it was intalled correctly with a simple `nvidia-smi` command.

3. Next, let's install NVIDIA CUDA. CUDA is a NVIDIA package that allows us to run TensorFlow models on our GPUs:

```
wget"http://developer.download.nvidia.com/compute/cuda/repos/ubuntu
1604/x86_64/cuda-repo-ubuntu1604_8.0.44-1_amd64.deb"
## Install the drivers
sudo chmod +x cuda_7.5.18_linux.run
./cuda_7.5.18_linux.run --driver --silent
./cuda_7.5.18_linux.run --toolkit --silent
./cuda_7.5.18_linux.run --samples --silent
```

4. Next, let's add the library to our system path:

```
echo 'export
LD_LIBRARY_PATH="$LD_LIBRARY_PATH:/usr/local/cuda/lib64:/usr/local/
cuda/extras/CUPTI/lib64"' >> ~/.bashrc
```

5. Lastly, we need to install a higher-level package called cuNN, which is a specific library that sits on top of CUDA and provides highly-tuned procedures for typical deep learning operations:

```
sudo scp cudnn-7.0-linux-x64-v4.0-prod.tgz
```

6. One last step to move the files to the correct place:

```
tar -xzvf cudnn-7.0-linux-x64-v4.0-prod.tgz
cp cuda/lib64/* /usr/local/cuda/lib64/
cp cuda/include/cudnn.h /usr/local/cuda/include/
```

7. And there you are, we're set up on Ubuntu for GPU acceleration. Our last step is to simply install the GPU-enabled version of TensorFlow with Python 3:

```
pip3 install tensorflow-gpu
```

With Windows

To set up your GPU for deep learning on Windows, you must be running Windows 7 or higher. You can verify that you have a CUDA-capable GPU through the **display adapters** section in the **Windows Device Manager**. Here, you will find the vendor name and model of your graphics card.

1. To see what type of GPU you have, open a command line prompt and run:

   ```
   control /name Microsoft.DeviceManager
   ```

2. If you do not have the driver installed for your NVIDIA GPU, or would like to update the drivers, you can find the correct driver based on your device on the NVIDIA website: `http://www.nvidia.com/Download/index.aspx?lang=en-us`.

3. Next, go ahead and grab the CUDA toolkit (`https://developer.nvidia.com/cuda-downloads`) form NVIDIA. Select **CUDA Version 8.0**. Go ahead and select your OS; it should look something this: **OS**: **Windows Architecture**: **x86_64 Version**: **10**.

4. After CUDA has finished downloading, we can go ahead and install the package. If your screen starts to flicker, do not worry! We're dealing with your graphics card directly, so it's just busy working.

5. Next, let's install cuNN; go ahead and download the file from NVIDIA. You should click on the following two items in sequential order:
   1. Download cuDNN v6.0 (April 27, 2017), for CUDA 8.0.
   2. cuDNN v6.0 library for Windows 10.

6. Unzip the file, and open the **CUDA** folder. You should see something such as this: `bin/include/lib/`.

7. Copy and paste these three folders into `C:\Program Files\NVIDIA GPU Computing Toolkit\CUDA\v8.0`.

8. Lastly, all we need to do is install the GPU-enabled TensorFlow:

   ```
   pip install tensorflow-gpu
   ```

You're now ready to start utilizing TensorFlow with your GPUs!

Basic GPU operations

Now that we have our GPUs set up for deep learning, let's learn how to utilize them. In TensorFlow, GPUs are represented as strings:

- /cpu:0: The CPU of your machine
- /device:GPU:0: The GPU of your machine, if you have one
- /device:GPU:1: The second GPU of your machine, and so on

Distributed training is the practice of training a network across several GPUs, and it's becoming an increasingly common way to train models in the AI field. TensorFlow, Keras, and PyTorch all support distributed training.

Logging is an operation in TensorFlow to assign a particular set of commands to a particular GPU or CPU on your system. With logging, we can also **parallelize** our operations, meaning that we can distribute training across several GPUs at the same time. To do this, we utilize a simple loop structure:

```
my_list = []
## Iterate through the available GPUs
for device in ['/gpu:0', '/gpu:1']:
    ## Utilize the TensorFlow device manager
    with tf.device(device):
        x = tf.constant([1,2,3], shape=[1,3])
        y = tf.constant([1,2,3],shape [3,1])
        my_list.append(tf.matmul(x, y))
    with tf.device('/cpu:0'):
        sum_operation = tf.add(x,y)
    ## Run everything through a session
    sess = tf.Session(config=tf.ConfigProto(log_device_placement=True))
    sess.run(sum_operation)
```

We first create an empty set, and use an iterator to assign the matrix multiplication procedure across two GPUs: GPU1 and GPU2. Another procedure, a simple sum, gets assigned to our CPU. We then run both through a TensorFlow session to execute the operations as we did before.

Keep in mind that this type of device management is for local devices, and that management is different for cloud architectures.

The future – TPUs and more

Google has recently released a new piece of hardware known as the **Tensor Processing Unit** (**TPU**), which is specifically designed for AI applications. These TPUs deliver 15-30x higher performance and 30-80x higher performance-per-watt than a CPU or GPU can deliver. Weights in large scale, production-level AI applications can number from five million to 100 million, and these TPUs excel in performing these operations.

TPUs are specifically tailored for TensorFlow processing, and are currently available on Google Cloud for use. If you're interested in exploring their functionality, GCP has a great tutorial (`https://cloud.google.com/tpu/docs/quickstart`) on how to get started.

Summary

The landscape for AI platforms and methods is diverse; in this chapter, we've outlined some of the most promising and well regarded technologies in the AI arena. For deep learning packages, we learned about TensorFlow, PyTorch, and Keras. TensorFlow, released by Google, is the most popular and robust of the deep learning libraries. It utilizes sessions and static graphs to compile to its underlying C++ code. PyTorch, on the other hand, is a newer library that features a dynamic graph for runtime execution, which allows it to feel like native Python. Lastly, Keras is a high-level library that runs on top of TensorFlow, and can be useful for creating straightforward networks where customization is not needed.

We also discussed cloud computing, utilizing AWS as the most popular cloud computing service, with its primary workhorses being the EC2 instance and the s3 Bucket. EC2 consists of virtual servers that can be used for scaling AI applications where hardware doesn't exist/is not needed. S3, Amazon's Simple Storage Service gives us the ability to store data and other resources that are necessary for running our applications. Lastly, we walked through enabling your computer and languages for GPU-accelerated deep learning. In the next chapter, we'll put this to use by creating our first ANNs.

In the next chapter, we'll put together the fundamental knowledge that learned in `Chapter 2`, *Machine Learning Basics*, with the platform knowledge from this chapter to create our first ANNs.

4
Your First Artificial Neural Networks

In the past few chapters, we learned about the basics of machine learning, and how to get our environments set up for creating **Artificial Intelligence** (**AI**) applications. Now that we've learned the basics, it's time to put our knowledge to use.

In this chapter, we'll focus on:

- How to construct basic AI applications, starting with constructing a basic feedforward network with TensorFlow
- We'll discuss the essential elements of **Artificial Neural Networks** (**ANNs**), and then code up an example of a basic feedforward network to illustrate this

ANNs allow us to define complex non-linear problems, and as we delve into the mechanics of true deep learning, you'll begin to see how powerful AI applications can be with deep learning at the core.

We'll get slightly technical dive in this section, and look at the concepts from a mathematical as well as a Python perspective. This is why I hope that you'll start to see deep learning as less of a *black box* and more of a set of mathematical tools that we can implement in the code to create amazing applications.

Technical requirements

We'll be utilizing the GPU-enabled TensorFlow environment that we developed in the previous chapter. You will need:

- Python 3.6
- GPU TensorFlow
- PyTorch

Network building blocks

The most basic form of an ANN is known as a **feedforward network**, sometimes called a **multi-layer perceptron**. These models, while simplistic in nature, contain the core building blocks for the various types of ANN that we will examine going forward.

In essence, a feedforward neural network is nothing more than a **directed graph**; there are no loops of recurrent connections between the layers, and information simply flows forward through the graph. Traditionally, when these networks are illustrated, you'll see them represented as in the following diagram:

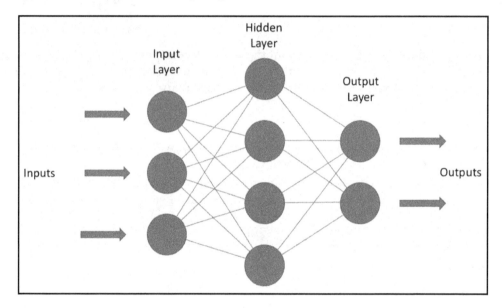

A feedforward neural network

In this most basic form, ANNs are typically organized into three basic layers; an **input layer**, a **hidden layer**, and an **output layer**, each made up of many basic input/output processing units commonly referred to as **neurons**. While it's helpful to view networks as basic structures such as this, the idea of neurons is a leftover term from the early days of AI research, when these networks were viewed from a different perspective. This perspective, sometimes called the **biological perspective**, viewed the task of AI as perfectly replicating the function of the human brain. Neurons were simply a way of trying to relate the processing within ANNs back to this neurological model. In this chapter, we're going to reject that old-school notion of modeling networks as neurological units, and instead model them as computational graphs while referring to neurons as **units**.

This layered structure of neural networks allows us to utilize the matrix math that we learned in the past chapters, which makes our network computations a lot easier and cleaner. Each layer performs some type of computation on the input from the previous layer.

As we go through the sections, we'll build a network along the way to do a simple classification problem: categorizing handwritten digits from the MNIST dataset. Collected by Deep Learning pioneer Yann LeCun, MNIST is a popular dataset for testing computer vision algorithms. It consists of a set of handwritten digits that can be classified by numerous means:

Y. LeCun, L. Bottou, Y. Bengio, and P. Haffner. Gradient-based learning applied to document recognition. Proceedings of the IEEE, 86(11):2278-2324, November 1998.

Before we start, let's import TensorFlow with the following code, and get our data properly set up:

```
import tensorflow as tf
from tensorflow.examples.tutorials.mnist import input_data
mnist = input_data.read_data_sets("/tmp/data/", one_hot=True)
```

Network layers

The **input layer** consists of the features that we are passing to our neural network. If we had, say, a *10 x 10* pixel image as our input, we would have 100 input units. Nothing is actually done in the input layer, but it is the connection between the input and hidden layers that is important.

Our input layer connections perform a linear transformation on the input vectors, and sends the results of that transformation to the hidden layer, through which the results are transformed through the **activation function**. Once we perform this computation, we pass the results onto the hidden layer. **Hidden layers** are where our activation functions live, and our network can have any number of them. Hidden layers are so called such because they compute values that are not seen in the training set; their job is to transform the network's input into something that the output layer can use. They allow us to learn more complicated features in a dataset.

The output of the last hidden layer gets sent to the final layer, the **output layer**. The output layer is the final layer in our network; it transforms the results of the hidden layers into whatever you'd like the output to be binary classification, real numbers, and so on. We do this by utilizing special types of activation function. In general:

- For classification problems, we'll often use a function called a **softmax**

- For regression tasks, we'll use a **linear** function

Your choice of activation function really depends on your loss function, as we'd like to make the derivative of the loss function easy to compute during training.

Naming and sizing neural networks

We refer to networks by the amount of **fully connected layers** that they have, minus the input layer. The network in the following figure, therefore, would be a two-layer neural network. A single-layer network would not have an input layer; sometimes, you'll hear logistic regressions described as a special case of a single-layer network, one utilizing a **sigmoid** activation function. When we talk about deep neural networks in particular, we are referring to networks that have several hidden layers as shown in the following diagram:

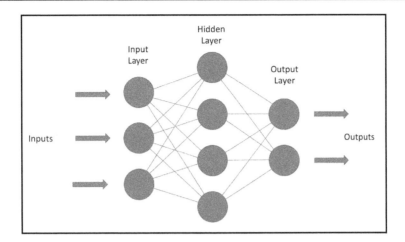

Networks are typically sized in terms of the number of parameters that they have (weights and biases). To determine the size of the network, we need simply to calculate the number of connections between each of the layers in the network, including the input layer. For the network shown in the preceding figure *A feedforward neural network*, we would have the number of units in the input layer (3) times the number in the hidden layer (4), plus the number in the output layer times the hidden layer, so:

$$(input \times hidden) + (hidden \times ouput)$$

$$(3 \times 4) + (4 \times 2) = 20$$

Therefore, the network has *20* learnable parameters. We'll want to keep this notion in mind, as the size of the network can greatly increase our computational load and affect training performance.

Setting up network parameters in our MNIST example

Looking at our MNIST example, we can now set up our overall network parameters. We'll define `input_layer_size` as the size of the incoming data, `784`. This will give us the number of neurons in the input layer. The parameters `hidden_one` and `hidden_two` will define the amount of neurons in the hidden layer. Meanwhile, `number_classes` constructs the output layer as the potential number of classes that a piece of input data could be classified as:

```
## Size of the input data
input_layer_size = 784
```

```
## Define the size of the hidden layers; We want them to be smaller than
the input
hidden_layer_one = 256
hidden_layer_two = 256

## Size of the potential output classes
number_classes = 10
```

In total, these will define the size of our network's input and output layers with respect to the size of the `MNIST` dataset's shape.

Activation functions

Activation functions are the building blocks that make neural networks able to do what they do: convert inputs into desired outputs within ANNs in a nonlinear fashion. As such, they are frequently referred to as **nonlinearities**. Putting this together with what we learned earlier, in a neural network we compute the sum of products of input (X) and their corresponding weights w, and apply an activation function $f(x)$ to it to get the output of that layer and feed it as an input to the next layer.

Without a nonlinearity, a unit would be just a simple linear function, and our network something such as a linear regression. When we think about traditional analytical models, such as linear regression or support vector machines, one of their primary limitations is their assumption of linearity or data being linearly separable. Part of the power of deep learning is our ability to move beyond these simple models into the world of **nonlinear functions**, and activation functions are our ticket there.

Another key property of activation functions that makes them a workhorse of deep learning is that they are **differentiable**. This allows us to use a technique called **backpropagation** to train neural networks, which we'll cover in an upcoming section.

Historically popular activation functions

Three activation functions that you will commonly see used are the `sigmoid`, `tanh`, and **Rectified Linear Unit (ReLU)** functions. While popular, each of these has a caveat that frequently comes with their use.

During the mid-early 2010s, it was popular to use sigmoids or tanh activation functions in the fully connected layers of a network. Sigmoids have fallen out of fashion, but you might still see them around. They are bounded between the values of 0 and 1 (that is: they can represent any value between that range).

```
import math
import numpy as np

def sigmoid(x):
  s_out = []
  for item in x:
      s_out.append(1/(1+math.exp(-item)))
  return s_out
```

We can easily plot a `sigmoid` function in Python to take a look:

```
x = np.arange(-10., 10., 0.2)
f = sigmoid(x)
plt.plot(f,sig)
plt.show()
```

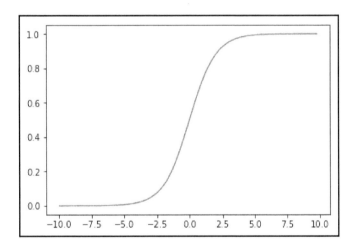

The function is also built into TensorFlow simply as `tf.sigmoid`. The `tanh` is a very similar function; it's simply a rescaled version of the sigmoid:

```
import numpy as np
import matplotlib.pyplot as plt

tanh = np.tanh(np.arange(-5, 5, .1))

fig = plt.figure()
ax = fig.add_subplot(111)
```

```
ax.plot(np.arange(-5, 5, .1), tanh)
ax.set_ylim([-1.0, 1.0])
ax.set_xlim([-5,5])
plt.show()
```

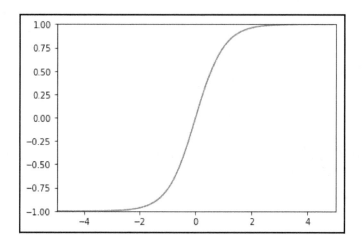

Likewise, the tanh function is available in TensorFlow simply as tf.tanh.

Both of these are prone to the vanishing gradient problem. Both sigmoid and tanh are both prone to what is known as **saturation**. When a unit saturates at either end of these functions, the gradient when weights are initialized too large, they become saturated.

Both the sigmoid and tanh functions are fundamentally bounded—they have limits. Nonlinearities become saturated when they take on values too close to the boundaries of these functions. Tanh, unlike sigmoid, is always centered on zero, and therefore, less likely to saturate. As such, it is always preferable to use tanh over sigmoid for your activation function.

As a result of the finicky nature of these activation functions, a new function began to be utilized in the late 2000s called **ReLU**:

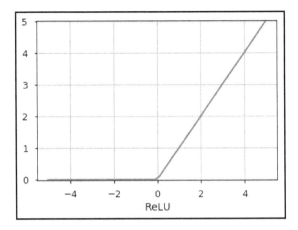

ReLU is a simple and efficient nonlinearity that computes the maximum:

$$f(x) = \max(0, x)$$

ReLU makes convergence (having a small error rate) much faster because of its linear and non-saturating nature, and its computational efficiency. ReLUs utilize matrices of zeros, which is significantly more efficient than the exponentials that sigmoids or tanh functions utilize, sometimes making them up to six times faster than tanh. ReLUs, on the other hand, run into an issue known as the *dying neuron problem*. ReLU nonlinearities can die in training when large gradients combined with odd weight updating causes the function to output a gradient of zero, as a result of having a large valued learning rate. Like the other activations function, ReLu is available in TensorFlow as `tf.nn.relu`.

In recent years, practitioners have backed away from the `sigmoid` and `tanh` functions and created more stable methods based on ReLU.

Modern approaches to activation functions

In recent years, several modifications have been made to the ReLU function to solve the dying neuron problem and make them more robust. Most notable of these is a solution called the **Leaky ReLU**. Leaky ReLU introduces a small slope to the ReLU function to keep potentially dead neurons alive, by allowing a small **gradient** to keep the units active. The Leaky ReLu function is available in TensorFlow as:

```
tf.nn.leaky_relu(features,alpha=0.2,name=None)
```

Another adaption, the **Parametric Rectified Linear Unit (PreLU)**, takes this further by making that small gradient a parameter that can be adjusted during training. Instead of predefining a slope of the function, the slope becomes an adaptable parameter, hence the *parametric* name. TensorFlow does not currently have a built-in implementation of PreLu, but we can easily create one ourselves. Let's define a function called `PreLu`:

```
## Parametric ReLu
def PreLu(x):
    alpha = tf.get_variable('alpha',x.get_shape()[-1],
initializer=tf.constant_initializer(0.0), dtype=tf.float32)
    p_bound = tf.nn.relu(x)
    n_bound = alpha * (x - abs(x)) * 0.5
    return p_bound + n_bound
```

Here, `alpha` is an array that is learned by the network as the adaptive slope. It has the same size as the input, x. The upper bound of our function is the same as standard ReLu—what we are really interested in is the lower bound where the activation functions can become saturated. That adaptive bound will be defined as:

$$a * (x - |x|) * 0.5$$

One last modern approach to prevent common faults with activation functions isn't an activation function at all it's a layer. Maxout layers are a new iteration on the traditional feedforward neural network that utilizes maxout units for activation functions. These maxout units are generalizations of the ReLUand Leaky ReLU functions.

Maxout computes:

$$\max(w_1^T x + b_1, w_2^T x + b_2)$$

ReLU and Leaky ReLU now become just special cases of `maxout`. While `maxout` units do not saturate and have mitigated the dying neuron problem, they double the number of parameters that each neuron has, leading to increasingly large parameter sets that can be hard to compute. Maxout layers are available in TensorFlow as:

```
tf.contrib.layers.maxout(inputs,num_units)
```

Where inputs are the `inputs` to the maxout layer, and `num_units` is the size of the layer.

So, what activation function should you use?

- When in doubt, utilize ReLU (just be careful with your learning rates)
- If you see dead neurons in your network, utilize Leaky ReLU or MaxOut
- Tanh is a valid option, but will work worse than ReLU, Leaky ReLU, or MaxOut
- Never use sigmoid

Weights and bias factors

Two key parts of ANNs are weights and biases. These elements help us squash and stretch our nonlinearities to help us better approximate a function.

Weights are applied at every transformation in a neural network, and help us stretch a function. They essentially change the steepness of the nonlinearity. **Bias factors** are important parts of ANNs as well; you've probably noticed them in the diagrams shown so far in this chapter. Bias factors are values that allow us to shift our activation function left or right to help us best approximate a natural function.

How does this work in practice? Let's say you have a simple two-neuron setup such as the one in the following diagram:

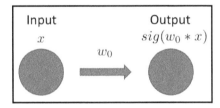

Let's see how adding weights into the mix can help change a function. In Python, we can represent this as a simple setup as a function that takes in the input data x, a weights matrix w, computes the dot product between them, and runs them through a non-linearity:

```
def single_output(x, w):
        return np.tanh(np.dot(x, w))
```

We can then run the function with various weight values, and plot it's output:

```
x = np.arange(-5, 5, .1)
f1 = single_output(x, 0.5)
f2 = single_output(x, 1.0)
f3 = single_output(x, 2.0)
plt.plot(x,f1)
plt.plot(x,f2)
```

```
plt.plot(x,f3)
plt.show()
```

If you run this code, you should see something such as the following chart:

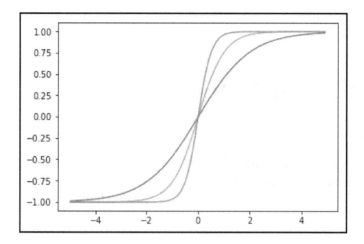

As you can see, the simple weight factor is bending our sigmoid depending on it's magnitude! Now, let's say that you want the network to output 0.5, when the input equals 5. With the help of a bias factor, we can achieve transformations of the sort:

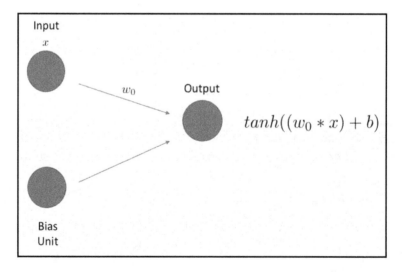

In Python, we simply have to add the bias factor to shift the output:

```
def single_output(x, w, b):
  return np.tanh(np.dot(x, w) + b)
```

Run the following code to see how different bias values can shift the curve from left and right; we'll set all of the weights to 1, so that we can clearly see the shift:

```
x = np.arange(-5, 5, .1)
f1 = single_output(x, 1.0, 2.0)
f2 = single_output(x, 1.0, 1.0)
f3 = single_output(x, 1.0, -2.0)
f4 = single_output(x, 1.0, 0.0)
plt.plot(x,f1)
plt.plot(x,f2)
plt.plot(x,f3)
plt.plot(x,f4)
plt.show()
```

The code should produce a curve such as the following. As you can see in the following graph, we've shifted the curve so that it better approximates the function we want:

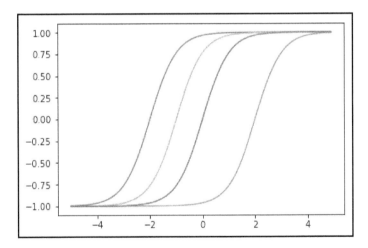

Weights and biases are updated during the training of a neural network. One of the goals of learning to adjust out weights and biases is so that our transformations throughout our network result in a value that is as close as possible to reality.

Utilizing weights and biases in our MNIST example

Let's get back to our MNIST example. Let's set up our weights and biases based on the network parameters that we defined before. We'll denote our weights for connections between our input layer and first hidden layer at `w1`, those between our first hidden layer and second hidden layer as `w2`, and those between our second hidden layer and output layer as `w_out`. Notice how the weights track the incoming size and the outgoing size of the data at a given layer:

```
weights = {
  'w1': tf.Variable(tf.random_normal([input_layer_size, hidden_layer_one])),
  'w2': tf.Variable(tf.random_normal([hidden_layer_one, hidden_layeR_two])),
  'w_out': tf.Variable(tf.random_normal([hidden_layer_two, number_classes]))
}

biases = {
  'b1': tf.Variable(tf.random_normal([hidden_layer_one])),
  'b2': tf.Variable(tf.random_normal([hidden_layer_two])),
  'b_out': tf.Variable(tf.random_normal([number_classes]))
}
```

Each of these will be be initialized as a TensorFlow variable whose value will be updated during training.

Loss functions

Loss functions are another essential building block of neural networks, and they measure the difference between our predictions and reality.

We tend to think of functions as mathematical expressions; which they are, but they also have a shape and surface, or topology. Topology in itself is an entire branch of mathematics and too much for the contents of this book, but the important takeaway is that these functions have topologies of peaks and valleys, much such as a real topological map would:

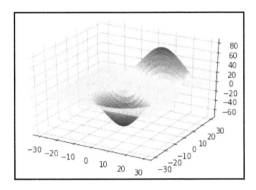

In the AI field, when creating neural networks, we seek to find the minimum point on these loss functions, called the **global minima**. This represents the point at which our rate of error (how far off we are) between our actual and predicted values is smallest. The process of getting to the global minima is called **convergence**.

Loss functions come in two variations:

- **Convex loss functions**: Loss functions that curve down, such as a bowl. These loss functions are the easiest way to find the global minima.
- **Non-convex loss functions**: Loss functions that look like the preceding example, with many peaks and valleys. These loss functions are the most difficult when it comes to finding the local minima.

Non-convex loss functions are difficult, because they may have two hazards called **local minima** and **saddle points**. Local minima are exactly what they sound such as: the valleys in the loss function that are not the lowest valleys across the entire topology:

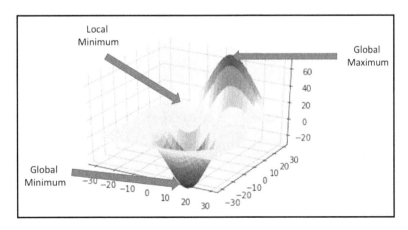

Saddle points are areas in the topology where the **gradient** is equal to zero. Learning algorithms get stuck at these points, and we'll address how to remedy this in our next section on the core learning algorithm of neural networks: **gradient descent**.

So, how do we choose a loss function for our network? The problem that we are trying to solve will determine which loss function we should choose for our network. Choosing an appropriate loss, function can be a lengthy task, so for now we'll focus on a few general rules. We can start with using the **mean square error** (**MSE**) loss function for regression problems.

Using a loss function for simple regression

Linear regression is one of the simplest models we can implement; you've probably used it before in your own job. Simple regression attempts to find the **line of best fit** for two linearly distributed variables. We can use all of the principles that we've precedingly learned about weights, biases, and loss functions, and apply them to a simple regression to see how they work together.

Now, let's get back to loss functions. MSE measures the average squared difference between an observation's actual and predicted values. The output is a single number representing the cost or score associated with our current set of weights:

$$MSE = 1\frac{1}{n}\sum_{t=1}^{n} e_2^t$$

Let's develop a linear regression in TensorFlow to see how `loss` functions, `weights`, and biases all work together. We are going to be using a small dataset on housing prices in Boston, which you can find in the folder that accompanies this chapter. Let's go ahead and import the data:

```
import pandas as pd
data = pd.read_csv('/users/patricksmith/desktop/housing-data.csv')
data.head()
```

Since this data is measured in all different types of units, let's go ahead and scale the data:

```
data = StandardScaler().fit_transform(data)
```

For our example, we are just going to conduct a simple regression, where we'll regress square footage against price. Let's go ahead and select those columns:

```
features = data[:,0]
labels = data[:,3]
```

At this point, let's quickly graph our data to ensure that it's linearly distributed:

```
plt.plot(features, labels, 'ro', label='Data')
plt.legend()
plt.show()
```

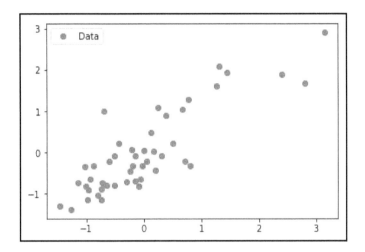

As you previously learned, all models in TensorFlow need to be initialized with placeholders. We'll initialize placeholders for the feature and label data, the weights of the network, and the bias factors:

```
X = tf.placeholder("float", name="X")
Y = tf.placeholder("float", name="Y")
W = tf.Variable(np.random.randn(), name="weights")
b = tf.Variable(np.random.randn(), name="biases")
```

Let's then setup our actual linear model. We'll be using a simple regression formula:

$$y = mx + b$$

You've probably seen this equation before; it's the general equation for a straight line, where *m* is the slope of the line, and *b* is the lines intercept on the *x*-axis. We are going to use it to find the line of best fit for our housing data. Remember how weights bend the slope of a function? In this example, we'll plug in the learned weights at *m* to help our algorithm learn the slope of the line of best bit. Our bias factor will become the *y*-intercept *b*:

```
linear_model = tf.add(tf.multiply(X, W), b)
```

1. Now that we have the linear model, we can define the MSE loss. Notice the `tf.reduce_mean` function - this is necessary with all `loss` functions in TensorFlow as it explicitly tells your algorithm to reduce the loss:

   ```
   loss = tf.reduce_mean(tf.square(linear_model - Y))
   ```

2. We'll then define an `optimizer`. While this may look unfamiliar at the moment, we'll go over it's function in a bit:

   ```
   optimizer =
   tf.train.GradientDescentOptimizer(learning_rate).minimize(loss)
   ```

3. Lastly, we'll define the training hyperparameters, just as we did with the machine learning models in Chapter 2, *Machine Learning Basics*. The parameter `epochs` will tell the model how long to train, `display` will tell it when to show the training information. The `learning_rate` function is a training hyperparameter that we'll be discussing in the next section:

   ```
   learning_rate = 0.001
   epochs = 1000
   display = 50
   job_dir = './'
   ```

If you recall TensorFlow sessions from Chapter 2, *Machine Learning Basics*, we'll have to initiate a session to run our computations through. In the session we'll initialize the variables, and run a training cycle for each of the training epochs that we precedingly defined. We then have to tell the session what to run; in this case, we feed it the optimization procedure, and give it the real values for the X and Y variable placeholders that we defined:

```
with tf.Session() as sess:
    sess.run(tf.global_variables_initializer())
    for epoch in range(epochs):
        sess.run(optimizer, feed_dict={X: features, Y: labels})
```

When constructing training processes in TensorFlow, it's helpful to write a handler that will calculate the loss at each `epoch` so that we know how our training is proceeding. This is a place where you can calculate and output accuracy or other metrics that you'd like to keep track of during training. For our case, we'll print out the loss, value of the weight at that iteration, and the value of the loss at that iteration:

```
if (epoch+1) % display == 0:
            c = sess.run(loss, feed_dict={X: features, Y: labels})
            print("Epoch:", '%04d' % (epoch+1), "loss=",
    "{:.9f}".format(c), \
                "Weight Value=", sess.run(W), "Bias Value=", sess.run(b))
```

Lastly, let's print out our best fit line. We'll need to run this operation within the session in order to access certain value and operations:

```
plt.plot(features, labels, 'ro', label='Data')
    plt.plot(features, sess.run(W) * features + sess.run(b),
label='Regression Line')
    plt.legend()
    plt.show()
```

Now, go ahead and run the training operation and take a look at how the loss, weight value, and bias value changed throughout the training:

```
Epoch: 0050 loss= 0.601646066 Weight Value= 0.43415096 Bias Value= -0.39439365
Epoch: 0100 loss= 0.541292369 Weight Value= 0.47423694 Bias Value= -0.35682642
Epoch: 0150 loss= 0.491888851 Weight Value= 0.51050466 Bias Value= -0.3228376
Epoch: 0200 loss= 0.451448590 Weight Value= 0.543318 Bias Value= -0.29208636
Epoch: 0250 loss= 0.418345660 Weight Value= 0.5730055 Bias Value= -0.26426417
Epoch: 0300 loss= 0.391248673 Weight Value= 0.59986526 Bias Value= -0.23909216
Epoch: 0350 loss= 0.369068146 Weight Value= 0.62416625 Bias Value= -0.21631786
Epoch: 0400 loss= 0.350911766 Weight Value= 0.64615273 Bias Value= -0.1957129
Epoch: 0450 loss= 0.336049646 Weight Value= 0.6660447 Bias Value= -0.1770706
Epoch: 0500 loss= 0.323883951 Weight Value= 0.68404204 Bias Value= -0.1602041
Epoch: 0550 loss= 0.313925475 Weight Value= 0.70032513 Bias Value= -0.14494416
Epoch: 0600 loss= 0.305773795 Weight Value= 0.7150573 Bias Value= -0.13113779
Epoch: 0650 loss= 0.299101114 Weight Value= 0.72838616 Bias Value= -0.11864646
Epoch: 0700 loss= 0.293639064 Weight Value= 0.74044544 Bias Value= -0.10734498
Epoch: 0750 loss= 0.289168060 Weight Value= 0.7513558 Bias Value= -0.097120024
Epoch: 0800 loss= 0.285508215 Weight Value= 0.7612271 Bias Value= -0.08786903
Epoch: 0850 loss= 0.282512337 Weight Value= 0.7701583 Bias Value= -0.07949924
Epoch: 0900 loss= 0.280060112 Weight Value= 0.7782385 Bias Value= -0.0719267
Epoch: 0950 loss= 0.278052747 Weight Value= 0.7855489 Bias Value= -0.065075435
Epoch: 1000 loss= 0.276409566 Weight Value= 0.7921633 Bias Value= -0.058876768
```

You'll want to pay attention to two things here. First, the loss - notice how it's continually going down? This means our model is in fact optimizing itself during the training cycle. Secondly, notice how the weights and bias values change? This the the regression model attempting to find the optimal slope/intercept combination for the line.

As you can see, our regression fit to the data quite well!

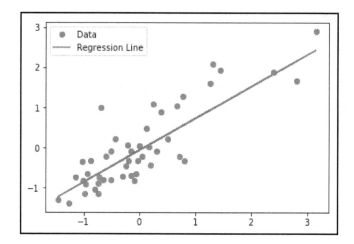

Congratulations! In this small example you successfully trained your first model in TensorFlow. Now, let's get back to learning about more essential model building blocks.

Using cross-entropy for binary classification problems

While we can use MSE for regression problems, we need to use a different type of loss for classification problems. For that, we use a function known as **cross-entropy**. Cross entropy measure the performance of a classification model whose outputs are between 0 and 1. A low cross entropy means that a predicted classification is similar to the actual classification. A high cross entropy, on the other hand, means that a predicted classification is different from the real classification.

It's also known as **Bernoulli negative log-likelihood** and **Binary cross-entropy**:

```
def CrossEntropy(yHat, y):
    if yHat == 1:
        return -log(y)
    else:
        return -log(1 - y)
```

Defining `loss` functions for classification problems with more than one right answer can be a bit more tricky; we'll cover this as we work through multi-class classification in the following chapters. We'll talk about customizing your `loss` functions towards the end of this book.

Defining a loss function in our MNIST example

Since we have a basic binary classification task of, recognizing digits, we're going to utilize `cross entropy` as our `loss` function. We can easily implement it with a built-in function in TensorFlow:

```
loss =
tf.reduce_mean(tf.nn.softmax_cross_entropy_with_logits(network_output, y))
```

Stochastic gradient descent

Gradient descent is the means by which we find the global minima in our loss function, and it's how neural networks learn. In gradient descent, we calculate the value of individual **gradients**, or slopes of the loss function. This helps us reach our minima. Think about descending a hill blindfolded; the only way you can reach the bottom is by feeling the slope of the ground. In gradient descent, we use calculus to feel what the slope of the ground is, to make sure we are headed in the right direction towards our minima's.

In bland old gradient descent, we have to calculate the loss of every single sample that is being passed into the network at a given time, resulting in many redundant calculations.

We can mitigate this redundancy by utilizing a method called **stochastic gradient descent**. Stochastic gradient descent is actually one of the simplest procedures available for optimization. It just so happens that it also works surprisingly well. Typically with deep learning, we are working with high-dimensional data. Unlike with vanilla gradient descent, with stochastic gradient descent we're able to approximate the gradient from a given pass by sampling the loss of one particular data point at a time, reducing redundancy.

Learning rates

Because stochastic gradient descent randomly samples, our location along the surface of our loss function jumps all over the place! We can mitigate this behavior by decreasing a parameter known as our **learning rate**. The learning rate is something called a **hyperparameter**, a parameter that controls the training process of the network. Learning rates control how much we are adjusting the weights of our network, with respect to the gradient of the loss function. In other words, it determines how quickly or slowly we descend while trying to reach our global minimum. The lower the value, the slower we descend downhill, just like on the right in the diagram as described as follows. Think of slowly rolling a tire down a hill - the more we control the movement, the more it will stay on track.

Now on the other hand, think of letting a tire free roll down a hill; the velocity combining with it's natural bounciness is going to send it all over the place! This is exactly what happens with a higher learning rate value; we proceed going downhill too quickly, and risk bouncing around to the wrong place, just like the left side of the diagram following.

In our MNIST example, we'll define the `learning_rate` as a parameter that the network will use during training:

```
learning_rate = 0.001
```

While it's tempting to utilize a small learning rate, this can lead to slow convergence, longer training times, and ultimately more expense (computational or real!) on our GPUs. We can overcome this problem with a common optimizer for stochastic gradient descent and our learning rate.

Utilizing the Adam optimizer in our MNIST example

The **adaptive gradient descent method** (**Adam**) takes an initial learning rate and adaptively computes updates to it. Adam stores an exponentially decaying average of past squared gradients and of past gradients, which amounts to measuring something similar to momentum. This helps us prevent overshooting or undershooting during our training process.

Adam is easily implemented in TensorFlow with the following command line:

```
tf.train.AdamOptimizer(learning_rate=learning_rate).minimize(loss_func)
```

The `tf.train` class contains various different optimizers that are executed at runtime and contain TensorFlow's version of the Adam optimizer; it takes our initially defined `learning_rate` as a parameter. We then call the `minimize` method and pass it to our `loss` function, wrapping up our learning processing into one object, called `optimizer`.

Regularization

Recall from the `Chapter 2`, *Machine Learning Basics* that overfitting and underfitting can happen when a machine learning model learns it's training dataset too well, or when it doesn't learn it well enough. Artificial neural networks are not immune from this problem! Overfitting often occurs in neural network because the amount of parameters that they have is too large for the training data. In other words, the model is too complex for the amount of data that it is being trained on.

One way that we can prevent overfitting in our networks is through a technique called **regularization**. Regularization works by shrinking the parameters of a model to create a less-complex model, thereby reducing overfitting. Let's say we have a loss function $f(\theta)$, regularization adds the penalty term λ so that that the entire loss function becomes:

$$error + \lambda(\theta)$$

There are three forms of regularization:

- **L1 Regularization**: Penalizes the absolute value of a weight; often forces weight values to be zero
- **L2 Regularization**: Penalizes the squared value of a weight; forces weight values to be smaller number
- **Dropout**: A method specific to ANNs that randomly cuts out nodes and their connections during different training cycles

Regularization can be used with the neural network models that we will be creating in the coming chapters. Now that we have the tools that we need to build ANNs let's go ahead and start assembling our MNIST network for training.

The training process

Training is the process by which we teach a neural network to learn, and it's controlled programmatically in our code. Recall, from `Chapter 2`, *Machine Learning Basics*, that there are two forms of learning in the AI world: supervised learning and unsupervised learning. In general, most ANNs are supervised learners, and they learn by example from a **training set**. A singular unit in a training cycle in a neural network is called an **epoch.** By the end of one epoch, your network has been exposed to every data point in the dataset once. At the end of one epoch, epochs are defined as a **hyperparameter** when first setting up your network. Each of these epochs contain two processes: **forward propagation** and **backpropagation**.

Within an epoch we have **iterations**, which tell us what proportion of the data has gone through both forward propagation and backpropagation. For instance, if we have a dataset with 1,000 data points and send them all through forward propagation and backpropagation at once, we would have one iteration within an epoch; however, sometimes, to speed up training, we want to break down the amount of data to go through in one pass, so we **minibatch** the data. We could minibatch the 1,000-point dataset into four iterations of 250 data points each, all within a singular epoch.

Putting it all together

Now that we've gone through all of the elements of a basic feedforward neural network, it's time to begin assembling the pieces. The first thing we'll do is define our **hyperparameters.** We'll train the network for 50 epochs, each time feeding a batch of 100 samples into the network. At the end of each epoch, the `batch_size` parameters will tell the network to print out the current value of the loss, as well as the accuracy of the network:

```
## Network Parameters
epochs = 15
batch_size = 100
display_step = 1
```

Next, we'll create `placeholders` for our MNIST data features (*x*) and their correct label (*y*), which we'll use to represent the data while constructing the network:

```
# Create the Variables
x = tf.placeholder("float", [None, input_layer_size])
y = tf.placeholder("float", [None, number_classes])
```

Now it's time to assemble our layers. We'll define the network, and give it the parameters of x for our training data, `weights`, and `biases`. The `tf.add` function adds a layer to our network, and `tf.matmul` defines the matrix multiplication operation that will happen between the layers. We then pass the results through the activation function with `tf.nn.relu`, and repeat for the next layers:

```
def feedforward_network(x, weights, biases):
    ## First layer; a hidden layer with RELU activation
    layer_1 = tf.nn.relu(tf.add(tf.matmul(x, weights['w1']), biases['b1']))

    ## Second layer; a hidden layer with RELU activation function
    layer_2 = tf.nn.relu(tf.add(tf.matmul(layer_1,
weights['w2']),biases['b2']))

    ## Output layer; utilizes a linear activation function
    outputLayer = tf.matmul(layer_2, weights['w_out']) + biases['b_out']
    ## Return the Last Layer
    return outputLayer
```

Forward propagation

Forward propagation is the process of how information flows through our network during the learning phase of training. Before we walk through the process, let's return to our MNIST example. First, we need to initialize the feedforward network that we precedingly created. To do that, we can simply create an instance of the function, and feed it the input placeholder, as well as the weight and bias dictionaries:

```
network_output = feedforward_network(x, weights, biases)
```

This model instance gets fed into our `loss` function that we preceedingly defined:

```
loss_func =
tf.reduce_mean(tf.nn.softmax_cross_entropy_with_logits(logits=network_outpu
t, labels=y))
```

Which subsequently gets fed into the optimizer we defined:

```
training_procedure =
tf.train.AdamOptimizer(learning_rate=learning_rate).minimize(loss_func)
```

With all of this defined, you can begin to see why placeholders are so essential in TensorFlow. The placeholders for the input, as well as the randomly initialized weights and biases, provide a basis for which TensorFlow builds the model from. Without these, the program wouldn't know how to compile the network because it wouldn't have any concept of the input, output, weight, and bias values.

Training happens behind the scenes in TensorFlow, so let's walk through the process manually to gain a better understanding of what's under the hood. At its simplest, forward propagation is just matrix multiplications offset by a bias unit, and then processed through activation functions. Let's look at the example of the following singular unit, where *X1:X3* represents our input layer (plus a bias value), and the empty unit represents a node in the hidden layer:

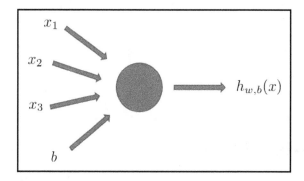

Each connection between an input value and a hidden layer unit represents a multiplication of the input value times the weight:

$$conn = x1 \cdot w1$$

Remember, both our inputs as well as our weights are matrices, so we represent their multiplication as the **dot product**. We take those values and sum them all together, so $(x1 \cdot w1) + (x2 \cdot w2) + (x3 \cdot w3)$. Finally, we take the result of that operation, and feed it through our hidden layer's activation function.

Let's say that we are utilizing a ReLU as the activation function of our hidden layer units; then our unit computes:

$$f(x) = \max(0, x) = \max(0, (x1 \cdot w1) + (x2 \cdot w2) + (x3 \cdot w3) + bias)$$

The output of this function is then multiplied by a second set of weight matrices, just as we did with the output of the first layer. This process can be repeated over and over depending on how many hidden layers are in our network:

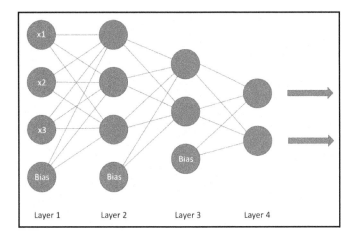

Our last layer of the network often contains a squashing function, such as a softmax to output prediction values. At the end of this whole process, our error from that pass is calculated, and the error is sent back through the network in a process called **backpropagation**.

Backpropagation

Backpropagation, or **Backprop**, is a core learning algorithm that we utilize in AI applications, and learning about it will be essential to creating and debugging your neural networks going forward. Short for **backpropagation of error**, it is the means by which ANNs calculate how erroneous they are with their predictions.

You can think of it as the complement to the gradient descent optimization algorithm that we precedingly discussed. Recall that at their core, ANNs seek to learn a set of weight parameters that help them approximate a function that replicates our training data. Backpropagation measures how error changes after each training cycle, and gradient descent tries to optimize the error. Backprop computes the gradient but doesn't know what to do with them. It doesn't learn from the gradients, it simply tells us what they are and those gradients can be learned from by gradient descent, however, and so to provide the necessary input for the gradient descent algorithm to run it's optimization, backpropagation needs to set up those gradients before a new training cycle begins. Those gradients will tell the gradient descent algorithm which direction to go when trying to minimize error, they are our map down the hill to the valley, and so the two methods work hand in hand to optimize a network.

Formally, Backprop is defined as:

> *"Backpropagation is the process of calculating the gradients of functions through the recursive application of the **chain rule**."*

Error is calculated at the output layer of the network, and is propagated back through the network. Recall that our loss function is a measure of the difference between the predicted distribution of our target data, and its actual distribution.

While we'll often have TensorFlow do most of the work with BackProp going forward, understanding what's under the hood here is important. Most explanations of BackProp tend to abstract away from the idea to a point where it is hard to understand the mechanics; in computer science terms, this is called a **leaky abstraction**.

Backpropagation sends our network's error back through our network by taking partial derivatives of the loss function. Basically, it's deciding how much the algorithm will need to change it's weights by in order to compensate for any bad predictions it just made on the forward pass. At each node in the network, it calculates the error with respect to the weights:

$$\frac{dE}{dw}$$

All we're doing here is simple calculus. Once we've calculated this derivative, we can then calculate how much that weight needs to be updated:

$$w = w - \alpha \frac{dE}{dw}$$

Let's break this down. Here, we are saying that the new weight, w, is equal to the derivative of the error with regards to the current weight, times the network's learning rate α. For each node, we also compute a derivative with respect the input to the node:

$$\frac{dE}{dx}$$

and another with respect to the output of the node:

$$\frac{dE}{dy}$$

In order to keep track of how error changes as data flows through. Starting with the output node of the network, this is calculated again and between each different function combination in the network, until all of the gradients have been calculated. Take the following example:

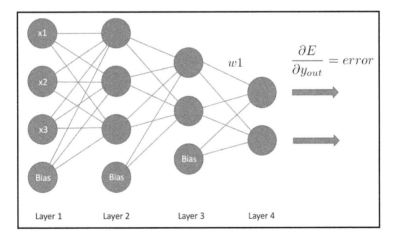

We calculating the gradients with the output layer of the network. Given that we know what the ending value of the network's error was, we can set that as the value of the derivative for the output. Now that we have a starting point, we can use the chain rule to calculate the derivative for the node's input:

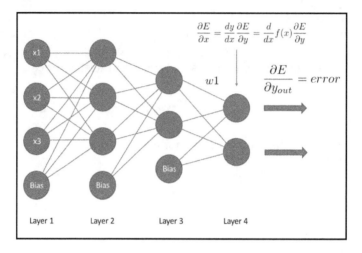

$$\frac{\partial E}{\partial x} = \frac{dy}{dx}\frac{\partial E}{\partial y} = \frac{d}{dx}f(x)\frac{\partial E}{\partial y}$$

Here, f(x) is the activation function for the node. From there, we can calculate the derivative for the corresponding weight:

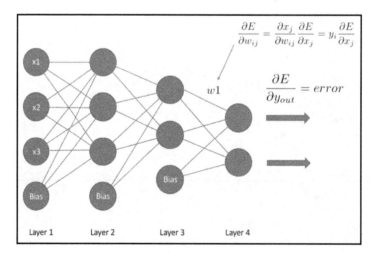

$$\frac{\partial E}{\partial w_{ij}} = \frac{\partial x_j}{\partial w_{ij}} \frac{\partial E}{\partial x_j} = y_i \frac{\partial E}{\partial x_j}$$

This output then becomes the starting point to take the derivatives of the next node down using the first equations precedingly defined, and so on all the way down the network until we reach the nodes of the input layer.

In recent years, many have become suspicious about backpropagation, including Geoffrey Hinton himself. Researchers have found that a method called **synthetic gradients** decouples layers so that backpropagation is not needed. Each layer uses data on the forward pass to try to estimate what the gradient will be, and hence each layer can learn in isolation from the other layers. This drastically speeds up training and stability. Although outside the context of this introductory book, Synthetic Gradients are an exciting invention in the AI world at the moment.

Forwardprop and backprop with MNIST

Remember that, to run a training process in TensorFlow, we run our computations through a session. To get started, let's open a new training session.

1. In TensorFlow, before we enter the training process, we need to initialize our model class as an object, and bring all of our variable placeholders online with the tf.global_variables_initializer() command:

```
with tf.Session() as sess:
    ## Initialize the variable
    sess.run(tf.global_variables_initializer())
```

2. Now, we can write the core of the training process, which is what we call the training loop. We'll define the loop by the number of training epochs for the model. In it, we'll first batch out our incoming data; our model cannot and should not handle all of the data at once, and so we define the total amount of the incoming samples by the batch size of 100 that we precedingly defined. So in this case, for each epoch in the 15 epochs that we've told the network to train, we'll run 100 samples of the training data through each time:

```
for epoch in range(epochs):

    ## Batch the incoming data
    total_batch = int(mnist.train.num_examples/batch_size)
```

3. Within the same loop, we'll create another loop that runs the training process by batch. We'll create a batch for the x and y data, and run those examples through a TensorFlow session that runs the training procedure and computes the loss:

```
for batch in range(total_batch):
            batch_x, batch_y = mnist.train.next_batch(batch_size)
            _, loss = sess.run([training_procedure, loss_func],
feed_dict={x: batch_x, y: batch_y})
```

4. So far, we've defined the bare minimum that's necessary to train a model in TensorFlow. In addition to the training procedure itself, you'll also often see a procedure to keep track of the current value of the loss, as well as accuracy metrics so that we know how well (or poorly) our model is training. For that, we'll define a loop that's at the level of the batching loop precedingly defined, so that it runs at the end of each training epoch. In it, fetch the predictions from the network at that epoch by running the output of the network through a `softmax` function. Softmax functions spit out probabilities for which class a sample potentially belongs to in a classification problem:

```
if epoch % display == 0:
            pred = tf.nn.softmax(network_output)
```

5. Once we have those probabilities, we need to select the highest probability from the tensor that's returned out of the softmax. Fortunately for us, TensorFlow has an easy function for this called `tf.argmax`. Once we have that, we can compare it against the actual value of y that we should have expected:

```
correct_prediction = tf.equal(tf.argmax(pred, 1), tf.argmax(y, 1))
```

6. Once we have the correct prediction, we can calculate the `accuracy`, save a model checkpoint, and return the current epoch, value of the loss function, and accuracy of the model at that step:

```
accuracy = tf.reduce_mean(tf.cast(correct_prediction, "float"))
saver.save(sess, save_model)
print("Epoch:", '%04d' % (epoch+1), "loss {:.9f}".format(loss),
"Accuracy:", accuracy.eval({x: mnist.test.images, y:
mnist.test.labels}))
```

7. At the end of the training process, you should see an output such as follows:

```
Epoch: 0001 loss=27.935014725 Accuracy: 0.8691
Epoch: 0002 loss=30.841621399 Accuracy: 0.9005
Epoch: 0003 loss=25.148893356 Accuracy: 0.9149
Epoch: 0004 loss=5.794556141 Accuracy: 0.9202
Epoch: 0005 loss=10.781435966 Accuracy: 0.926
Epoch: 0006 loss=6.771206856 Accuracy: 0.9327
Epoch: 0007 loss=3.539288044 Accuracy: 0.9327
Epoch: 0008 loss=13.814244270 Accuracy: 0.9349
Epoch: 0009 loss=3.350750446 Accuracy: 0.9355
Epoch: 0010 loss=0.000006614 Accuracy: 0.9401
Epoch: 0011 loss=0.319492191 Accuracy: 0.9366
Epoch: 0012 loss=1.493563175 Accuracy: 0.9419
Epoch: 0013 loss=0.963657975 Accuracy: 0.9403
Epoch: 0014 loss=0.722837269 Accuracy: 0.9431
Epoch: 0015 loss=0.000000000 Accuracy: 0.9429
```

Now that we've setup our network and trained it, let's go ahead and look at a few tools that can help us inspect it's training progress.

Managing a TensorFlow model

TensorBoard is a tool built into TensorFlow that visualizes the values of your network's parameters over the coarse of the training process. It can also help to visualize data, and can run several exploratory analysis algorithms. It helps you explore the underlying TensorFlow graph in a simple, easy to use graphical interface.

Once a TensorFlow model is trained, say the MNIST example defined precedingly, TensorFlow allows us to create something called a **Model Summary**. Summaries are, as you probably guessed, condensed versions of a model that contain the necessary key aspects that we need to use TensorBoard.

1. To create a summary, we first need to initialize the `writer`; we'll insert the line preceding just before we start the training loop in the preceding example:

```
with tf.Session() as sess:
    writer = tf.summary.FileWriter("output_directory", sess.graph)
```

2. Then, add the following line as follows, which tells TensorBoard to launch utilizing the your model. In this case, `network_output` is the end output of our feedforward network:

```
print(sess.run(network_output))
writer.close()
```

3. Then, in your terminal, run the following command, replacing `file_name` with the name of your program, and `output_directory` with the name of the directory where you plan to save the model summary:

```
python file_name.py
tensorboard --logdir="./output_directory"
```

Saving model checkpoints

In Tensorflow, a checkpoint is a binary file that contains the model weights and gradients that were calculated during training. Should you want to load up a model for further training, or access the model at a certain point during training, we can save and restore checkpoints with all of the training information that we need. To save a checkpoint, we can use a saver utility that is provided to us in native TensorFlow:

```
save_model = os.path.join(job_dir, 'saved_mnist.ckpt')
saver = tf.train.Saver()
```

Then, during the training cycle, we can periodically save checkpoints by calling the `saver`:

```
saver.save(sess, save_model)
```

Note that you can choose to save the model checkpoints in whatever directory that you wish. A TensorFlow saver will create three files:

- A `.meta` file that describes the structure of the saved graph
- A `.data` file that stores the values of all of the variables in the graph (The weights and gradients)
- A `.index` file which identifies the particular checkpoint

To re-load a TensorFlow model from it's checkpoints, we load the meta graph, and then restore the values of the graph's variables within a TensorFlow session. Here, `meta_dir` is the location of the `.meta` file, and `restore_dir` is the location of the `.data` file:

```
init = tf.global_variables_initializer()
saver = tf.train.import_meta_graph(meta_dir)
with tf.Session() as sess:
    sess.run(init)
    saver.restore(sess, restore_dir)
```

TensorFlow checkpoints can only be used in training, not for deploying a model. There is a separate process for readying a model for deployment, and we will cover it in `Chapter 13`, *Deploy and Maintaining AI Applications*.

Summary

Feedforward networks are a basic and essential class of network. This chapter has helped us study the building blocks of neural networks, and will help illuminate network topics going forward.

Feedforward neural networks are best represented as directed graphs; information flows through in one direction and is transformed by matrix multiplications and activation functions. Training cycles in ANNs are broken into epochs, each of which contains a forward pass and a backwards pass. On the forward pass, information flows from the input layer, is transformed via its connections with the output layers and their activation functions, and is put through an output layer function that renders the output in the form we want it; probabilities, binary classifications, so on. At the end of one of these training cycles, we calculate our error rate based on our loss function; how far are we from producing the correct answer? The error is backpropagated through the network with the chain rule of calculus, and we begin another training epoch.

When it comes to activation functions, remember that ReLU and its variations are your best bet for success. Recall that we should almost never use the sigmoid activation function in practice, as the `tanh` function is much less prone to saturation.

We've covered the basics of ANNs, but this is only the beginning. Throughout the rest of this book, we'll expand upon this knowledge by learning about individual networks and their functions, as well as, toward the end of the book, talking about advanced optimization techniques. In the next chapter, we'll touch upon the basic building blocks of convolutions, pooling layers, and other elements, and also construct a Convolutional Neural Network for image tagging.

Convolutional Neural Networks 5

Convolutional Neural Networks (**CNNs**), or **ConvNets**, are a special class of feedforward networks; they are primarily used for computer vision tasks, but have also been adapted to other domains with unstructured data, such as natural language processing. As they are feedforward networks, they are very similar to the simple networks that we just learned about; information passes through them in one direction, and they are made up of layers, weights, and biases.

CNNs are the image recognition methods used by Facebook for image tagging, Amazon for product recommendations, and by self-driving cars for recognizing objects in their field of vision. In this chapter, we'll discuss the functions that make CNNs different from standard feedforward networks, and then jump into some examples of how to apply them to a variety of tasks.

In this chapter, we will be covering the following topics:

- Convolutions
- Pooling layers
- Fully formed convolutional neural networks
- Convolutional neural networks for image tagging

Overview of CNNs

CNNs are one of the most influential classes of networks in the history of deep learning. Invented by Yann LeCun (now head of **Facebook Artificial Intelligence Research**), CNNs really came into their own in 2012, with the introduction of deep Convolutional Neural Networks by Alex Krizhevsky.

Plain old neural networks don't scale well to images; CNNs adapt regular old feedforward neural networks by adding one or more convolutional layers as the input layer to the network. These convolutions are specifically designed to take in two-dimensional input, such as images or even sound, as illustrated in the following diagram:

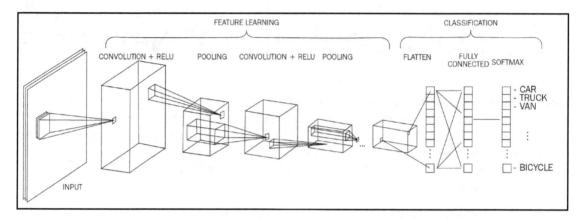

As you can see, CNNs add these layers of convolutions together with something called, appropriately **pooling layers** in order to insert an image. The second part of the network is nothing more than the standard feedforward network that we've already discussed.

Convolutional layers

Suppose we have an image recognition program to identify objects in an image, such as the example we referred to previously. Now imagine how hard it would be to try and classify an image with a standard feedforward network; each pixel in the image would be a feature that would have to be sent through the network with its own set of parameters. Our parameter space would be quite large, and we could likely run out of computing power! Images, which in technical terms are just high-dimensional vectors, require some special treatment.

What would happen if we were to try and accomplish this task with a basic feedforward network? Let's recall that basic feedforward networks operate on top of vector spaces. We start with an image, which is made up of independent pixels. Let's say our image is 32 pixels by 32 pixels; the input to our convolutional layer would be *32 x 32 x 3*, where *3* represent the RGB color scale of images. To translate this to vector space, we'd end up with a *3072 x 1* vector to represent the entire image:

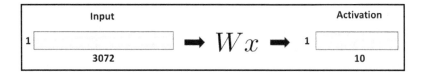

Let's also say our network has **10** neuron units; using the simple feedforward model, our weight matrix alone would have **30,720** learnable parameters. CNNs mitigate this problem, as well as others, with their convolutional layers.

Convolutional layers have four parameters that we have to define when we create a CNN:

- The number of filters, K
- The size of each filter, F
- The stride, S
- The amount of zero padding, P

In the next section, we'll walk through each of these and look at how they play into the structure of the network.

Layer parameters and structure

Convolutional layers allow us to preserve the original image dimensions, thereby improving our ability to learn features and reduce our computational load. They do this by utilizing something called a **filter,** which slides across the image, learning features by computing dot products. For example, a typical filter on the first layer of a CNN might have size *5 x 5 x 3* (namely, *5* pixels width and height, and *3* because images have a depth of three colors, RGB).

Mathematically, it's done as follows:

$$w^T x + b$$

Here, w represents our filter, but it also represents our learnable weights. We take a transpose of our input filter, multiply it by our input x, and add our bias term b. In our case, the *5 x 5 x 3* filter would result in a *75–* dimensional dot product, plus a bias term. Each of our filters will be looking for different characteristics of the image, which we'll then aggregate into a full view of the sample.

During the forward pass of the network we slide, or **convolve**, each of the convolutional layers filters over the height and weight of the input volume for that filter. Imagine that the following grid represents an image; our filter would be the *3 x 3* blue squares. We will move this filter across the image grid one unit at a time, computing dot products at each move:

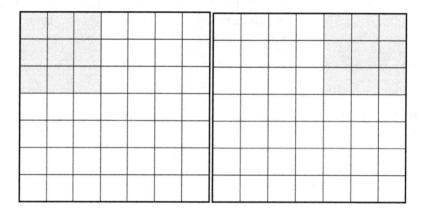

The length that we move the filter across the image is called its **stride**. If we use a stride of 1 on this image, we will end up with a 5 x 5 output from our original 7 x 7 frame; our filter will have moved five spatial locations horizontally, and five spatial locations vertically. Stride is limited by the dimensions of our image; we can't use a stride of 3 on the preceding image, as it would not match up with the image's dimensions:

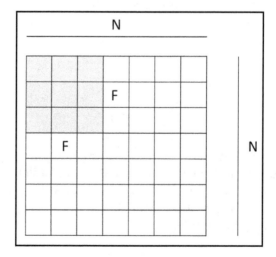

We can determine the output of a given filter by a simple formula, where N and F represent the length of the axes in the preceding diagram:

$$\frac{N - F}{stride + 1}$$

It's common practice to pad the borders of our images with zeros, colloquially known as **zero padding**, which allows us to control the input spatial size of our image. It's most common to see convolutional layers with a stride of one filters of an F x F size, and zero padding of $\frac{f - 1}{2}$. It's important to select a filter size that is not too large, as it will shrink the input over the convolutional layers too quickly, and we might potentially lose out on information. One of the great features of these convolutional layers is that they are stackable – you can feed the output of one convolutional layer into another, all the while extracting different features from your sample.

Pooling layers

Convolutional layers are often intertwined with **pooling layers**, which down sample the output of the previous convolutional layer in order to decrease the amount of parameters we need to compute. A particular form of these layers, **max pooling layers**, has become the most widely used variant. In general terms, max pooling layers tell us if a feature was present in the region, the previous convolutional layer was looking at; it looks for the most significant value in a particular region (the maximum value), and utilizes that value as a representation of the region, as shown as follows:

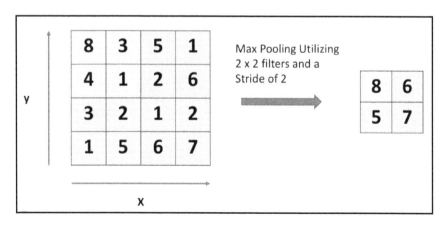

Max pooling layers help subsequent convolutional layers focus on larger sections of the data, providing abstractions of the that help both reduce overfitting and the amount of hyperparameters that we have to learn, ultimately reducing our computational cost. This form of automatic feature selection also helps prevent overfitting by preventing the network from focusing on too-specific areas of the image.

Fully connected layers

The **fully connected layer** of a CNN works in the same manner as that of a vanilla feedforward network. This layer maps the outputs extracted from the image to the outputs that we desire from the network, such as a label for an image:

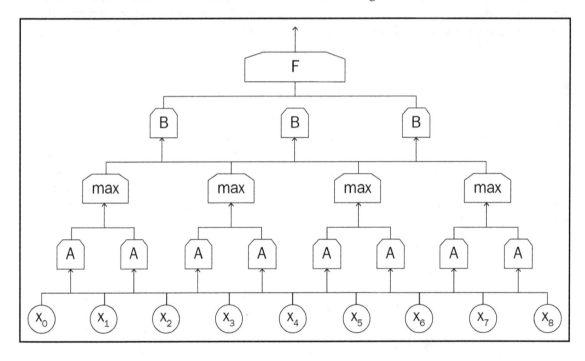

In the preceding diagram, our inputs are represented by the blue nodes, which are fed into the first convolutional layer, A. We then have a max pooling layer, a second convolutional layer, and finally the fully connected layer, which transforms our output into human–readable output. As with vanilla feedforward networks, we typically use a cross-entropy loss function for classification tasks.

The training process

When we connect convolutional layers, a hyperparameter known as the **receptive field** or **filter size** prevents us from having to connect the unit to the entire input, but rather focuses on learning a particular feature. Our convolutional layers typically learn features from simple to complex. The first layer typically learns low-level features, the next layer learns mid-level features, and the last convolutional layer learns high-level features. One of the beautiful features of this is that we do not explicitly tell the network to learn different features at these various levels; it learns to differentiate its task in this manner through the training process:

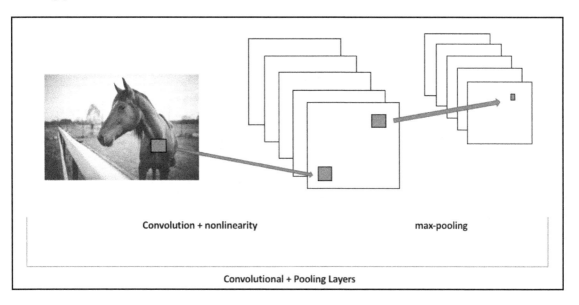

Convolution + nonlinearity   max-pooling

Convolutional + Pooling Layers

As we pass through this process, our network will develop a two-dimensional **activation map** to track the response of that particular filter at a given position. The network will learn to keep filters that activate when they reach an edge of a shape, or perhaps the color of an object. Sometimes, these will be lines and smaller pieces of the puzzle, or perhaps a filter will learn entire subsections of the image, maybe the horses' ears, in the preceding diagram. Each filter for a specific convolutional layer leaves us with individual activation maps. If we have six filters for the image, we would have six activation maps, each focusing on something different within the image:

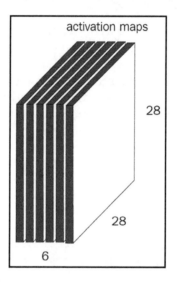

Our convolutional layers then become a sequence of stacked individual layers, interspersed by ReLU activation functions. We typically use ReLU or Leaky ReLU here to increase the training speed:

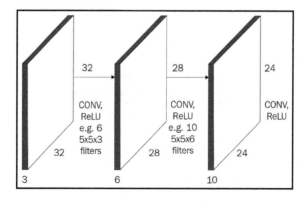

Between these convolutional layers, we add in our max pooling layers. The output of these combined convolutional + max pooling layers will be sent to a fully connected layer, which will contain our transformation for classification and other tasks. Once we reach the end of a forward pass, the error is backpropagated through the network in the same manner as vanilla feedforward networks.

CNNs for image tagging

Let's work on putting our new knowledge of CNNs to the test. We're going to work through one of the most popular tasks for CNNs: image classification.

In an image classification task, our horse looks at a given image and determines the probability that a certain object is an image. In the following example, the image is 248 pixels wide, 400 pixels tall, and has three color channels: **red**, **green**, and **blue** (RGB). Therefore, the image consists of *248 x 400 x 3* numbers, or a total of 2,97, 600 numbers. Our job is to turn these numbers into a single classified label; is this horse?

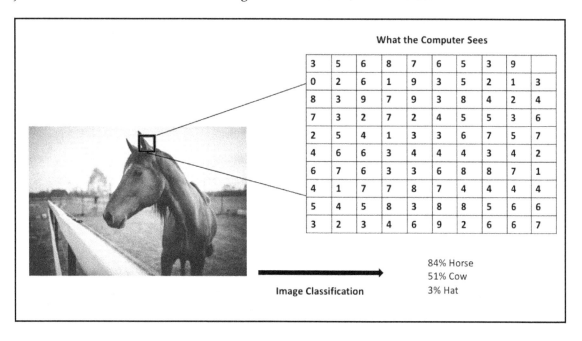

While this might seem a simple task for a human to perform, there are many challenges in trying to complete this with a computer:

- **Clouded vision**: An image of an object could be blurry
- **Variation in point of view**: An object could be seen from a variety of 360-degree views
- **Illumination inconsistencies**: Light could be shining on an object in a certain manner
- **Variations in scale**: Objects could be large or small
- **Variations in type**: Objects of certain types take lots of forms

When problems such as a classification task are solved by a network, however, the tasks are often performed immensely faster than if a human were performing them.

 For this example, we are going to utilize an open dataset that contains images of cats and dogs. We'll have 25,000 training images and 12,500 test images.

Now onto the code. We're going to try and classify images as containing a cat or a dog. Let's get started with our imports. As usual, I'll walk through the code by providing comments alongside each piece:

We'll be creating a deep CNN with three convolutional layers and two fully connected layers, with a binary classifier as our output layer, to tell us whether an image contains a cat or dog. The data for this exercise is available in the GitHub folder for this chapter.

1. First, let's start with our imports. You've seen each of these before with the exception of the cv2 package; this will help us process the image files:

```
import pandas as pd
import numpy as np
import tensorflow as tf
import os
import cv2
```

2. First, we need to import and prepare our training data. Since we are dealing with image files, we'll have to do some heavy pre-processing to get them ready for training. The first things we'll do is get a list of file paths to all of the cats/dogs training data, and store those in two lists, which we'll name *cats* and *dogs*:

```
dogs_dir = '/data/training/dogs/'
cats_dir = '/data/training/cats/'
```

3. With the directories in hand, we can do ahead and grab the list of full file paths:

```
dog_images = [dogs_dir + i for i in os.listdir(dogs_dir)]
cat_images = [cats_dir + i for i in os.listdir(cats_dir)]
```

4. Now let's get on to the pre-processing; we'll need to convert each of the images into a numerical representation of itself:

```
def process_image(img, img_size, pixel_depth):
    img = cv2.imread(img, cv2.IMREAD_COLOR)
 if (img.shape[0] >= img.shape[1]):
    resizeto = (img_size, int(round(img_size *
(float(img.shape[1]) / img.shape[0])))))
 else:
    resizeto = (int(round(img_size * (float(img.shape[0])
img.shape[1]))), img_size)

    img = cv2.resize(img, (resizeto[1], resizeto[
0]), interpolation=cv2.INTER_CUBIC)

    img = cv2.copyMakeBorder(img, 0, img_size - img.shape[0], 0,
img_size - img.shape[1], cv2.BORDER_CONSTANT, 0)

    img = normalize_image(img, pixel_depth)

    return img[:, :, ::-1]
```

6. We'll also use a function to normalize the newly created numerical representation of the images:

```
def normalize_image(image, pixel_depth):
    image_data = np.array(image, dtype=np.float32)
    image_data[:, :, 0] = (image_data[:, :, 0].astype(
        float) - pixel_depth / 2) / pixel_depth
    image_data[:, :, 1] = (image_data[:, :, 1].astype(
        float) - pixel_depth / 2) / pixel_depth
    image_data[:, :, 2] = (image_data[:, :, 2].astype(
        float) - pixel_depth / 2) / pixel_depth

    return image_data
```

Now that we've defined our pre-processing functions, we can actually go ahead and run these on the data itself. We'll define two lists, one for the cats and one for the dogs, pull our information from each of the images, and append them to the list. We'll need to define two parameters to accomplish this; depth and image_size. Image size is the standardized size that we reformatted all of our images to the preceding parameters. Depth, on the other hand, represents what's known in image processing at the **color depth**. Color depth measures how many bits it takes to measure the color of a single pixel in an image:

```
depth = 255.0
image_size = 64
```

Now that we have these defined, let's process all of our cat and dog images into lists for each. We'll process each file using the scripts that we defined precedingly, and then append those file representations to the respective lists:

```
training_dogs = []
training_cats = []

for dog in dog_images:
    p_image = process_image(dog, image_size, depth)
    training_dogs.append([np.array(p_image), 1])

for cat in cat_images:
    p_image = process_image(cat, image_size, depth)
    training_cats.append([np.array(p_image), 0])
```

Next, we'll split our dataset into equal parts:

```
dog_data = np.array(np.array_split(training_dogs, 12500 / (batch_size /
2)))
cat_data = np.array(np.array_split(training_cats, 12500 / (batch_size / 2))
```

Now that we have a dataset that is evenly divided between cats and dogs, we'll go ahead and create batches for each. First, we'll initialize a blank array called total_batch. Then we zip together (combine) the dog and cat data, and iterate through the combined data in order to create batches:

```
total_batch = []
for dog_image, cat_image in zip(dog_data, cat_data):
    batch = np.concatenate([dog_image, cat_image])
    total_batch.append(batch)
```

What we now have are training batches of images that contained our combined cat/dog data. Now, we can actually construct our network! We are going to be constructing a standard CNN. While in the `Chapter 4`, *Your First Artificial Neural Networks*, we manually created our network layers, this time around, we are going to use a higher-up TensorFlow library called `tf.layers` to construct the network layers. Instead of have to manually define the weights, biases, and actual mathematical operations of the layers, `tf.layers` allows us to just pass in parameters to the network to define the layer. With that, let's start by building our actual network as a function, which we'll define as `convolutional_network`. The first layer we'll define manually as to handle the input shape for the image data. This layer will take in the x data, `image_size`, and a variable called `color_channels`. This variable measure what it sounds like, the color channels of a standard image, which in this case are the standard **red**, **green**,and **blue** (**RGB**) channels for a colored image. We'll also define the `dropout_rate`, which will tell our network what proportion of the time it should apply the dropout procedure:

```
color_channels = 3
dropout_rate = 0.5

def convolutional_network(x, image_size, color_channels):

    ## Input Layer
    input_layer = tf.reshape(x, [-1, image_size, image_size,
color_channels])
```

Next, let's define our first convolutional layer. Using the `tf.layers` library, we'll define the layer as `convolution_one` and pass in it's parameters. Let's walk through them one-by-one:

- `inputs`: Takes in the result of the input layer
- `filters`: The number of filters in each convolution of the layer
- `kernel_size`: Specifies the dimensions of the convolutional sliding window
- `padding`: The type of padding
- `kernal_initializer`: An initializer for the convolution, which we will define as follows
- `kernal_regularizer`: The regularization method, which we'll define as follows

- `bias_initializer`: An initializer for the layer's bias factors
- `bias_regularization`: A regularization method for the bias factors, which we will define as follows
- `activation`: An activation function for the layer

```
convolution_one = tf.layers.conv2d(inputs=input_layer, filters=32,
kernel_size=[3, 3],
 padding="same", kernel_initializer=initializer,
kernel_regularizer=regularizer,
 use_bias=True, bias_initializer=initializer, bias_regularizer=regularizer,
 activation=tf.nn.relu)
```

Once we have the layer defined, we can define our pooling layer. We can also use the `tf.layers` library here to easily define a layer without have to write out all of the transformations manually:

```
pooling_one = tf.layers.max_pooling2d(inputs=convolution_one, pool_size=[2,
2], strides=(2, 2))
```

Since we have three layers in this network, we'll repeat the process for the next two layers:

```
## Second convolutional layer with pooling
convolution_two = tf.layers.conv2d(inputs=pooling_one, filters=32,
kernel_size=[3, 3],
          padding="same", kernel_initializer=initializer,
kernel_regularizer=regularizer,
          use_bias=True, bias_initializer=initializer,
bias_regularizer=regularizer,
          activation=tf.nn.relu)
pooling_two = tf.layers.max_pooling2d(inputs=convolution_two, pool_size=[2,
2], strides=(2, 2))
## Third Convolutional layer with pooling
convolution_three = tf.layers.conv2d(inputs=pooling_two, filters=64,
kernel_size=[3, 3],
          padding="same", kernel_initializer=initializer,
kernel_regularizer=regularizer,
          use_bias=True, bias_initializer=initializer,
bias_regularizer=regularizer,
          activation=tf.nn.relu)
pooling_three = tf.layers.max_pooling2d(inputs=convolution_three,
pool_size=[2, 2], strides=(2, 2))
```

We'll use the layer-flattening function that we used before to morph the output of our convolutional layers from a four-dimensional tensor to a two-dimensional tensor, and feed that into our first fully connected layer:

```
flatten_layer = tf.reshape(pooling_three, [-1, 8 * 8 * 64])
```

At the output of the network, we'll create a fully connected layer to take the results of the preceding three layers, and output the potential classes that the image could be classified into:

```
fc_layer = tf.layers.dense(inputs=flatten_layer, units=1024,
activation=tf.nn.relu,
          kernel_initializer=initializer, kernel_regularizer=regularizer,
          use_bias=True, bias_initializer=initializer,
bias_regularizer=regularizer)
```

As part of the fully connected layer, we'll add a `dropout_layer` for regularization. Remember that `dropout` helps prevent overfitting by randomly shutting off nodes and connections in the network so that the network can learn different connections. Dropout helps out network to generalize:

```
dropout_layer = tf.layers.dropout(inputs=fc_layer, rate=dropout_rate,
training=True)
```

Lastly, we'll define the output layer as a simple dense layer with a sigmoid `activation` function, which will give us probabilities for each of the potential classes that the image could be. In our case, that would be cat or dog:

```
output = tf.layers.dense(inputs=dropout_layer, units=1,
activation=tf.nn.sigmoid)
```

Now that our network is defined, we can go ahead and begin to prepare for training. First, we'll want to setup the `placeholders` for our x and y inputs:

```
x = tf.placeholder(shape=[None, image_size, image_size, color_channels],
dtype=tf.float32)
y = tf.placeholder(shape=[None, 1], dtype=tf.float32, name='labels')
```

Next, let's go ahead and define the parameters for the training cycle. We'll define the `learning_rate`, the number of `training_epochs`, simple training parameters that will tell us when to `display` training reports, and a `threshold` for accuracy (The lowest amount of accuracy we will accept for a decision):

```
lr = 0.0001
training_epochs = 20
display = 1
threshold = 0.7
```

Now, let's start defining the pieces of our network. First, we'll define an `initializer`, in particular with a method called **Glorot Initialization**. Invented by Xavier Glorot, this method initializes the values of our weights and biases with a small value sampled from a Gaussian (normal) distribution, and helps with efficient training. Glorot initialization is available in TensorFlow as `xavier_initializer`. We'll also define a basic `l2_regularizer` method for our network:

```
initializer = tf.contrib.layers.xavier_initializer()
regularizer = tf.contrib.layers.l2_regularizer(0.001)
```

Lastly, we'll define the model, our `loss` function, and an `optimizer`. In this case, we'll be using a `log_loss`, or logarithmic loss. Closely related to cross-entropy, it is also used for binary classification problems, and will converge to give us a binary output (cat or dog) in the same manner. We'll then use Adam to optimize the `loss`:

```
model_output = convolutional_network(x)

loss = tf.losses.log_loss(labels=y, predictions=model_output)

optimizer = tf.train.AdamOptimizer(learning_rate=lr).minimize(loss)
```

We have to do one more operation before we start training, which is to define the accuracy metric that our model will be using while it trains. Using the `threshold` that we defined previously, we define what an acceptable prediction is from the model output. We'll then take that prediction tensor, grab the `correct_prediction`, and compute `accuracy`. This accuracy operations will be computed during each training epoch, and will be run in a session along with the `loss` and `optimization` method:

```
thresholds = tf.fill([batch_size], threshold)
predictions = tf.greater_equal(model_output, thresholds)
correct_prediction = tf.equal(predictions, tf.cast(y, tf.bool))
accuracy = tf.reduce_mean(tf.cast(correct_prediction, tf.float32))
```

Now, we're finally ready to start training! We'll start a `Session`, batch out our images and their correct labels, and run the training procedure. After each epoch, we'll print out a report on how the training procedure is performing:

```
with tf.Session() as sess:
    sess.run(tf.global_variables_initializer())
    for epoch in range(training_epochs):
        for batch in training_batches:
            batch_images, batch_labels = map(list, zip(*batch))
            batch_images = np.array(batch_images)
            batch_labels = np.array(batch_labels).reshape(-1, 1)
            ## Run the training procedures
            _, l, acc = sess.run([optimizer, loss, accuracy], feed_dict={x:
batch_images, y: batch_labels})
        if epoch % display == 0:
            print('\nEpoch: %d, Loss: %f, Accuracy: %f' % (epoch + 1, l,
acc))
```

That's it! You've trained your first CNN.

How many parameters do we have in this network? Each filter has 3 x 3 x 3 + 1 = 54 parameters; *54 x 60 = 3,240* parameters in total.

Summary

CNNs have been seminal in solving many computer vision tasks. In this chapter, we learned about how these networks differ from our basic feedforward networks, what their structures are, and how we can utilize them. CNNs are primarily used for computer vision tasks, although they can be adapted for use in other unstructured domains, such as natural language processing and audio signal processing.

CNNs are made up of convolutional layers interspersed with pooling layers, all of which output to a fully connected layer. CNNs iterate over images using filters. Filters have a size and a stride, which is how quickly they iterate over an input image. Input consistency can be better guaranteed by utilizing the zero padding technique.

In the next chapter, we'll learn about another important class of networks, called **Recurrent Neural Networks**.

6
Recurrent Neural Networks

Recurrent Neural Networks (**RNNs**) are the most flexible form of networks and are widely used in **natural language processing** (**NLP**), financial services, and a variety of other fields. Vanilla feedforward networks, as well as their convolutional varieties, accept a fixed input vector and output a fixed vector; they assume that all of your input data is independent of each other. RNNs, on the other hand, operate on sequences of vectors and output sequences of vectors, and allow us to handle many exciting types of data. RNNs are actually turing-complete, in that they can simulate arbitrary tasks, and hence are very appealing models from the perspective of the Artificial Intelligence scientist.

In this chapter, we'll introduce the core building blocks of RNNs, including special RNN units called **Gated Recurrent Units** (**GRU**) and **Long short-term memory units** (**LSTMs**). We'll then focus on practical applications of RNNs in Python, building models for NLP, and financial service tasks.

In this chapter, we will be covering the following topics:

- Building blocks of RNNs
- Memory units - LSTMs and GRUs
- Sequence processing with RNNs
- Extensions of RNN

Technical requirements

This chapter will be utilizing TensorFlow in Python 3. The corresponding code for this chapter is available in the book's GitHub repository.

The building blocks of RNNs

When we think about how a human thinks, we don't just observe a situation once; we constantly update what we're thinking based on the context of the situation. Think about reading a book: each chapter is an amalgamation of words that make up its meaning. Vanilla feedforward networks don't take sequences as inputs, and so it becomes very difficult to model unstructured data such as natural language. RNNs can help us achieve this.

Basic structure

RNNs differ from other networks in the fact that they have a recursive structure; they are recurring over time. RNNs utilize recursive loops, which allow information to persist within the network. We can think of them as multiple copies of the same network, with information being passed between each successive iteration. Without recursion, an RNN tasked with learning a sentence of 10 words would need 10 connected copies of the same layer, one for each word. RNNs also share parameters across the network. Remember in the past few chapters how the number of parameters we had in our network could get unreasonably large with complex layers? With recursion and parameter sharing, we are able to more effectively learn increasingly long sequence structures and minimize the amount of overall parameters that we have to learn.

Basically, recurrent networks take in items from a sequence and recursively iterate over them. In the following diagram, our sequence x gets fed into the network:

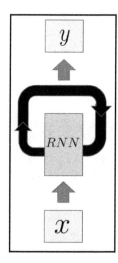

RNNs have memory, or **hidden states**, which help them manage and learn complex knowledge; we represent them with the variable h. These hidden states capture important information from the previous pass, and store it for future passes. RNN hidden states are initialized at zero and updated during the training process. Each pass in an RNN's is called a **time step**; if we have a 40-character sequence, our network will have 40 time steps. During an RNN time step, our network takes the input sequence x and returns both an output vector y as well as an updated hidden state. After the first initial time step, the hidden state h also gets fed into the network at each new step along with the input x. The output of the network is then the value of the hidden state after the last time step.

While RNNs are recursive, we could easily unroll them to graph what their structure looks like at each time step. Instead of viewing the RNN as a box, we can unpack its contents to examine its inner workings:

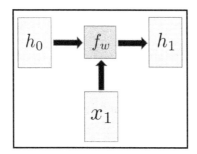

In the preceding diagram, our RNN is represented as the function f to which we apply the weights w, just as we would with any other neural network. In RNNs, however, we call this function the **recurrence formula**, and it looks something such as this:

$$h_t = f_w(h_{t-1}, x)$$

Here, h_t represents our new state that will be the output of a single time step. The h_{t-1} expression represents our previous state, and x is our input data from the sequence. This recurrence formula gets applied to an element of a sequence until we run out of time stamps.

Let's apply and dissect how a basic RNN works by walking through its construction in TensorFlow.

Vanilla recurrent neural networks

Let's walk through the architecture of a basic RNN; to illustrate, we are going to create a basic RNN that predicts the next letter in a sequence. For our training data, we will be using the opening paragraph of Shakespeare's Hamlet. Let's go ahead and save that corpus as a variable that we can use in our network.

```
corpus = "Hamlet was the only son of the King of Denmark.
He loved his father and mother dearly--and was happy in the love
of a sweet lady named Ophelia. Her father, Polonius, was the King's
Chamberlain. While Hamlet was away studying at Wittenberg, his father died.
Young Hamlet hastened home in great grief to hear that a serpent had stung
the King, and that he was dead. The young Prince had loved his father so
tenderly that you may judge what he felt when he found that the Queen,
before yet the King had been laid in the ground a month, had determined to
marry again--and to marry the dead King's brother.Hamlet refused to put off
mourning for the wedding."
```

At it's very basis, all natural language processing techniques require us to clean up the text in the corpus. Since our text above is messy, we'll want to strip and split the corpus into individual words, and group these words as a set of vocab. We can use the .strip() and .split() methods from python to easily handle this for us.

```
corpus = [x.strip() for x in corpus]
corpus = [x.split() for x in corpus]
corpus = np.hstack(corpus)
vocab = set(corpus)
```

Now that we've created a vocabulary, we can create a dictionary that gives us the count of every characters in the vocab. We'll call this dictionary letter_dict.

```
letter_dict = {letters: i for i, letters in enumerate(vocab)}
reverse_dict = {i: letters for i, letters in enumerate(vocab)}
```

Lastly, we just need to create a variable, vocab_size, that will store the length of this vocab dictionary so that we can use it later.

```
vocab_size = len(letter_dict)
```

To get started with building a basic recurrent network, let's first initialize our hidden state variable, h_t. We've initialized the state as a `placeholder` in TensorFlow, and passed it a batch size and state size. We'll also initialize our weights and bias factors:

Let's take a look at our recurrence formula again; we can break down our generic function fw and actually examine its parts:

This looks scarier than it is. Our formula f has been replaced by something you're familiar with: a tanh nonlinearity. Inside that nonlinearity, our input x gets multiplied by a weight matrix W_{xh}. On the other side of the expression, our previously hidden state h_{t-1} is multiplied by another weight matrix. These two products are then added together and put through the nonlinearity function. We can add this process easily in TensorFlow:

Remember, this recurrence function gets applied again and again for as many time stamps as we have defined:

```
def simple_rnn(input_data):
    ## RNNs need to take in data in sequences, so here we will split the
data into a sequence
    input_data = tf.reshape(input_data, [-1, 4])
    input_data = tf.split(input_data, 4 , 1)

    ## Creates the basic RNN cell that will be used throughout the network
    cell = tf.nn.rnn_cell.BasicRNNCell(50)

    ## Creates the actual RNN with the supplied celler
    output, hidden_state = tf.nn.static_rnn(cell, input_data,
dtype=tf.float32)

    return output
```

Before we get to training the network, we are going to set just a few training parameters. Most of these should be self explanatory to you by now! Here, our bias factors, `bias` and `end_bias`, are actually variables called offsets that help model where letters should be placed in a sequence.

```
learning_rate = 0.001
n_input = 4
epochs = 10
display = 1
bias = random.randint(0, 4)
end_bias = 4
n_hidden = 512
```

As usual, we'll need to create placeholders for the input and output data to our network.

```
input_data = tf.placeholder("float", [None, n_input, 1])
output = tf.placeholder("float", [None, vocab_size])
```

Before we run our network, we'll initialize the network itself, the loss, and the optimization procedure just as we'e done with different networks in previous chapters.

```
logits = simple_rnn(input_data)

loss =
tf.reduce_mean(tf.nn.softmax_cross_entropy_with_logits(logits=logits[-1],
labels=output))

optimizer =
tf.train.AdamOptimizer(learning_rate=learning_rate).minimize(loss)
```

Now that we have completed the setup, it is time to train the model. We first create a session to serve as an environment in which all operations will be executed. We then initialize all the parameters (for example, the weight matrices contained in BasicRNNCell) of our network by calling tf.global_variable_initializer(). Next, we prepare the input data (symbol_in_keys) and target data (symbols_out_onehot) that will be passed into each RNN cell. We then continue by passing that data to our placeholders through feed_dict and specifying that TensorFlow evaluate optimizer, loss, and logits. Note that by evaluating optimizer we are instructing TensorFlow to perform a learning step for the entire network as specified above. Finally, we accumulate and print the loss to allow us to track the performance of the model:

```
with tf.Session() as sess:
    ## Initialize the variables
    sess.run(tf.global_variables_initializer())
    for epoch in range(epochs):
        if offset > (len(corpus) - end_offset):
            offset = random.randint(0, 5)

        symbols_in_keys = [[word_dict[str(corpus[i])]] for i in
range(offset, offset + n_input) ]
        symbols_in_keys = np.reshape(np.array(symbols_in_keys), [-1,
n_input, 1])

        symbols_out_onehot = np.zeros([vocab_size], dtype=float)
        symbols_out_onehot[word_dict[str(corpus[offset + n_input])]] = 1.0
        symbols_out_onehot = np.reshape(symbols_out_onehot, [1, -1])
        _, n_loss, preds = sess.run([optimizer, loss, logits],
feed_dict={input_data: symbols_in_keys, output: symbols_out_onehot})
        loss_total += n_loss
```

```
acc_total += acc
if epoch % display == 0:
    print("Iter= " + str(step+1) + ", Average Loss= " + \
        "{:.6f}".format(loss_total/display))
```

The output of our network then becomes the value of the hidden state at the last time step; however, to finish this structure, we need to have a good understanding of what type of task we're completing. RNN structures vary slightly depending on what type of task they are performing. In reality, there are three different tasks/sub-architectures for RNNs:

- **One-to-many**: An RNN that takes a single vector input and outputs a variable output. Example: image captioning.
- **Many-to-one**: An RNN that takes in a variable input and outputs a single prediction. Example: sentiment analysis.
- **Many-to-many**: An RNN that takes in variable input and outputs variables at each time step. Example: classifying someone's expression throughout a video.

Let's briefly go over these other types of task, and how their architectures vary.

The corresponding code for each of these examples can be found in the book's GitHub repository.

One-to-many

Image captioning represents a **one-to-many** scenario. We take in a single vector that represents that input image, and output a variable length description of the image. One-to-many scenarios output a label, word, or other output at each time step:

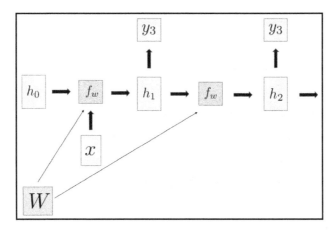

Music generation is another example of a one-to-many scenario, where we output a variable set of notes.

Many-to-one

In cases such as sentiment analysis, we are interested in a single and final hidden state for the network. We call this a **many-to-one** scenario. When we arrive at the last time step, we output a classification or some other value, represented in the computational graph by y_t:

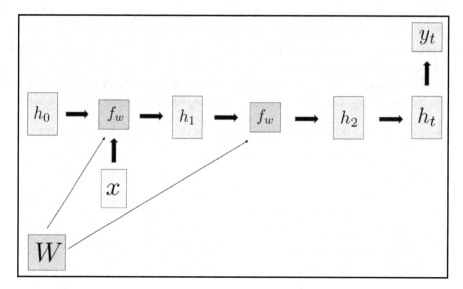

Many-to-one scenarios can also be used for tasks such as music genre labeling, where the network takes in notes and predicts a genre.

Many-to-many

If we wanted to classify the expression of a person during a video, or perhaps label a scene at any given time, or even for speech-to-text recognition, we would use a **many-to-many** architecture. Many-to-many architectures take in a variable's length sequence while also outputting a variable length sequence:

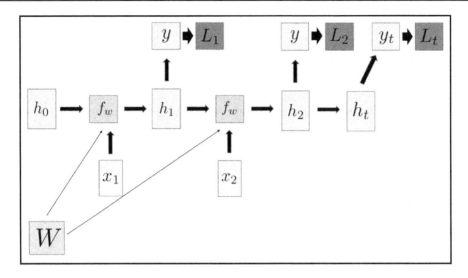

An output vector is computed at every step of the process, and we can compute individual losses at every step in the sequence. Frequently, we utilize a softmax loss for explicit labeling tasks. The final loss will be the sum of these individual losses.

Backpropagation through time

RNN utilizes a special variation of regular backpropagation called **backpropagation through time**. Like regular old backpropagation, this process is often handled for us in TensorFlow; however, it's important to note how it differs from standard backpropagation for feedforward networks.

Let's recall that RNNs utilize small *copies* of the same network, each with its own weights and bias factors. When we backpropagate through RNNs, we calculate the gradients at each time step, and sum the gradients across the entire network when computing the loss. We'll have a separate gradient from the weight that flows to the computation that happens at each of the time steps, and the final gradient for W will be the sum of the gradients from each of the individual timesteps.

Backpropagation through time (BPTT) can get computationally expensive as our number of timestamps increases. To remedy this, we use a variation called **truncated backpropagation through time**, where we conduct backpropagation over chunks of the sequence, not the entire sequence at a time. This helps improve computational efficiency.

Memory units – LSTMs and GRUs

While regular RNNs can theoretically ingest information from long sequences, such as full documents, they are limited in *how far back* they can look to learn information. To overcome this, researchers have developed variants on the traditional RNN that utilize a unit called a **memory cell**, which helps the network *remember* important information. They were developed as a means to solve the vanishing gradient problem that occurs with traditional RNN models. There are two main variations of RNN that utilize memory cell architectures, known as the **GRU** and the **LSTM**. These architectures are the most widely used RNN architectures, so we'll pay some what attention to their mechanics.

LSTM

LSTMs are a special form of RNN that excel at learning long-term dependencies. Developed by Hochreiter and Schmidhuber in 1997, LSTMs have several different layers that information passes through to help them keep what is important and jettison the rest. Unlike vanilla recurrent networks, the LSTM has not one but two states; the standard hidden state that we've been representing as h_i, as well as a state that is specific to the LSTM cell called the **cell state**, which we will denote with c_t. These LSTM states are able to update or adjust these states with **gating mechanisms**. These gates help to control the processing of information through the cell, and consist of an activation function and a basic **point wise operation**, such as vector multiplication. Let's examine this a bit more closely:

- The activation decides something, such as how much of a data component should be allowed into the cell's internal state. This can take on any continuous value between 0 and 1, with zero on one end of the scale meaning *let nothing in*, and 1 meaning *let everything in*.
- The pointwise operation is a basic mathematical operation (addition, subtraction, multiplication, division) between two functions.

We can take a look at how data flows through LSTMs to examine this process in more detail. The LSTM's four gates can easily be remembered by their initials, with the acronym **IFOG**:

- **I**: The **information gate** or **input gate**, which tells us how much information we want to allow into the cell
- **F**: The **forget gate**, which tells us how much information we want to erase or forget from the previous time step iteration

- **O**: The **output gate**, which controls how much information we want to flow out of the cell
- **G**: The **write gate**, which tells us how much information we want to write into our input cell

We take our hidden state h_t and our input x, and multiply them by four different weight matrices to compute the value of the four different LSTM gates:I, F, O, and G. Sometimes, you will see the weight matrix written as one large matrix – it's the same thing as the four-matrix representation:

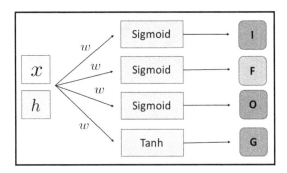

Let's break down this process. Information first hits the **forget gate**; this will tell us what information to forget from our past subject. As it utilizes a sigmoid function, it outputs a value between zero and 1. For instance, let's say we are doing some NLP and are ingesting a sequence about politics. Take a look at this sentence:

The French president supports the international agreement. The American president does not support it. Other countries are split on their decisions.

If one sentence has to do with European politics, we would want to remember that throughout the ingest of the sentence as a phenomenon that is happening *there*; however, *if* the next sentence is to do with American politics, we would want to know that the event is happening *here*. The forget gate can help contextualize the location, a subject's gender, or other relevant information. In this example, the forget gate will forget that we are talking about European politics, and change the LSTM's internal state with the function:

$$f_t = \sigma(W_f \bullet [h_{t-1} x_t] + b_f)$$

$$f_t = Sigmoid(Weights \bullet [HiddenState \bullet Input] + bias)$$

Remember, the LSTM's internal state is what helps us better contextualize information over longer inputs. In this example, it's helping us with nuance and context:

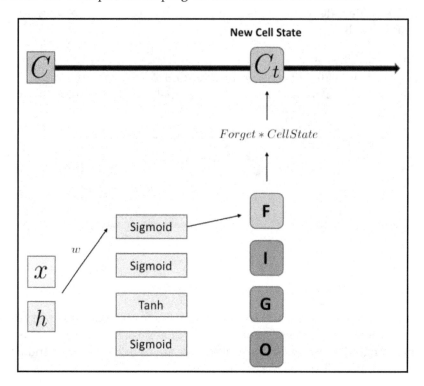

Our data next flows into the two update states: the **input gate** and the **write gate**. In the context of the preceding example, as we process the second sentence, our input gate will remember that we are now talking about American politics, not French politics. Meanwhile, our write gate will ingest the fact that we are discussing American politics in the context of international agreements. While these gates have decided *what* they will want to do, they haven't actually done it. The outputs of both of these operations are combined in a point wise operation, which, in this case, is a multiplication between these two gating functions:

The update:

$$i_t = \sigma(W_i \bullet [h_{t-1} x_t] + b_i)$$

The write:

$$C_t = tanh(W_C \bullet [h_{t-1} x_t] + b_C)$$

Then, we add the results of the multiplication between the update function and write function to the cell state that we updated earlier with the forget gate. Our new state then becomes as follows:

$$C_t = (f_t * C_{t-1}) + (i_t * \widetilde{C_t})$$

$$NewCellState = (Forget * OldCellState) + (Update * Write)$$

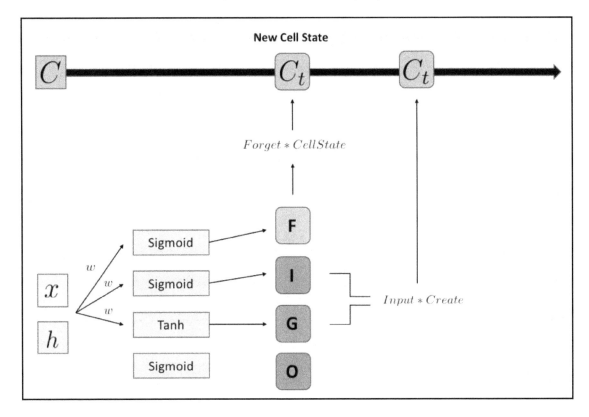

Finally, we come to the output gate. Remember our hidden state? We take that same hidden state/input combination that has fed into the last three gates, and feed it into the output gate. Its form looks pretty similar to the other gates:

$$O_t = \sigma(W_O \bullet [h_{t-1}x_t] + b_O)$$

Simultaneously, we take the cell state **C** that we've just calculated, and push it through a tanh function. The results of the tanh operations are then multiplied with the results of the output gate; this way, we only output information that's important:

$$h_t = tanh(W\binom{h_{t-1}}{x_t}))$$

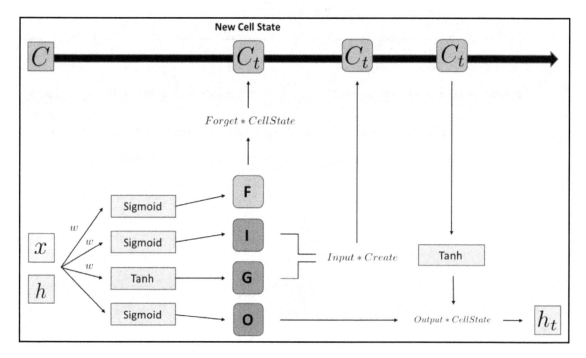

In the context of our example, the output might be action items in the sentence, such as the phrase does not support. In this way, at the end of a single pass through the LSTM, our internal cell state knows what we are talking about, the President of the United States, while the outputted hidden state knows that he/she does not support the agreement.

GRUs

GRUs were developed in 2014 as a new take on the classic LSTM cell. Instead of having four separate gates, it combines the forget and input gates into a single update gate; you can think of this in the sense of: whatever is not written, gets forgotten. It also merges the cell state c_t from the LSTM with the overall hidden state h_t. At the end of a cycle, the GRU exposes the entire hidden state:

- **Update gate**: The update gate combines the forget and input gates, essentially stating that whatever is not written into memory is forgotten. The update gate takes in our input data x and multiplies it by the hidden state. The result of that expression is then multiplied by the weight matrix and fed through a sigmoid function:

$$u_t = \sigma(W_u \cdot [h_{t-1}, x_t])$$

- **Reset gate**: The reset gate functions similarly to the output gate in the LSTM. It decides what and how much is to be written to memory. Mathematically, it is the same as the update gate:

$$r_t = \sigma(W_r \cdot [h_{t-1}, x_t])$$

- **Memory gate**: A tanh operation that actually stores the output of the reset gate into memory, similar to the write gate in the LSTM. The results of the reset gate are combined with the raw input, and put through the memory gate to calculate a provisional hidden state:

$$\tilde{h}_t = tanh(W \cdot [r_t * h_{t-1}, x_t])$$

Our end state is calculated by taking the provisional hidden state and conducting an operation with the output of the update gate:

$$h_t = (1 - u_t) * h_{t-1} + u_t * \widetilde{h_t}$$

The performance of a GRU is similar to that of the LSTM; where GRUs really provide benefit is that they are more computationally efficient due to their streamlined structure. In language modeling tasks, such as the intelligent assistant that we will create in a later chapter, GRUs tend to perform better especially in situations with less training data.

Sequence processing with RNNs

Now that we've learned about the components of RNNs, let's dive into what we can do with them. In this section, we'll look at two primary examples: **machine translation** and **generating image captions**. Later on in this book, we'll utilize RNNs to build a variety of end-to-end systems.

Neural machine translation

Machine translation represents a sequence-to-sequence problem; you'll frequently see these networks described as **sequence-to-sequence** (or **Seq2Seq**) models. Instead of utilizing traditional techniques that involve feature engineering and n-gram counts, neural machine translation maps the overall meaning of a sentence to a singular vector, and we then generate a translation based on that singular meaning vector.

Machine translation models rely on an important concept in artificial intelligence known as the **encoder/decoder** paradigm. In a nutshell:

- **Encoders** parse over input and output a condensed, vector representation of the input. We typically use a GRU or LSTM for this task
- **Decoders** take the condensed representation, and extrapolate to create a new sequence from it

These concepts are extremely import in understanding generative adversarial networks, which we will learn about in a coming chapter. The first part of this network acts as an encoder that will parse over your sentence in English; it represents the summarization of the sentence in English.

Architecturally, neural machine translation networks are many-to-one and one-to-many, which sit back-to-back with each other, as demonstrated in the following diagram:

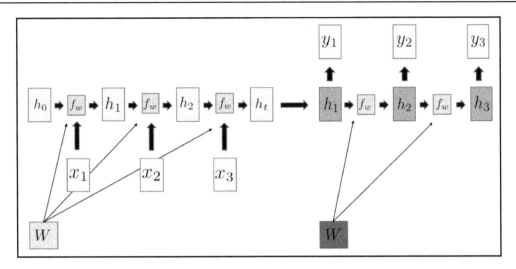

This is the same architecture that Google uses for Google Translate.

Attention mechanisms

Neural machine translation (**NMT**) models suffer from the same long-term dependency issues that RNNs in general suffer from. While we saw that LSTMs can mitigate much of this behavior, it still becomes problematic with long sentences. Especially in machine translation, where the translation of the sentence is largely dependent on how much information is contained within the hidden state of the encoder network, we must ensure that those end states are as rich as possible. We solve this with something called **attention mechanisms**.

Attention mechanisms allow the decoder to select parts of the input sentence based on context and what has generated thus far. We utilize a vector called a **context vector** to store scores from the hidden states at each time step. We then use a softmax function to normalize all scores, which generates a probability distribution over all the hidden states. This distribution helps the decoder decide what information to focus on.

Neural machine translation models can be robust; for an example of an NMT model in TensorFlow, please check the corresponding GitHub repository for this chapter.

Generating image captions

RNNs can also work with problems that require fixed input to be transformed into a variable sequence. Image captioning takes in a fixed input picture, and outputs a completely variable description of that picture. These models utilize a CNN to input the image, and then feed the output of that CNN into an RNN, which will generate the caption one word at a time:

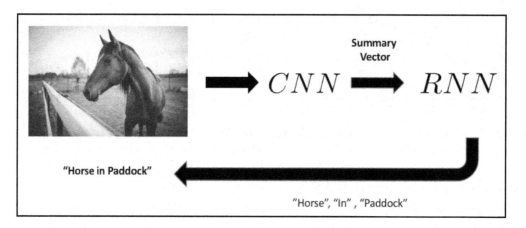

We'll be building a neural captioning model based on the Flicker 30 dataset, provided by the University of California, Berkley, which you can find in the corresponding GitHub repository for this chapter. In this case, we'll be utilizing pretrained image embeddings for the sake of time; however you can find an example of an end-to-end model in the corresponding GitHub repository.

1. Let's start with our imports:

```
import math
import os
import tensorflow as tf
import numpy as np
import pandas as pd

import tensorflow.python.platform
from keras.preprocessing import sequence
```

2. Next, let's load the image data from the files you've downloaded from the repository. First, let's define a path to where we can find the images.

```
captions = 'image_captions.token'
features = 'features.npy'
```

3. Next, we can actually load in the images and the various captions. We'll call these captions and images.

```
annotations = pd.read_table(captions, sep='\t', header=None,
names=['image', 'caption'])
images = np.load(features,'r'),
captions = annotations['caption'].values
```

4. Next, we'll have to store the occurrence count for the number of times the words appear:

```
occuranceDict = {} ## This Dictionary will store the occurance
count of our words
wordCount = 0 ## wordCount is a value that we will use to keep
track of the number of occurances of a word
```

5. First, we'll have to construct a vocabulary to draw from; we'll need to do a bit of preprocessing for our captions beforehand. You can go through the following code:

```
def ConstructVocab(captions):
    '''Function to Construct the Vocab that we will be generating
from'''
    occuranceDict = {} ## This Dictionary will store the occurance
count of our words
    wordCount = 0 ## wordCount is a valuee that we will use to keep
track of the number of occurances of a word
    ## Iterate over the captions to split them into individuals
words to construct the vocab
    for item in captions:
        wordCount += 1
        for word in item.lower().split(' '):
            occuranceDict[word] = occuranceDict.get(word, 0) + 1
    vocab = [word for word in occuranceDict if occuranceDict[word]
>= 20]
    ## Set a dictionary to set a word for each index
    IndexesToWords = {} ##
    ixtoword[0] = '.'
    ## Set a dictionary to the indexes of each word at each steps
    WordsToIndexes = {}
    WordsToIndexes['#START#'] = 0
    index = 1
    ## Iterate over the words in the vocab to store them and index
their position.
    for word in vocab:
      WordstoIndexes[word] = index
      IndexestoWords[index] = word
      index += 1
```

```
## Set the wordcount for the occurance dictionary
occuranceDict['.'] = wordCount
## Initiative the word bias vectors
biasVector = np.array([1.0*occuranceDict[IndexestoWords[i]] for
i in IndexestoWords])
biasVector = biasVector / np.sum(biasVector)
biasVector = np.log(biasVector)
biasVector = biasVector - np.max(biasVector)
## Return the dictionarties, as well as the bias vector
return WordstoIndexes, IndexestoWords,
biasVector.astype(np.float32)
```

6. Now we can construct the model itself. Follow the comments below to understand what each section is doing:

```
def captionRNN():
    ''' RNN for Image Captioning '''
    ## Define our Networks Parameters
    dim_embed = 256
    dim_hidden = 256
    dim_in = 4096
    batch_size = 128
    momentum = 0.9
    n_epochs = 150
    ## Initialize the embedding distribution and bias factor as a
random uniform distribution.
    captionEmbedding = tf.Variable(tf.random_uniform([n_words,
dim_embed], -0.1, 0.1))
    captionBias = tf.Variable(tf.zeros([dim_embed]))

    ## Initialize the embedding distribution and bias for the
images
    imgEmbedding = tf.Variable(tf.random_uniform([dim_in,
dim_hidden], -0.1, 0.1))
    imgBias = tf.Variable(tf.zeros([dim_hidden]))

    ## Initialize the encodings for the words
    wordEncoding = tf.Variable(tf.random_uniform([dim_hidden,
n_words], -0.1, 0.1))
    wordBias = tf.Variable(init_b)
    ## Initialize the variables for our images
    img = tf.placeholder(tf.float32, [batch_size, dim_in]) ##
Placeholder for our image variables
    capHolder = tf.placeholder(tf.int32, [batch_size,
n_lstm_steps]) ## Placeholder for our image captions
    mask = tf.placeholder(tf.float32, [batch_size, n_lstm_steps])
    ## Compute an initial embedding for the LSTM
    imgEmbedding = tf.matmul(img, imgEmbedding) + imgBias
```

```
## Initialize the LSTM and its starting state
lstm = tf.contrib.rnn.BasicLSTMCell(dim_hidden)
state = self.lstm.zero_state(batch_size, dtype=tf.float32)

## Define a starting loss
totalLoss = 0.0
```

7. Now, we will train the cycle for the model:

```
## Training Cycle for the Model
    with tf.variable_scope("RNN"):
        for i in range(n_lstm_steps):
            ## Tell the model to utilizing the embedding
corresponding to the appropriate caption,
            ## if not, utilize the image at the first embedding
            if i > 0:
                current_embedding =
tf.nn.embedding_lookup(captionEmbedding, capHolder[:,i-1]) +
captionBias
                tf.get_variable_scope().reuse_variables()
            else:
                current_embedding = imgEmbedding
            out, state = lstm(current_embedding, state) ## Output
the current embedding and state from the LSTM

            if i > 0:

                labels = tf.expand_dims(capHolder[:, i], 1)
                ix_range = tf.range(0, batch_size, 1) ## get the
index range
                indexes = tf.expand_dims(ix_range, 1) ## get the
indexes
                concat = tf.concat([indexes, labels],1) ##
Concatonate the indexes with their labels
                ## Utilizng a "One Hot" encoding scheme for the
labels
                oneHot = tf.sparse_to_dense(concat,
tf.stack([batch_size, n_words]), 1.0, 0.0)

                ## Run the results through a softmax function to
generate the next word
                logit = tf.matmul(out, wordEncoding) + wordBias
                ## Utilizing Cross Entropy as our Loss Function
                crossEntropyLoss =
tf.nn.softmax_cross_entropy_with_logits(logits=logit,
labels=oneHot)
                crossEntropyLoss = crossEntropyLoss * mask[:,i]
```

```
                              ## Tell Tensorflow to reduce our loss
                              loss = tf.reduce_sum(crossEntropyLoss)
                              ## Add the loss at each iteration to our total loss
                              totalLoss = totalLoss + loss

                         totalLoss = totalLoss / tf.reduce_sum(mask[:,1:])
                         return totalLoss, img, capHolder, mask
```

During training, we utilize a separate weight matrix to help model the image information, and utilize that weight matrix to ingest the image information at every RNN time step cycle.

At each step, our RNN will compute a distribution over all scores in the network's vocabulary, sample the most likely word from that distribution, and utilize that word as the input for the next RNN time step. These models are typically trained end-to-end, meaning that backpropagation for both RNN and the CNN happens simultaneously. In this case, we only need to worry about our RNN:

```
    def trainNeuralCaption(learning_rate=0.0001):
      '''Function to train the Neural Machine Translation Model '''

      ## Initialize a Tensorflow Session
      sess = tf.InteractiveSession()

      ## Load the images and construct the vocab using the functions we
    described above
      images, captions = load_images('path/to/captions', 'path/to/features')
      WordstoIndexes, IndexestoWords, init_b = constructVocab(captions)

      ## Store the indexes
      index = (np.arange(len(images)).astype(int))
      np.random.shuffle(index)
      n_words = len(WordstoIndexes)
      maxlen = np.max( [x for x in map(lambda x: len(x.split(' ')), captions) ]
    )
```

Now, let's initialize the caption RNN model and start building the model. The code for that is as follows:

```
    ## Initialize the Caption RNN model function and build the model
    nc = neuralCaption(dim_in, dim_hidden, dim_embed, batch_size, maxlen+2,
    n_words, init_b)
    loss, image, sentence, mask = nc.build_model()

    ## Define our timestep and the overall learning rate
    global_step = tf.Variable(0,trainable=False)
```

```
learning_rate = tf.train.exponential_decay(learning_rate, global_step,
int(len(index)/batch_size), 0.95)

## Utilize Adam as our optimization function
train_op = tf.train.AdamOptimizer(learning_rate).minimize(loss)

## Initialize all our variables
tf.global_variables_initializer().run()

## Run the training cucle
for epoch in range(n_epochs):
for start, end in zip( range(0, len(index), batch_size), range(batch_size,
len(index), batch_size)):

## Current Images and Captions
currentImages = images[index[start:end]]
currentCaptions = captions[index[start:end]]
current_caption_ind = [x for x in map(lambda cap: [WordstoIndexes[word]
for word in cap.lower().split(' ')[:-1] if word in WordstoIndezes],
current_captions)]

## Pad the incoming sequences
current_caption_matrix = sequence.pad_sequences(current_caption_ind,
padding='post', maxlen=maxlen+1)
current_caption_matrix = np.hstack( [np.full(
(len(current_caption_matrix),1), 0), current_caption_matrix] )

current_mask_matrix = np.zeros((current_caption_matrix.shape[0],
current_caption_matrix.shape[1]))
nonzeros = np.array([x for x in map(lambda x: (x != 0).sum()+2,
current_caption_matrix )])

for ind, row in enumerate(current_mask_matrix):
row[:nonzeros[ind]] = 1

## Run the operations in a TensorFlow session
_, currentLoss = sess.run([train_op, loss], feed_dict={
image: current_feats.astype(np.float32),
sentence : current_caption_matrix.astype(np.int32),
mask : current_mask_matrix.astype(np.float32)
})

print("Loss: ", currentLoss)
```

The last thing we need to do is train the model; we can do that by simply calling the `training` function:

```
trainNeuralCaption()
```

Often, you may see many variants of RNNs for text generation called the **character-level RNN**, or **ChaRnn**. It's advisable to stay away from character-level RNN models.

Extensions of RNNs

There have been many extensions of vanilla RNNs over the past several years. This is by no means an exhaustive list of all of the great advances in RNNs that are happening in the community, but we're going to review a couple of the most notable ones: Bidirectional RNNs, and NTM.

Bidirectional RNNs

In recent years, researchers have developed several improvements on the traditional RNN structure. **Bidirectional RNNs** were developed with the idea that they may not only depend on the information that came before in a sequence, but also the information that comes afterwards. Structurally, they are just two RNNs that are stacked on top of each other, and their output is a combination of the hidden states of each of the individual networks.

Neural turing machines

Neural turing machines (NTM) are a form of RNN that were developed by Alex Graves of DeepMind in 2014. Instead of having an internal state such as an LSTM, NTMs have external memory, which increases their ability to handle complex computational tasks.

NTMs consist of two main components: a **controller** and a **memory bank**.

- **NTM controller**: The controller in an NTM is the neural network itself; it manages the flow of information between input and memory, and learns to manage its own memory throughout
- **NTM memory bank**: The actual external memory, usually represented in tensor form

Provided there's enough memory, an NTM can replicate any algorithm by simply updating its own memory to reflect that algorithm. The architecture combines that of a traditional, programmable computer with that of a neural network in order to harness the power of both.

Summary

RNNs are the primary means by which we reason over textual inputs, and come in a variety of forms. In this chapter, we learned about the recurrent structure of RNNs, and special versions of RNNs that utilize memory cells. RNNs are used for any type of sequence prediction, generating music, text, image captions, and more.

RNNs are different from feedforward networks in that they have recurrence; each step in the RNN is dependent on the network's memory at the last state, along with its own weights and bias factors. As a result, vanilla RNNs struggle with long-term dependencies; they find it difficult to remember sequences beyond a specific number of time steps back. GRU and LSTM utilize memory gating mechanisms to control what they remember and forget, and hence, overcome the problem of dealing with long-term dependencies that many RNNs run into. RNN/CNN hybrids with attention mechanisms actually provide state-of-the-art performance on classification tasks. We'll create one of these in the `Chapter 9`, *Deep Learning for Intelligent Assistants* about creating a basic agent.

In the next chapter, we'll move beyond RNNs into one of the most exciting classes of networks, **generative networks**, where we'll learn how to use unlabeled data, and how to generate images and paintings from scratch.

Generative Models

7

Generative models are the most promising push toward enabling computers to have an understanding of the world. They are true unsupervised models, and are able to perform those tasks that many today consider to be at the cutting edge of **artificial intelligence** (**AI**). Generative models are different for precisely the reason as it sounds: they generate data. Centered mostly around computer vision tasks, this class of network has the power to create new faces, new handwriting, or even paintings.

In this section, we'll introduce generative models and their foundations, focusing specifically on the two most popular types of model, the **variational autoencoder** (**VAE**), and the **generative adversarial network** (**GAN**), where you'll learn how to generate pictures and faces with these networks. We'll also touch upon other common generative models, and finish up with several related exercises, depending on how comfortable you are with the material. Later on in this book, you'll work more with integrating generative models into larger systems.

Technical requirements

In this chapter, we will be utilizing Python 3. You'll need the following packages to be installed:

- NumPy
- TensorFlow
- PyTorch

It will be helpful if your machine is GPU enabled, as discussed in `Chapter 3`, *Platforms and Other Essentials*.

Getting to AI – generative models

Generative models are a class of neural networks that are wholly different from what we have discussed thus far. The networks that we've discussed hitherto are feedforward networks. CNNs and RNNs are all discriminatory networks, in that they try to classify data. Given a specific input, they can predict classes or other labels. Generative models, on the other hand, try to predict features given a certain label. They do this by having a parameter set that is much smaller than the amount of data they are learning, which forces them to comprehend the general essence of the data in an efficient manner.

There are two main types of generative model, VAE and GAN. First, we'll start with the motivations for generative models. Then, we'll discuss the architecture and inner workings of each, and work through a practical example for each model.

Autoencoders

Autoencoders, and their encoder/decoder frameworks, are the inspiration behind generative models. They are a self-supervised technique for representation learning, where our network learns about its input so that it may generate new data just as input. In this section, we'll learn about their architecture and uses as an introduction to the generative networks that they inspire.

Network architecture

Autoencoders work by taking an input and generating a smaller vector representation for later *reconstructing its own input*. They do this by using an encoder to impose an information bottleneck on incoming data, and then utilizing a decoder to recreate the input data based on that representation. This is based on the idea that there are *structures* within data (that is, correlations, and so on) that exist, but that are not readily apparent. Autoencoders are a means of automatically learning these relationships without explicitly doing so.

Structurally, autoencoders consist of an **input layer**, a **hidden layer**, and an **output layer**, as demonstrated in the following diagram:

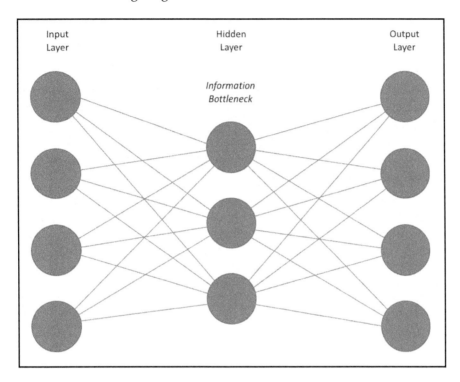

The encoder learns to preserve as much of the relevant information as possible in the limited encoding, and intelligently discards irrelevant parts. This forces the network to maintain only the data required to recreate the input; we do this by using a reconstruction loss with a regularization term to prevent overfitting. As the task of autoencoders is to recreate their output, they utilize a type of loss function known as **reconstruction loss**. These loss functions are usually **mean squared error** or **cross entropy** loss functions that penalize the network for creating an output that is markedly different from the input.

The information bottleneck is the key to helping us to minimize this reconstruction loss; if there was no bottleneck, information could flow too easily from the input to the output, and the network would likely overfit from learning generic representations. The ideal autoencoder is both of the following:

- Sensitive enough to its input data that it can accurately reconstruct it
- Insensitive enough to its input data that the model doesn't suffer from overfitting that data

The process of going from a high input dimension to a low input dimension in the encoder process is a dimensionality reduction method that is almost identical to **principal component analysis** (**PCA**), which we discussed in previous chapter. The difference lies in the fact that PCA is restricted to **linear manifolds**, while autoencoders can handle **non-nonlinear manifolds**. A manifold is a continuous, non-intersecting surface.

Remember when we talked about the topology of loss functions? Those loss functions are a manifold. A sphere is a manifold; really, any surface in space that doesn't intersect with itself could be a manifold. For the sake of neural networks, learning, and loss functions, be sure to always think of manifolds as a topological map.

Building an autoencoder

If you're thinking that the task of reconstructing an output doesn't appear that useful, you're not alone. What exactly do we use these networks for? Autoencoders help to extract features when there are no known labeled features at hand. To illustrate how this works, let's walk through an example using TensorFlow. We're going to reconstruct the MNIST dataset here, and, later on, we will compare the performance of the standard autoencoder against the variational autoencoder in relation to the same task.

Let's get started with our imports and data. MNIST is contained natively within TensorFlow, so we can easily import it:

```
import tensorflow as tf
import numpy as np

from tensorflow.examples.tutorials.mnist import input_data
mnist = input_data.read_data_sets("/tmp/data/", one_hot=True)
```

For ease, we can build the auto-encoder with the `tf.layers` library. We'll want our Autoencoder architecture to follow the convolutional/de-convolutional pattern, where the input layer of the decoder matches the size of the input and the subsequent layer squash the data into a smaller and smaller representation. The decoder will be the same architecture reversed, starting with the small representation and working larger.

All together, we want it to look something like the following:

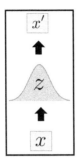

Let's start with the encoder; we'll define an initializer for the the weight and bias factors first, and then define the encoder as a function that takes and input, x. we'll then use the `tf.layers.dense` function to create standard, fully connected neural network layers. The encoder will have three layers, with the first layer size matching the input dimensions of the input data (784), with the subsequent layers getting continually smaller:

```
initializer = tf.contrib.layers.xavier_initializer()

def encoder(x):
    input_layer = tf.layers.dense(inputs=x, units=784,
activation=tf.nn.relu,
                            kernel_initializer=initializer,
bias_initializer=initializer
                    )
    z_prime = tf.layers.dense(inputs=input_layer, units=256,
activation=tf.nn.relu,
                            kernel_initializer=initializer,
bias_initializer=initializer
                    )
    z = tf.layers.dense(inputs=z_prime, units=128, activation=tf.nn.relu,
                    kernel_initializer=initializer,
bias_initializer=initializer
                    )
        return z
```

Next, let's let's build our decoder; it will be using the same layer type and initializer as the encoder, only now we invert the layers, so that the first layer of the decoder is the smallest and the last is the largest.

```
def decoder(x):
    x_prime_one = tf.layers.dense(inputs=x, units=128,
activation=tf.nn.relu,
                            kernel_initializer=initializer,
```

```
    bias_initializer=initializer
                                )
    x_prime_two = tf.layers.dense(inputs=x_prime_one, units=256,
activation=tf.nn.relu,
                               kernel_initializer=initializer,
    bias_initializer=initializer
                                )
    output_layer = tf.layers.dense(inputs=x_prime_two, units=784,
activation=tf.nn.relu,
                               kernel_initializer=initializer,
    bias_initializer=initializer
                                )
    return output_layer
```

Before we get to training, let's define some hyper-parameters that will be needed during the training cycle. We'll define the size of our input, the learning rate, number of training steps, the batch size for the training cycle, as well as how often we want to display information about our training progress.

```
input_dim = 784
learning_rate = 0.001
num_steps = 1000
batch_size = 256
display = 1
```

We'll then define the placeholder for our input data so that we can compile the model:

```
x = tf.placeholder("float", [None, input_dim])
```

And subsequently, we compile the model and the optimizer as you've seen before in previous chapter:

```
# Construct the full autoencoder
z = encoder(x)

## x_prime represents our predicted distribution
x_prime = decoder(z)

# Define the loss function and the optimizer
loss = tf.reduce_mean(tf.pow(x - x_prime, 2))
optimizer = tf.train.RMSPropOptimizer(learning_rate).minimize(loss)
```

Lastly, we'll code up the training cycle. By this point, most of this should be fairly familiar to you; start a TensorFlow session, and iterate over the epochs/batches, computing the loss and accuracy at each point:

```
with tf.Session() as sess:
    sess.run(tf.global_variables_initializer())

    ## Training Loop
    for i in range(1, num_steps+1):
        ## Feed Batches of MNIST Data
        batch_x, _ = mnist.train.next_batch(batch_size)

        ## Run the Optimization Process
        _, l = sess.run([optimizer, loss], feed_dict={x: batch_x})

        ## Display the loss at every 1000 out of 30,000 steps
        if i % display == 0 or i == 1:
            print('Step %i: Loss: %f' % (i, l))
```

For this particular example, we'll add in a little something more to this process; a way to plot the reconstructed images alongside their original versions. Keep in mind that this code is still contained within the training session, just outside of the training loop:

```
n = 4
canvas_orig = np.empty((28 * n, 28 * n))
canvas_recon = np.empty((28 * n, 28 * n))

for i in range(n):

    batch_x, _ = mnist.test.next_batch(n)

    # Encode and decode each individual written digit
    g = sess.run(decoder, feed_dict={x: batch_x})

    # Display original images
    for j in range(n):

        # Draw the original digits
        canvas_orig[i * 28:(i + 1) * 28, j * 28:(j + 1) * 28] =
batch_x[j].reshape([28, 28])

    # Display reconstructed images
    for j in range(n):

        # Draw the reconstructed digits
        canvas_recon[i * 28:(i + 1) * 28, j * 28:(j + 1) * 28] =
g[j].reshape([28, 28])
```

```
# Plot the original image vs the reconstructed images.
print ("Original Images")
plt.figure(figsize=(n, n))
plt.imshow(canvas_orig, origin="upper", cmap="gray")
plt.show()

print ("Reconstructed Images")
plt.figure(figsize=(n, n))
plt.imshow(canvas_recon, origin="upper", cmap="gray")
plt.show()
```

After training, you should end up with a result along the lines of the following, with the actual digits on the left, and the reconstructed digits on the right:

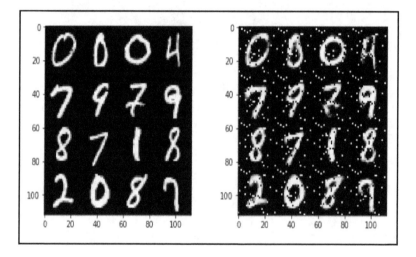

So what have we done here? By training the autoencoder on unlabeled digits, we've done the following:

- Learned the latent features of the dataset without having explicit labels
- Successfully learned the distribution of the data and reconstructed the image from scratch, from that distribution

Now, let's say that we wanted to take this further and generate or classify new digits that we haven't seen yet. To do this, we could remove the decoder and attach a classifier or generator network:

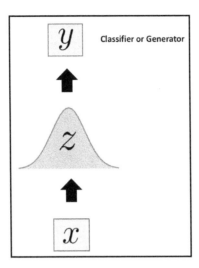

The encoder therefore becomes a means of initializing a supervised training model. Standard autoencoders have been used in a variety of tasks. In the supplementary code for this chapter, we'll walk through an example where we utilize autoencoders for visual anomaly detection.

Variational autoencoders

Variational autoencoders (**VAEs**) are built on the idea of the standard autoencoder, and are powerful generative models and one of the most popular means of learning a complicated distribution in an unsupervised fashion. VAEs are **probabilistic models** rooted in Bayesian inference. A probabilistic model is exactly as it sounds:

Probabilistic models incorporate random variables and probability distributions into the model of an event or phenomenon.

VAEs, and other generative models, are probabilistic in that they seek to learn a distribution that they utilize for subsequent sampling. While all generative models are probabilistic models, not all probabilistic models are generative models.

The probabilistic structure of VAEs comes into play with their encoders. Instead of building an encoder that outputs a single value to describe the input data, we want to learn the latent variables by generating a probability distribution for each of those variables. VAEs have a constraint on the encoding network that forces it to generate vectors that roughly follow a standard normal distribution. This is what makes VAEs unique: they generate from continuous space, which means that we can easily sample and interpret from that space. We'll see how this unique probabilistic structure helps us to overcome the limitations of standard autoencoders.

Structure

Like standard autoencoders, VAEs utilize the same encoder/decoder framework, but, that aside, they are mathematically different from their namesake. VAEs take a probabilistic perspective in terms of guiding the network:

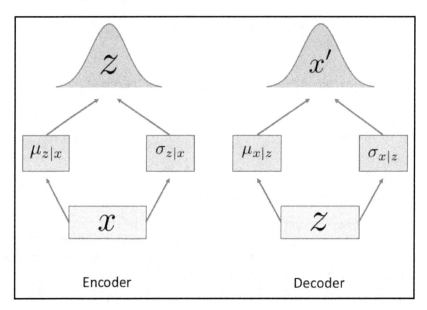

Both our **encoder** and **decoder** networks are generating distributions from their input data. The encoder generates a distribution from its training data, **Z**, which then becomes the input distribution for the decoder. The decoder takes this distribution, **Z**, and tries to replicate the original distribution, **X**, from it.

Encoder

The encoder generates its distribution by first defining its prior as a standard normal distribution. Then, during training, this distribution becomes updated, and the decoder can easily sample from this distribution later on. Both the encoder and the decoder are unique in terms of VAEs in that they output two vectors instead of one: a vector of means, μ, and another vector of standard deviation, σ. These help to define the limits for our generated distributions. Intuitively, the mean vector controls where the encoding of an input should be centered, while the standard deviation controls the extent to which the encoding may vary from the mean. This constraint on the encoder forces the network to learn a distribution, thereby taking it beyond the vanilla autoencoder that simply reconstructs its output.

Decoder

Like the standard autoencoder, the decoder in the VAE is a backward convolutional network, or a deconvolutional network. In processing the decoding, data is sampled from the generation stochastically (randomly), making the VAE one of the few models that can directly sample a probability distribution without a Markov chain Monte Carlo method. As a result of the stochastic generation process, the encoding that we generate from each pass will be a different representation of the data, all while maintaining the same mean and standard deviation. This helps with the decoder's sampling technique; because all encodings are generated from the same distribution, the decoder learns that a latent data point and its surrounding points are all members of the same class. This allows the decoder to learn how to generate from similar, but slightly varying, encodings.

Training and optimizing VAEs

VAEs utilize a negative log-likelihood loss as their reconstruction loss to measure how much information is lost during the reconstruction phase of the decoder. If the decoder does not reconstruct the input satisfactorily, it will incur a large reconstruction loss. VAEs also introduce something called **Kullback–Leibler (KL)** divergence into their loss functions. KL divergence simply measures how much two probability distributions diverge; in other words, how different they are from one another. We want to minimize the KL distance between the mean and standard deviation of the target distribution and that of a standard normal. It is properly minimized when the mean is zero and the standard deviation is one. The log-likelihood loss with KL divergence forms the complete loss function for VAEs.

$$l_i(\theta, \phi) = -E_{z \sim q_\theta(z|x_i)}[\log p_\phi(x_i|z)] + KL(q_\theta(z|x_i)||p(z)) l i (\theta, \phi) = -E z \sim q \theta (z \mid x i) [log p \phi (x i \mid z)] + KL(q \theta (z \mid x i) \mid\mid p(z))$$

When training VAEs, there is an implicit trade-off between the accuracy of the model and how close it can model the normal distribution. On its own, KL loss results in encoded data that is densely clustered near the center of the distribution, with little iteration with other potentially similar encoded data. A decoder wouldn't be able to decode anything from the space, because it wouldn't be particularly continuous! By combining the losses and optimizing them, we are able to preserve the dense nature of encoded data created by the KL loss function, as well as the clustered data produced by the reconstruction loss. What we then end up with are tight clusters that are easy for the decoder to work with. We wanted our generated distribution Z to resemble a standard normal distribution as closely as possible, and the more efficiently we can encode the original image, the closer we can push the standard deviation of the generated distribution toward one, the standard deviation of the targeted normal distribution.

Utilizing a VAE

We can construct a variational autoencoder in TensorFlow to see how it compares to it's simpler, standard autoencoder cousin. In this section, we'll be using the same MNIST dataset so that we can standardize our comparison across methods. Let's walk through how to construct a VAE by utilizing it to generate handwriting based on the `MNIST` dataset. Think of x as being the individual written characters and z as the latent features in each of the individual characters that we are trying to learn.

First, let's start with our imports:

```
import numpy as np
import tensorflow as tf
from tensorflow.examples.tutorials.mnist import input_data
```

As before, we can import the `'MNIST_data'` directly from the TensorFlow library:

```
mnist = input_data.read_data_sets('MNIST_data', one_hot=True)
```

Next, we can start to build the encoder. We're going to be utilizing the same `tf.layers` package as we did before. Here, our encoder will look fairly similar to how it did in the previous example, our layers will take in an input and gradually compress that input until we generate a latent distribution, z:

```
def encoder(x):
    input_layer = tf.layers.dense(inputs=x, units=784,
activation=tf.nn.elu,
                                  kernel_initializer=initializer,
bias_initializer=initializer,
                                  name='input_layer'
```

```
                                           )
    hidden_1 = tf.layers.dense(inputs=input_layer, units=256,
activation=tf.nn.elu,
                               kernel_initializer=initializer,
bias_initializer=initializer
                                  )
    hidden_2 = tf.layers.dense(inputs=hidden_1, units=128,
activation=tf.nn.elu,
                         kernel_initializer=initializer,
bias_initializer=initializer
                                  )
```

Here's where we start to diverge from the standard autoencoder, however. While the last layer in the encoder will give us the potential z-distribution that represents our data, we'll need to calculate the values of μ and σ that will help define that distribution. We can do that by creating two new layers that take in the potential distribution z, and output out values of mu and sigma:

```
mu = tf.layers.dense(inputs=z, units=10, activation=None)
sigma = tf.layers.dense(inputs=z, units=10, activation=None)
```

Next, we'll use these values to go ahead and calculate the KL divergence for the encoder, which will eventually go into constructing our final loss function:

```
kl_div = -0.5 * tf.reduce_sum( 1 + sigma - tf.square(mu) - tf.exp(sigma),
axis=1)

kl_div = tf.reduce_mean(latent_loss)
```

Let's go ahead and create the decoder portion of the variational autoencoder now; we'll create a deconvolutional pattern that reverses the dimensions of the encoder. All of this will be contained under a function called decoder(z):

```
def decoder(z, initializer):
    layer_1 = fully_connected(z, 256, scope='dec_l1',
activation_fn=tf.nn.elu,
                         kernel_initializer=initializer,
bias_initializer=initializer
                                  )
    layer_2 = fully_connected(layer_1, 384, scope='dec_l2',
activation_fn=tf.nn.elu,
                         kernel_initializer=initializer,
bias_initializer=initializer
                                  )
    layer_3 = fully_connected(layer_2, 512, scope='dec_l3',
activation_fn=tf.nn.elu,
                         kernel_initializer=initializer,
```

```
bias_initializer=initializer
                                )
    dec_out = fully_connected(layer_3, input_dim, scope='dec_14',
activation_fn=tf.sigmoid,
                            kernel_initializer=initializer,
bias_initializer=initializer
                                )
```

Also under the decoder function, we'll use the decoder output to calculate the reconstruction loss:

```
epsilon = 1e-10

rec_loss = -tf.reduce_sum(x * tf.log(epsilon + dec_out) + (1 - x) *
tf.log(epsilon + 1 - dec_out), axis=1)

rec_loss = tf.reduce_mean(rec_loss)
```

As usual, we'll prepare our training parameters before we start initializing the model. We'll define a learning rate, batch size for our training, the number of training epochs, dimension of the input, and the size of our total training sample:

```
learning_rate = 1e-4
batch_size = 100
epochs = 100
input_dim = 784
num_sample = 55000
n_z = 10
```

We'll also define the placeholder for our input data, x:

```
x = tf.placeholder(name='x', dtype='float', shape=[None, input_dim])
```

Before we start training, we'll initialize the model, loss, and `optimizer`:

```
## initialize the models
z, kl_div = encoder(x)
dec_out, rec_loss = decoder(x)

## Calculate the overall model loss term
loss = tf.reduce_mean(rec_loss + kl_div)

## Create the optimizer
optimizer = tf.train.AdamOptimizer(learning_rate).minimize(loss)

## Create the weight initializer
initializer = tf.contrib.layers.xavier_initializer()
```

Finally, we can run the actual training process. This we be similar to the training processes that we've already built and experienced:

```
with tf.Session() as sess:
    sess.run(tf.global_variables_initializer())
    for epoch in range(epochs):
        for iter in range(num_sample // batch_size):

            batch_x = mnist.train.next_batch(batch_size)
            _, l, rl, ll = sess.run([optimizer, loss, rec_loss, kl_div],
feed_dict={x: batch_x[0]})

            if epoch % 5 == 0:
                print('[Epoch {}] Total Loss: {}, Reconstruction Loss: {},
Latent Loss: {}'.format(epoch, l, rl, ll))
```

Lastly, we can use the bit of code following code to generate new samples from our newly trained model:

```
z = np.random.normal(size=[batch_size, n_z])
x_generated = x_hat = self.sess.run(dec_out, feed_dict={z: z})

n = np.sqrt(batch_size).astype(np.int32)
I_generated = np.empty((h*n, w*n))
for i in range(n):
    for j in range(n):
        I_generated[i*h:(i+1)*h, j*w:(j+1)*w] = x_generated[i*n+j,
:].reshape(28, 28)

plt.figure(figsize=(8, 8))
plt.imshow(I_generated, cmap='gray')
```

Ultimately, you should end up with an image such as the following, with the original digits on the left and the generated digits on the right:

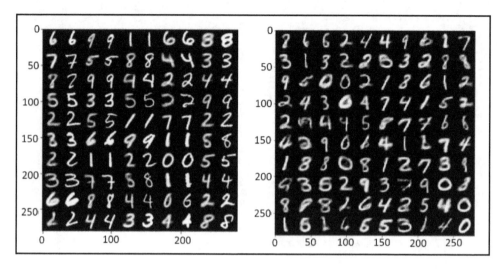

Observe how much clearer the digits are compared to the original autoencoder:

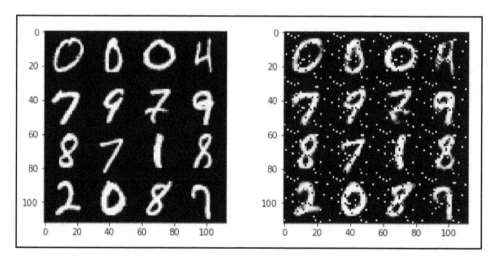

Now, let's see how we can take this further with GANs.

Generative adversarial networks

Generative adversarial networks (**GANs**) are a class of networks that were introduced by Ian Goodfellow in 2014. In GANs, two neural networks play off against one another as adversaries in an **actor-critic model**, where one is the creator and the other is the scrutinizer. The creator, referred to as the **generator network**, tries to create samples that will fool the scrutinizer, the discriminator network. These two increasingly play off against one another, with the generator network creating increasingly believable samples and the discriminator network getting increasingly good at spotting the samples. In summary:

- The generator tries to maximize the probability of the discriminator passing its outputs as real, not generated
- The discriminator guides the generator to create ever more realistic samples

All in all, this process is represented as follows:

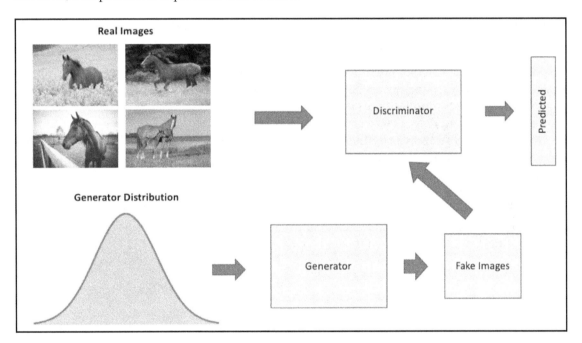

GANs can be used for a variety of tasks, and, in recent years, many GAN varieties have been created. As they were originally built for image-related tasks, we will focus our architecture discussions on image-based GANs. A larger list of GANs is available at the end of the section. Throughout, we'll follow along in TensorFlow to illuminate the topics. As before, we'll be utilizing the same MNIST data in order to compare the frameworks with our previous ones:

```
import tensorflow as tf
import numpy as np

from tensorflow.examples.tutorials.mnist import input_data
mnist = input_data.read_data_sets("MNIST_data/", one_hot=True)
training_data = (mnist.train.images - 0.5) / 0.5
```

With that, let's walk through the pieces of the network one at a time. By this point, you should be pretty familiar with this process in TensorFlow.

Discriminator network

The discriminator network in image-related GANs is a standard convolutional neural network. It takes in an image and outputs a single number that tells us whether the image is *real* or *fake*. The discriminator takes in an image, and learns the attributes of that image so that it may be a good *judge* vis-à-vis the outputs of the generator. In TensorFlow, we can create the discriminator as a function that we will then run in a TensorFlow session later on. This framework is more or less the same as you've seen in the previous sections with autoencoder and variational autoencoders; we'll use the higher level tf.layers api to create three main network layers and an output layer. After each of the main network layers, we'll add a dropout layer for regularization. The last layer will be slightly different, as we'll want to squash the output. For this, we'll use a sigmoid activation function that will give us a final output saying if an image is believed to be fake or not:

```
def discriminator(x, initializer, dropout_rate):
    layer_1 = tf.layers.dense(x, units=1024, activation=tf.nn.relu,
kernel_initializer=initializer,
                              bias_initializer=initializer,
name='input_layer')
    dropout_1 = tf.layers.dropout(inputs=layer_1, rate=dropout_rate,
training=True)

    layer_2 = tf.layers.dense(dropout_1, units=512, activation=tf.nn.relu,
kernel_initializer=initializer,
                              bias_initializer=initializer,
name='disc_layer_1')
    dropout_2 = tf.layers.dropout(inputs=layer_2, rate=dropout_rate,
```

```
training=True)
    layer_3 = tf.layers.dense(dropout_2, units=256, activation=tf.nn.relu,
kernel_initializer=initializer,
                              bias_initializer=initializer,
name='disc_layer_2')
    dropout_3 = tf.layers.dropout(inputs=layer_3, rate=dropout_rate,
training=True)
    output_layer = tf.layers.dense(dropout_3, units=1,
activation=tf.sigmoid, kernel_initializer=initializer,
                              bias_initializer=initializer,
name='disc_output')
    return output_layer
```

Now that we have this discriminator defined, let's go ahead and move on to the generator.

Generator network

You can think of the `generator` portion of the GAN as a reverse convolutional neural network. Like a VAE, it uses generic normal distribution, the only difference being that it up samples the distribution to form an image. This distribution represents our prior, and is updated during training as the GAN improves at producing images that the discriminator is unable to determine whether they are fake.

In between each layer, we utilize a `ReLu` activation function and `batch _normalization` to stabilize each layer's outputs. As the discriminator starts inspecting the outputs of `generator`, `generator` will continually adjust the distribution from which it's drawing to closely match the target distribution. The code will look fairly familiar to what you've seen in previous sections:

```
def generator(x, initializer):
    layer_1 = tf.layers.dense(x, units=256, activation=tf.nn.relu,
kernel_initializer=initializer,
                              bias_initializer=initializer,
name='input_layer')
    layer_2 = tf.layers.dense(layer_1, units=512, activation=tf.nn.relu,
kernel_initializer=initializer,
                              bias_initializer=initializer,
name='hidden_layer_1')
    layer_3 = tf.layers.dense(layer_2, units=1024, activation=tf.nn.relu,
kernel_initializer=initializer,
                              bias_initializer=initializer,
name='hidden_layer_2')
    output_layer = tf.layers.dense(layer_3, units=784,
activation=tf.nn.tanh, kernel_initializer=initializer,
                              bias_initializer=initializer,
```

```
    name='generator_output')
        return output_layer
```

Now that we have our model set up, let's get into the training process!

Training GANs

GANs are easy to train, but difficult to optimize due to a number of unstable dynamics in their training processes. To train a GAN, we train the generator on sub samples of a high-dimensional training distribution; since this does not innately exist, we initially sample from a standard normal (Gaussian) distribution.

Both the generator and the discriminator are trained jointly in a minimax game using an objective function, also referred to as the `minimax` function:

$$min \ max \left[\mathbb{E}_{x \sim p_d} \log D_{\theta_d}(x) + \mathbb{E}_{z \sim p(z)} \log(1 - D_{\theta_d}(G_{\theta_d}(z))) \right]$$

Let's break this down a bit. The function is telling us what happens where. Let's look at the initial bit of the first expression:

$$\mathbb{E}_{x \sim p_d}$$

The $\mathbb{E}$ notation means expectation, so we are saying that the expected output, x, of the discriminator for real images drawn from the actual distribution of will be:

$$\log D_{\theta_d}(x)$$

Likewise, here's the second expression:

$$\mathbb{E}_{z \sim p(z)}$$

It's telling us that the expected value of the output of the discriminator for fake images drawn from the generated distribution will be as follows:

$$\log(1 - D_{\theta_d}(G_{\theta_d}(z)))$$

The discriminator wants to maximize (max) the objective so that its output for real data $D(x)$ is as close to one as possible, while its output for fake data $D(G(z))$ is as close to zero as possible. Meanwhile, the generator seeks the opposite, to minimize (min) the objective function so that $D(x)$ is as close to zero as possible, while $D(G(z))$ is as close to one as possible. Mathematically, this is how the generator and the discriminator play off against one another.

When training GANs, we train to minimize the objective function so that the generator can win. We want the generator to be able to create examples that are realistic enough to fool the discriminator. To do this, we train and optimize the discriminator and the generator in parallel using gradient ascent. For each iteration of training, we are going to train the discriminator network in small batches, and then train the generator network in small batches, alternating between the two paradigms. Gradient ascent for the discriminator computes the following:

$$max \left[\mathbb{E}_{x \sim p_d} \log D_{\theta_d}(x) + \mathbb{E}_{z \sim p(z)} \log(1 - D_{\theta_d}(G_{\theta_d}(z))) \right]$$

Training both the discriminator and the generator jointly can be challenging. If we tried to actually minimize the loss function for the generator, as follows, we would run into some issues:

$$min \left[\log(1 - D_{\theta_d}(G_{\theta_d}(z))) \right]$$

If we look at a plot of the `minimax` function, we can see why this is:

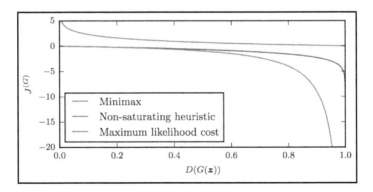

Optimization procedures look for gradient signals, which more or less tell gradient descent which way to go. In the `minimax` function, the biggest signals for gradient descent are to the right, but we actually want to to learn values to the left of the function, where it's minimized to zero and the generator is fooling the discriminator. However, as the generator optimizes, it will move away from its optimal point, taking us away from where it should be. To solve this, we can flip the paradigm of the generator. Instead of focusing on what it did right, we can make it focus on what it did wrong:

$$max \left[\log(1 - D_{\theta_d}(G_{\theta_d}(z))) \right]$$

By taking the maximum of the generator's objective, we're maximizing the likelihood of being wrong. This parallelized training process can still be unstable, however, and stabilizing GANs is a very active area of research at the moment.

Let's get back to the TensorFlow process. We'll start by defining our network's training parameters:

```
learning_rate = 0.0002
batch_size = 100
epochs = 100
dropout_rate=0.5
```

We then need to define our placeholders, both for the input x, as well as the z distribution which the generator will generate from:

```
z = tf.placeholder(tf.float32, shape=(None, 100))
x = tf.placeholder(tf.float32, shape=(None, 784))
```

Like before, we'll create a Glorot `Initializer` that will initialize our weight and bias values for us:

```
initializer = tf.contrib.layers.xavier_initializer()
```

Once we have all of this, we can go ahead and actually define our network pieces. You'll notice that for the discriminator, we're using something called a scope. Scopes allow us to reuse items from the TensorFlow graph without generating an error - in this case, we want to use the variables from the discriminator function twice in a row, so we use the `tf.variable_scope` function that TensorFlow provides us. Between the two, we simply use the `scope.reuse_variables()` function to tell TensorFlow what we're doing:

```
G = generator(z, initializer)

with tf.variable_scope('discriminator_scope') as scope:
```

```
        disc_real = discriminator(x, initializer, 0.5)
        scope.reuse_variables()
        disc_fake = discriminator(G, initializer, 0.5)
```

Lastly, we'll define the loss functions for both the generator and discriminator, and set the optimizer:

```
epsilon = 1e-2
disc_loss = tf.reduce_mean(-tf.log(disc_real + epsilon) - tf.log(1 -
disc_fake + epsilon))
gen_loss = tf.reduce_mean(-tf.log(disc_fake + epsilon))

disc_optim = tf.train.AdamOptimizer(lr).minimize(disc_loss)
gen_optim = tf.train.AdamOptimizer(lr).minimize(gen_loss)
```

We can the run the training cycle just as we have in the previous two examples. The only two differences you'll see here is that we run two optimization processes, one for the generator and one for the discriminator:

```
with tf.Session() as sess:
    sess.run(tf.global_variables_initializer())
    for epoch in range(epochs):
        ## Define the loss to update as a list
        gen_loss = []
        disc_loss = []
        ## Run the training iteration
        for iter in range(training_data.shape[0] // batch_size):
            ## Batch the input for the discriminator
            x_prime = training_data[iter*batch_size:(iter+1)*batch_size]
            z_prime = np.random.normal(0, 1, (batch_size, 100))

            ## Run the discriminator session
            _, DLoss = sess.run([disc_optim, disc_loss], {x: x_prime, z:
z_prime, drop_out: 0.3})
            disc_loss.append(DLoss)

            ## Run the generator session
            z_prime = np.random.normal(0, 1, (batch_size, 100))
            _, GLoss = sess.run([gen_optim, gen_loss], {z: z_prime,
drop_out: 0.3})
            gen_loss.append(GLoss)
        if epoch % 5 == 0:
            print('[%d/%d] - loss_d: %.3f, loss_g: %.3f' % ((epoch + 1),
epochs, np.mean(D_losses), np.mean(G_losses)))
```

GANs are fairly computational expensive, so training this network may take a while unless you scale with a web services platform.

As you can see, all of the models that we've run thus far have built upon each other. Even with advanced generative models like GANs, we can use certain recipes to create powerful neural networks, and larger AI applications, quickly and efficiently.

Other forms of generative models

While we've only covered two types of generative model, there are many different types that you may encounter in the literature. The following chart is not exhaustive, but does provide a general overview of the types of generative models out there:

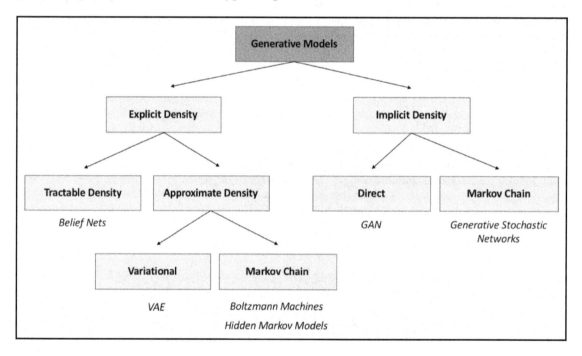

Let's break this down:

- **Explicit density models**: Model our data directly from a probability distribution. We explicitly define the probability and solve for it
- **Implicit density models**: Learn to sample from a probability distribution without defining what that distribution is

Within explicit density models, we have **tractable density** models and **approximate density** models. Here, tractable is related to defined computational time; we can calculate the computational complexity of a tractable problem. Approximate density relates to **intractability**—a computer science term that means that there is no defined computational time or algorithm. In practice, an intractable problem utilizes too many computational resources in order to be useful. Therefore, approximate density models use probabilistic approximation techniques to estimate the solution.

We'll briefly touch upon three notable classes: fully visible belief nets, Hidden Markov models, and Boltzmann machines. While each of these could be a chapter on its own, we'll touch on them briefly. Examples of each of these networks in Python are available in the code accompanying this chapter.

Fully visible belief nets

Fully visible belief networks are a class of explicit density models and a form of deep belief network. They use the chain rule to decompose a probability distribution $p(x)$ over a vector, into a product over each of the members of the vector, represented between by $p(x_i | x_1, \cdots)$. All together, it's formula is:

$$p(x) = \prod_{i=1}^{n} p(x_i | x_1, \ldots\ldots, x_{i-1})$$

The most popular model in this family is PixelCNN, an **autoregressive** generative model. Pixels approach image generation problems by turning them into a sequence modeling problem, where the next pixel value is determined by all the previously generated pixel values. The network scans an image one pixel at a time, and predicts conditional distributions over the possible pixel values. We want to assign a probability to every pixel image based on the last pixels that the network saw. For instance, if we're looking at the same horse images as in the previous example, we would be consistently predicting what the next anticipated pixel looks such as follows:

Based on the features that we've seen, will the next pixel still contain the horse's ear, or will it be background? While their training cycles are more stable than GANs, the biggest issue with the networks is that they generate new samples extremely slowly; the model must be run again fully in order to generate a new sample. They also block the execution, meaning that their processes cannot be run in parallel.

Hidden Markov models

A hidden Markov model is a type of **Markov model**, which is itself a subclass of **Dynamic Bayesian Networks**. Markov models are used to model randomly changing systems called **Markov processes** also called **Markov chains**. Simply put, a Markov process is a sequence of events where the probability of an event happening solely depends on the previous event.

Markov chains appear as follows:

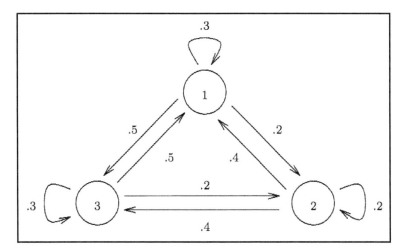

In this simple chain, there are three states, represented by the circles. We then have probabilities for transitioning to another state, as well as probabilities of staying in a current state. The classic example of a Markov chain is that of the taxi driver, where the driver finds himself currently solely depends on where he was last, in other words, his most recent fare. If we were to apply this example to the preceding Markov chain, the driver would have three possible locations to pick up or drop off customers; the associated probabilities between locations would represent the chance of him going to the other location or staying put.

Hidden Markov models are used to model Markov processes that we can't observe; what if the driver's route structure of where he would like to pick up customers is secret? There is likely some logic to the scenario, and we can try and model that process with a Hidden Markov model.

Boltzmann machines

Boltzmann machines are a general class of models that contain take binary vectors as input and units that assign a probability distribution to each of those binary vectors. As you can see in the following diagram, each unit is dependent on every other unit:

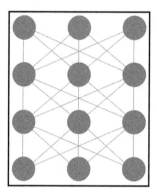

A Boltzmann machine uses something called an **energy function**, which is similar to a loss function. For any given vector, the probability of a particular state is proportional to each of the energy function values. To convert this to an actual probability distribution, it's necessary to renormalize the distribution, but this problem becomes another intractable problem. Monte Carlo methods are again used here for sampling as a workaround, hence making Boltzmann machines a Monte Carlo-based method.

Let's say we have documents that are represented by binary features. A Boltzmann machine can help us determine whether a particular word or phrase came from a particular document. We can also use Boltzmann machines for anomaly detection in large, complex systems. They work well up to a point, although this method does not work well in high dimensional spaces.

Summary

In this chapter, we learned about some of the most exciting networks in AI, variational autoencoders and GANs. Each of these relies on the same fundamental concepts of condensing data, and then generating from again from that condensed form of data. You will recall that both of these networks are probabilistic models, meaning that they rely on inference from probability distributions in order to generate data. We worked through examples of both of these networks, and showed how we can use them to generate new images.

In addition to learning about these exciting new techniques, most importantly you learned that the building blocks of advanced networks can be broken down into smaller, simpler, and repetitive parts. When you think about writing advanced models in TensorFlow, you need to remember what kind of layers you need, what type of activation functions you need, how to shape your data through the network, as well other procedures like choosing loss functions and optimizers. From basic autoencoders to advanced GANs, you have begun to learn certain tools that you can use to build advanced AI applications.

In the next chapter, we'll be taking a look at another excited field of AI, reinforcement learning, and how it is reshaping our day-to-day lives.

References

1. statisticshowto.com
2. Figure adapted from Ian Goodfellow, Tutorial on GANs, 2017

8
Reinforcement Learning

Along with generative networks, reinforcement learning algorithms have provided the most visible advances in **Artificial Intelligence** (**AI**) today. For many years, computer scientists have worked toward creating algorithms and machines that can perceive and react to their environment like a human would. Reinforcement learning is a manifestation of that, giving us the wildly popular AlphaGo and self-driving cars. In this chapter, we'll cover the foundations of reinforcement learning that will allow us to create advanced artificial agents later in this book.

Reinforcement learning plays off the human notion of learning from experience. Like generative models, it learns based on **evaluative feedback**. Unlike instructive feedback in supervised learning where the network learns by us telling it how to do something, evaluative feedback helps algorithms learn by telling them how well they did something.

In this section, we'll introduce two methods for reinforcement learning:

- Deep Q-learning
- Policy gradients

Technical requirements

In this chapter, we will be utilizing TensorFlow in Python. We will also be using the OpenAI gym to test our algorithms.

OpenAI gym is an open source toolkit for developing and testing reinforcement learning algorithms. Written in Python, there are environments from Atari games to robot simulations. As we develop reinforcement learning algorithms in this chapter and later chapters, gym will give us access to test environments that would otherwise be very complicated to construct on our own.

You will need either a macOS or Linux environment to run gym. You can install gym by running a simple `pip install` command:

```
pip install gym
```

You should now have gym installed! If you've run into an error, you may have dependency issues. Check the official gym GitHub repo for the latest dependencies (`https://github.com/openai/gym`).

Principles of reinforcement learning

Reinforcement learning is based on the concept of learning from interaction with a surrounding environment and consequently rewarding positive actions taken in that environment. In reinforcement learning, we refer to our algorithm as the **agent** because it takes action on the world around it:

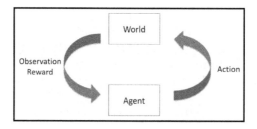

When an agent takes an action, it receives a reward or penalty depending on whether it took the *correct* action or not. Our goal in reinforcement learning is to let the agent learn to take actions that maximize the rewards it receives from its environment. These concepts are not at all new; in fact, they've been around for quite some time. What has allowed reinforcement learning to achieve such great heights has been the combination of new advances in deep learning, coupled with the computing power to handle increasingly complex scenarios.

There are two forms of environments in which reinforcement learning algorithms can act:

- **Deterministic environments**: Finite amount of actions. These environments are easier for reinforcement learning to solve.
- **Stochastic environments**: Many possible actions. These environments are harder to solve with many methods.

Reinforcement learning methods can be used to solve a variety of problems. To illustrate the effectiveness of various algorithms, we'll walk through examples to solve a classic problem known as the **cartpole** problem. This scenario is exactly as it sounds; a moving cart has a weighted, teetering pole on the top, and needs to balance the pole by making the correct movements.

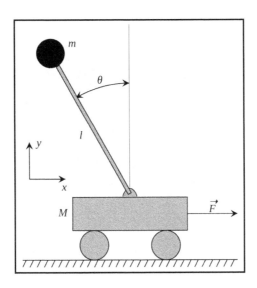

Reinforcement learning methods generally fall into two categories: policy optimization methods and dynamic programming methods. In this chapter, we'll cover an example of both, starting with using the dynamic programming methods of basic value iteration and Deep Q-learning, and then moving on to policy gradient methods for direct policy optimization.

Markov processes

At the crux of reinforcement learning is the **Markov Decision process (MDP)**. Markov processes are random strings of events where the future probabilities of events happening are determined by the probability of the most recent event. They extend the basic Markov Chain by adding rewards and decisions to the process. The fundamental problem of reinforcement learning can be modeled as an MDP. **Markov models** are a general class of models that are utilized to solve MDPs.

Markov models rely on a very important property, called the **Markov property**, where the current state in a Markov process completely characterizes and explains the state of the world at that time; everything we need to know about predicting future events is dependent on where we are in the process. For instance, the following Markov process models the state of the stock market at any given time. There are three states– a **Bull market**, a **Bear market**, or a **Stagnant market** – and the respective probabilities for staying in each **state** or transitioning to another state:

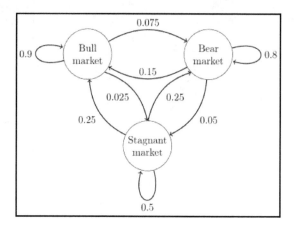

The entity that navigates an MDP is called an **agent**. In this case, the agent would be the stock market itself. We can remember the parameters of the Markov process by SAP:

- **Set of possible states (S)**: The possible states of being that an agent can be in at any given time. When we talk about states in reinforcement learning, this is what we are referring to.
- **Set of possible actions (A)**: All of the possible actions that an agent can take in its environment. These are the lines between the states; what actions can happen between two states?
- **Transition probability (P)**: The probability of moving to any of the new given states.

The goal of any reinforcement learning agent is to solve a given MDP by maximizing the **reward** it receives from taking specific actions.

Rewards

As we mentioned previously, reinforcement learning algorithms seek to maximize their potential future reward. In deep learning languages, we call this the expected **reward**. At each time step, *t*, in the training process of a reinforcement learning algorithm, we want to maximize the return, *R*:

$$Rt = rt + 1 + \gamma rt + 2 + \gamma^2 rt + 3 + \gamma^3 rt + 4 + \cdots = \sum_{k=0}^{\infty} \gamma^k rt + k + 1$$

Our final reward is the summation of all of the expected rewards at each time step – we call this the **cumulative reward**. Mathematically, we can write the preceding equation as follows:

$$\sum_{k=0}^{\infty} r_{t+k+1}$$

Theoretically, this process could go on forever; the termination for our ultimate reward depends on the problem we are trying to solve. To make the equation more robust to general circumstances, we will introduce something called the **discount factor**, which we represent with the Greek letter gamma, γ. We can introduce the discount factor at each time step for the **cumulative discounted reward**:

$$Rt = rt + 1 + \gamma rt + 2 + \gamma^2 rt + 3 + \gamma^3 rt + 4 + \cdots = \sum_{k=0}^{\infty} \gamma^k rt + k + 1$$

The discount factor can be any value between 0 and 1, and it represents the relative importance between a current reward and a future reward. If we set that discount factor to 0, we would be making our agent focus greedily on the present, there by giving greater weight to rewards that will happen sooner rather than later. If we set the discount factor to 1, our agent would look at both the past and present equally, just as if there was no discount factor at all. If you think about this in the context of a self-driving car, a value of 0 would cause the car to focus its immediate field of vision on the road, not what's several miles in the distance, while a value of 1 would not give it enough focus on its immediate surroundings. Ideally, we'd want a discount that is somewhere in the middle.

Rewards relate back to a MDP in that any potential action has a reward attached to it. The process now becomes SARP:

- Set of possible states (S)
- Set of possible actions (A)
- Distribution of the reward (R)—what reward an agent will receive when it is in a given state
- Transition probabilities between states (P)

Summarizing this process in simpler words, the process becomes:

- The agent selects an action
- The environment samples a reward and the next state
- The agent receives the reward as well as the next state

Reinforcement learning algorithms achieve their maximum reward by finding an optimal **policy** that tells the agent how to achieve the maximum award at each step.

Policies

A policy, simply stated, is a way of acting; your place of employment or education has policies about how, what, and when you can do things. This term is no different when used in the context of reinforcement learning. We use policies to map states to potential actions that a reinforcement learning agent can take. Mathematically speaking, policies in reinforcement learning are represented by the Greek letter π, and they tell an agent what action to take at any given state in an MDP. Let's look at a simple MDP to examine this; imagine that you are up late at night, you are sleepy, but maybe you are stuck into a good movie. Do you stay awake or go to bed? In this scenario, we would have three states:

- Your initial state of sleepiness
- Being well rested
- Being sleep deprived

Each of these states has a transition probability and reward associated with taking an action based on them.

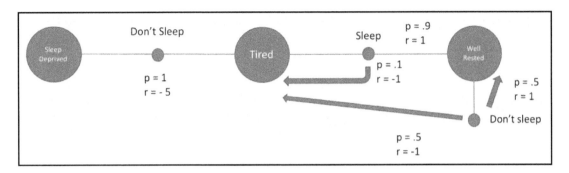

For example, Let's say you decide to stay up. In this scenario, you'll find yourself in the **Don't Sleep** transition state. From here, there is only one place to go - a 100% chance of ending up in the **Sleep Deprived** State.

If you slept, there is a 90% chance of you being well rested and a 10% chance of you still being tired. You could return to your tired state by not sleeping as well. In this scenario, we'd want to choose the actions (sleeping) that maximize our rewards. That voice in your head that's telling you to go to sleep is the policy.

Our objective is to learn a policy (π^*) that maximizes the network's reward; we call this the **optimal policy**. In this case, the optimal policy is **deterministic**, meaning that there is a clear optimal action to take at each state. Policies can also be **stochastic**, meaning that there is a distribution of possible actions that can be drawn from.

Reinforcement learning agents can learn **on-policy** or **off-policy**; when an algorithm is on-policy, it learns the policy from all of the agent's actions, including exploratory actions that it may take. It improves the *existing policy*. Off-policy learning is *off from the previous policy*, or in other words, evaluating or learning a policy that was different from the original policy. Off-policy learning happens independent of an agent's previous. Later on in this chapter, we'll discuss two different approaches to reinforcement learning – one on-policy (policy gradients) and one off-policy (Q-learning).

To help our algorithm learn an optimal policy, we utilize **value functions**.

Value functions

A value function helps us measure the expected reward at certain states; it represents the expected cumulative reward from following a certain policy at any given state. There are two types of value functions used in the field of reinforcement learning; **state value functions** $V(s)$ and **action value functions** $Q(s, a)$.

The state value function describes the value of a state when following a policy. It is the expected return that an agent will achieve when starting at state s under a policy π. This function will give us the expected reward for an agent given that it starts following a policy at states:

$$V^{\pi}(s) = \mathbb{E}\left[\sum_{t \geq 0} \gamma^t r_t \mid s_0 = s, \pi\right]$$

Let's break down what this function is telling us:

$$V\pi(S)$$

V is representing our value function, and we are simply stating that it follows a policy π based on states. We're not raising the function to π, we're simply stating that π is an optimal policy:

$$\mathbb{E}\left[\sum_{t \geq 0} \gamma^t r_t \mid s_0 = s, \pi\right]$$

Here, the large $\mathbb{E}$ is stating that the expected value of the function is the summation of all the possible values of the discounted cumulative rewards $\gamma^t r_t$ for all of the states.

The difference between the action value function and the state value function lie in its name; action value functions describe the value of taking a certain action while in a specific state. It measures the cumulative reward from a pair of states and actions; for a given state and action we take, how much will it increase our reward? It lets us postulate what would happen by taking a different action in the first time step than what the agent may want to do, and then afterward follow the policy. The action value function is also often called the Q-function, because of the Q that we use to represent it:

$$Q^{\pi}(s, a) = \mathbb{E}\left[\sum_{t \geq 0} \gamma^t r_t \mid s_0 = s, a_0 = a, \pi\right]$$

The form is similar to the state value function, only that we are introducing the variable *a* to account for actions in a given environment as well.

To solve reinforcement learning problems utilizing value functions, we use the **Bellman equation**.

The Bellman equation

As one of the most important equations in the entire field of reinforcement learning, the Bellman equation is the cornerstone of solving reinforcement learning problems. Developed by applied mathematician Richard Bellman, it's less of a equation and more of a condition of optimization that models the reward of an agent's decision at a point in time based on the expected choices and rewards that could come from said decision. The Bellman equation can be derived for either the state value function or the action value function:

$$V^{\pi}(s) = \sum_{a} \pi(s, a) \sum_{s'} P^{a}_{ss'} \left[R^{a}_{ss'} + \gamma V^{\pi}(s') \right]$$

$$Q^{\pi}(s, a) = \sum_{s'} P^{a}_{ss'} \left[R^{a}_{ss'} + \gamma \sum_{a'} Q^{\pi}(s', a') \right]$$

As usual, let's break down these equations. We're going to focus on the state value function. First, we have the summation of all policies for every state/action pair:

$$\sum_{a} \pi(s, a)$$

Next, we have the transition probability; it's the probability of being in state *s*, taking action *a*, and ending up in state s':

$$P^{a}_{ss'}$$

Next is the cumulative reward that we discussed earlier:

$$R^{a}_{ss'}$$

Lastly, we have the discounted value of the function:

$$\gamma V^{\pi}(s')$$

Altogether, we're describing the entire reinforcement learning process; we want to find a state value function or an action value function that satisfies the Bellman equation. We're missing one key part here; how do we solve this in practice? One option is to use a paradigm called **dynamic programming,** which is an optimization method that was also developed by Bellman himself. One means of solving for the optimal policy with dynamic programming is to use the **value iteration method**. In this manner, we use the Bellman equation as an iterative update function. We want to converge from Q to Q* by enforcing the Bellman equation:

$$Q * (s, a) = max E[\sum_{t \geqslant 0} \gamma^2 rt | s_0 = s, a_0 = a\pi]$$

Let's see how this would work in Python by trying to solve the cartpole problem. With value iteration, we start with a random value function and then find an improved value function in an iterative process until we reach an optimal value function.

We can attempt this on the cartpole problem. Let's import gym and generate a random value function to begin with:

```
import gym
import numpy as np

def gen_random_policy():
    return (np.random.uniform(-1,1, size=4), np.random.uniform(-1,1))
```

Next, let's turn that policy into an action:

```
def policy_to_action(env, policy, obs):
    if np.dot(policy[0], obs) + policy[1] > 0:
    return 1
    else:
    return 0
```

Lastly, we can run the training process:

```
def run_episode(env, policy, t_max=1000, render=False):
    obs = env.reset()
    total_reward = 0
    for i in range(t_max):
    if render:
    env.render()
```

```
selected_action = policy_to_action(env, policy, obs)
obs, reward, done, _ = env.step(selected_action)
total_reward += reward
if done:
break
return total_reward

if __name__ == '__main__':
env = gym.make('CartPole-v0')

n_policy = 500
policy_list = [gen_random_policy() for _ in range(n_policy)]

scores_list = [run_episode(env, p) for p in policy_list]

print('Best policy score = %f' %max(scores_list))

best_policy= policy_list[np.argmax(scores_list)]
print('Running with best policy:\n')
run_episode(env, best_policy, render=True)
```

While value iterations work in this simplistic environment, we can quickly run into problems when utilizing it in larger, more complex environments. As we have to individually compute the value for every state/value pair, many unstructured inputs such as images become impossibly large. Imagine how expensive it would be to compute this function for every single pixel in an advanced video game, every time our reinforcement learning algorithm tried to make a move!

For this reason, we utilize deep learning methods to do these computations for us. Deep Neural Networks can act as function approximators. There are two primary methods, called **Deep Q-learning** and **policy gradients**.

Q–learning

Q-learning is a reinforcement learning method that utilizes the action value function, or Q function, to solve tasks. In this section, we'll talk about both traditional Q-learning as well as Deep Q-learning.

Standard Q-learning works off the core concept of the Q-table. You can think of the Q-table as a reference table; every row represents a state and every column represents an action. The values of the table are the expected future rewards that are received for a specific combination of actions and states. Procedurally, we do the following:

1. Initialize the Q-table
2. Choose an action
3. Perform that action
4. Measure the reward that was received
5. Update the Q- value

Let's walk through each of these steps to better understand the algorithm. First, we initialize the Q-table as zeros, and it is subsequently updated throughout the Q-learning training process. We then have to choose a starting action. Since the entire table is full of zeros and there is no logical starting point, we utilize a trick called the **epsilon greedy strategy** to point us in the right direction. In this strategy, we use a basic inequality:

$$n > \epsilon$$

We set the epsilon variable as 1, and draw random numbers from a distribution. If the number doesn't satisfy the inequality and is less than epsilon, our agent **explores** the space, meaning it seeks to figure out more information about where it is in order to start choosing state/action pairs so that we can calculate the Q-value. If the number is in fact larger than epsilon, we **exploit** the information that we already know to choose a Q-value to calculate. Exploration typically happens earlier in training when the algorithm knows less about the environment, and exploitation happens later in the training process when the algorithm has some information to rely on. Recall how this goes directly back to the unique nature of the action value function over the state value function. Action value functions help us postulate what would happen by taking a different action in the first time step than what the agent may want to do, and then afterward follow the policy.

After choosing and performing an action, it's time to update the Q-table. Updates are computed by using the Bellman equation:

$$Q^*(s, a) = max\mathbb{E}\left[\sum_{t \geq 0} \gamma^t r_t | s, a\right]$$

Recall that, here, we are simply stating that each Q-value in the table is the max of the expected value or the cumulative discounted reward that is the state/action combination. Over training time, the algorithm obtains accurate measures of expected future rewards for given actions at a given state. Let's walk through an example of how we would implement this process in Python to play cartpole, as we did with value iteration methods. As always, let's start with our imports:

```
import numpy as np
import gym
import random
import math
```

We'll start by creating the environment in which the agent will act. To do this, we'll simply define it as a variable that we will call environment.

```
environment = gym.make("CartPole-v0").unwrapped
```

Before we do anything else, we'll also initialize our Q-table with zeros. These zeros will be replaced during the training procedure. To do that, we can use the np.zeros function and make the q-table the size of the gym environment's action space.

```
q_table = np.zeros(10 + (env.action_space.n, ))
```

Since our Q-Learning agent relies on epsilon greedy strategy as we described above, we'll want to create a function that we can access to executes the strategy for us. The get_explore_rate function will dynamically set the exploration rate parameter for the pre-learning stage:

```
def epsilon_greedy(episode):
    return max(0.01, min(1, 1.0 - math.log10((episode+1)/25)))
```

Our model also uses an adaptive learning rate, which we can programmatically create with a function called `learning_rate()`. This function will look similar to the epsilon greedy strategy, only with slightly different values that are used within the function.

```
def learning_rate(episode):
    return max(0.1, min(0.5, 1.0 - math.log10((episode+1)/25)))
```

Next, let's define our a pythonic function to represent the Bellman Equation in our program; we'll call this function bellman(). The bellman function that we define here will not only compute the Bellman Equation below:

$$Q^*(s, a) = max\mathbb{E}\left[\sum_{t \geq 0} \gamma^t r_t | s, a\right]$$

It will also take the output of the equation and update the q-table for us. The function will take in the current state of the cartpole agent, it's new state, an action and reward pair, and finally, the episode that the agent is currently in. The function will use the `new_state` parameter in the bellman equation with `best_q = np.amax(q_table[new_state])`, and then compute an update using the `get_learning_rate` function.

```
def bellman(current_state, new_state, action, reward, episode):
    best_q = np.amax(q_table[new_state])
    q_table[current_state + (action,)] +=
get_learning_rate(episode)*(reward + 0.99*(best_q) - q_table[current_state
+ (action,)])
```

Next, we'll create a function to create the states for our Q-table:

```
def bucket(state, bucket_len_arr):
    bucket_indice = []
    bounds = list(zip(env.observation_space.low,
env.observation_space.high))
    bounds[1] = [-0.5, 0.5]
    bounds[3] = [-math.radians(50), math.radians(50)]
    for i in range(len(state)):
        if state[i] <= bounds[i][0]:
            bucket_index = 0
        elif state[i] >= bounds[i][1]:
            bucket_index = bucket_len_arr[i] - 1
        else:
            bound_width = bounds[i][1] - bounds[i][0]
            offset = (bucket_len_arr[i]-1)*bounds[i][0]/bound_width
            scaling = (bucket_len_arr[i]-1)/bound_width
            bucket_index = int(round(scaling*state[i] - offset))
        bucket_indice.append(bucket_index)
    return tuple(bucket_indice)
```

We'll also have to create a function to choose the initial action because of the algorithm's exploration.

```
def choose_action(state, episode):
    if random.uniform(0,1) < epsilon_greedy(episode):
        action = env.action_space.sample()
    else:
        action = np.argmax(q_table[state, :])
    return action
```

Lastly, we simply have to create a function to run the whole process. This code block iterates over the number of training episodes, and uses each of the functions that we defined about in order to learning how to keep to cart's pole from falling down.

```
total_reward = []
for episode in range(episodes):
    current_state = bucket(env.reset(), (1,1,6,3))
    ## Initialize the reward
    episode_reward = 0
    for leng in range(episode_length):
        env.render()
        action = choose_action(current_state, episode)
        obv, reward, done, _ = env.step(action)
        new_state = bucket(obv, (1,1,6,3))
        ## Update the q-table using the bellman equation
        print(new_state)
        bellman(current_state, new_state, action, reward, episode)
        ## Update the current state to the new selected state
        current_state = new_state
        ## Set the current reward as the episode reward
        episode_reward += reward
        if done:
            break

total_reward.append(episode_reward)
```

Let's break down this block a bit; `current_state = bucket(env.reset(), (1,1,6,3))` will take a state from the bucket of states. From there, this block below will compute the action, reward, state iterative process that we described earlier.

```
for leng in range(episode_length):
        env.render()
        action = choose_action(current_state, episode)
        obv, reward, done, _ = env.step(action)
        new_state = bucket(obv, (1,1,6,3))
```

We than update the q-table:

```
## Update the q-table using the bellman equation
        print(new_state)
        bellman(current_state, new_state, action, reward, episode)
```

Then, update the current state:

```
## Update the current state to the new selected state
        current_state = new_state
```

Finally, we set the reward and update the total reward:

```
## Set the current reward as the episode reward
        episode_reward += reward
        if done:
            break

total_reward.append(episode_reward)
```

Standard Q-learning can become challenging; the sheer fact that our algorithm must learn every Q-value pair makes for an incredibly difficult problem set! As you've probably noticed by this point in the book, when problems get difficult in AI, we often generalize or approximate them to make them easier to solve. Instead, we can use **Deep Q-learning,** which is where we replace the process of individually calculating values in a Q-table with a neural network that approximates these values.

Architecturally, Deep Q-learning utilizes a Convolutional Neural Network to take in states and approximate actions based on those states.

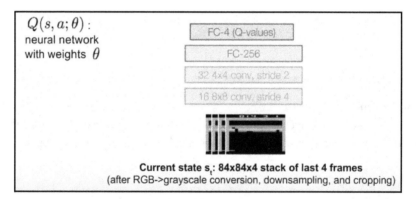

Current state s_t: 84x84x4 stack of last 4 frames
(after RGB->grayscale conversion, downsampling, and cropping)

As we now have a neural network, we'll have to create a loss function and optimization procedure for it as well. In Deep Q-learning, we create a loss function that minimizes the error of the Bellman equation:

$$L_i(\theta_i) = \mathbb{E}_{s,a \sim p(\cdot)}[(y_i - Q(s, a; \theta_i))^2]$$

Here, $y(i)$ is the convergence equation:

$$y_i = [r + \gamma max Q(s', a'; \theta_{i-1}|s, a]$$

In our backward pass, we compute our gradient update with respect to the parameters of the Q-function. The last layer's outputs are approximations of the Q-values for each possible action given the current state.

There are still problems with this that we have to overcome, however, learning from consecutive samples is bad practice. These samples are going to be correlated, and they can easily lead us off course. Think for a moment about how easily a game character could walk in the wrong direction based on immediate feedback from the area around it. This can lead to biased samples and negative feedback loops.

We can remedy this with a technique known as **experience replay**. Experience replay essentially consists of a table of transitions from state to action, reward, and onto a new state. In a way, this table becomes the network's memory of experiences that it can draw from when facing a situation. During training, we take random mini batches of these transitions from memory so that the network can learn distinct experiences.

Policy optimization

Policy optimization methods are an alternative to Q-learning and value function approximation. Instead of learning the Q-values for state/action pairs, these methods directly learn a policy π that maps state to an action by calculating a gradient. Fundamentally, for a search such as for an optimization problem, policy methods are a means of learning the correct policy from a stochastic distribution of potential policy actions. Therefore, our network architecture changes a bit to learn a policy directly:

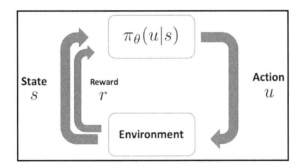

Because every state has a distribution of possible actions, the optimization problem becomes easier. We no longer have to compute exact rewards for specific actions. Recall that deep learning methods rely on the concept of an episode. In the case of deep reinforcement learning, each episode represents a game or task, while **trajectories** represent plays or directions within that game or task. We can define a trajectory as a path of state/action/reward combinations, represented by the Greek letter tau (T):

$$\tau = (s_0, a_0, r_0, s_1, a_1, r_1, \ldots, s_{T-1}, r_{T-1}, S_T)$$

Think about a robot learning to walk; if we used Q-learning or another dynamic programming method for this task, our algorithms would need to learn exactly how much reward to assign to every single joint movement for every possible trajectory. The algorithm would need to learn timings, exact angles to bend the robotic limbs, and so on. By learning a policy directly, the algorithm can simply focus on the overall task of moving the robot's feet when it walks.

When utilizing policy gradient methods, we can define an individual policy in the same simple manner as we did with Q-learning; our policy is the expected sum of future discounted rewards:

$$J(\theta) = \mathbb{E}\left[\sum_{t \geq 0} \gamma^t r_t \,|\, \pi_\theta\right]$$

Therefore, the goal of our network becomes to *maximize* some policy, J, in order to maximize our expected future reward:

$$\theta^* = argmax\, J(\theta)$$

One way to learn a policy is to use gradient methods, hence the name *policy* gradients. Since we want to find a policy that maximizes reward, we perform the opposite of gradient descent, *gradient ascent*, on a distribution of potential policies:

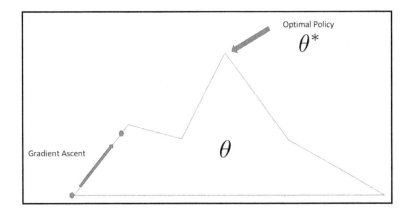

The parameters of the new neural network become the parameters of our policy, so by performing gradient ascent and updating the network parameters, π^* becomes θ^*. Fully deriving policy gradients is outside the scope of this book, however, let's touch upon some high-level concepts of how policy gradient methods work in practice. Take a look at the following landscape; there are three potential paths with three potential end rewards:

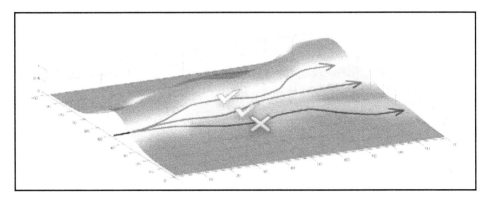

Policy gradient methods seek to increase the probability of taking the path that leads to the highest reward. Mathematically, the standard policy gradient method looks as follows:

$$\hat{g} = \hat{E}_t[\nabla \circ log\pi_0(a_t|s_t)\hat{A}t]$$

As usual, let's break this down a bit. We'll start by saying that our gradient, g, is the expected value of the gradient *times* the log of our policy for a given action/state pair, times the **advantage**. Advantage is simply the action value function minus the state value function:

$$A(s, a) = Q(s, a) - V(s)$$

In implementation, vanilla policy gradient methods still run into problems. One particularly notable issue is called the credit assignment problem, in which a reward signal received from a long trajectory of interaction happens at the end of the trajectory. Policy gradient methods have a hard time ascertaining which action caused this reward and finds difficulty *assigning credit* for that action.

Policy gradients are an outline for an entire class of algorithms that can be built around this idea. The key to optimizing these methods is in the details of individual optimization procedures. In the next section, we'll look at several means to improve on vanilla policy gradient methods.

Extensions on policy optimization

One common way to compute policy gradients is with the **Reinforce algorithm**. Reinforce is a Monte-Carlo policy gradient method that uses likelihood ratios to estimate the value of a policy at a given point. The algorithm can lead to high variance.

Vanilla policy gradient methods can be challenging as they are extremely sensitive to what you choose for your step size parameter. Choose a step size too big and the correct policy is overwhelmed by noise – too small and the training becomes incredibly slow. Our next class of reinforcement learning algorithms, **proximal policy optimization** (PPO), seeks to remedy this shortcoming of policy gradients. PPO is a new class of reinforcement learning algorithms that was released by OpenAI in 2017 that makes computation and optimization more effective by **clipping** its loss function:

$$L^{CLIP}(\theta) = \hat{E}_t[min(r_t(\theta)\hat{A}_t, clip(r_t(\theta), 1 - \epsilon, 1 + \epsilon)\hat{A}_t)]$$

You can see the clipping in action on the right-hand side of the loss function. We bring back the ϵ as our clipping parameter:

$$clip(r_r(\theta), 1 - \epsilon, 1 + \epsilon)A_t$$

The clipping expression tells us that if the reward for optimal policy parameters causes the loss to increase past a certain threshold, it will be clipped. Looking at the full expression, if the value of:

$$A(s, a) = Q(s, a) - V(s)$$

is greater than 0, this means that an individual action was better than the average of all the other possible actions for that state. Therefore, the clipping function will encourage that action by increasing the reward, thereby encouraging that action to be adopted. Likewise, a value of *A* less than *0* will decrease the reward and discourage the action. Essentially, this restricts the range that the new policy can vary from the old one, overcoming the step size issue seen with vanilla policy gradients.

Summary

In this chapter, we learned the important foundations of reinforcement learning, one of the most visible practices in the AI field.

Reinforcement learning is based on the concepts of agents acting in an environment and taking action based on what it sees in its surrounding environment. An agent's actions are guided by either policy optimization methods or dynamic programming methods that help it learn how to interact with its environment. We use dynamic programming methods when we care more about exploration and off-policy learning. On the other hand, we use policy optimization methods when we have dense, continuous problem spaces and we only want to optimize for what we care about.

We'll look at several different real-world applications of reinforcement learning in the upcoming chapter.

Deep Learning for Intelligent Agents

9

Intelligent Assistants are one of the most visible forms of **Artificial Intelligence** (**AI**) that we see in our daily lives. Siri, Alexa, and other systems have come to be commonplace in day-to-day life in the 21st century. This chapter will commence our section of chapters that dive deeply into the application of **Artificial Neural Networks** (**ANNs**) for creating AI systems. In this chapter, we will cover one new topic, word embeddings, and then proceed to focus on the application of **Recurrent Neural Networks** (**RNNs**) and generative networks to natural language processing tasks. While an entire book could have been written about deep learning for natural language processing, as is already the case, we'll touch upon the core concepts that you'll need to get started in building natural language AI platforms.

We will be covering the following topics in this chapter:

- Word embeddings
- Constructing a basic agent

Technical requirements

In this chapter, we will be using Python 3 with a few standard python packages that you've seen before:

- Numpy
- TensorFlow
- A GPU-enabled computer, or an AWS account for cloud computing, as described in Chapter 3, *Platforms and Other Essentials*

Word embeddings

So far, in our discussion of AI and deep learning, we've focused a lot on how rooted this field is in fundamental mathematical principles; so what do we do when we are faced with an unstructured source data such as text? In the previous chapters, we've talked about how we can convert images to numbers via convolutions, so how do we do the same thing with text? In modern AI systems, we use a technique called **word embedding**.

Word embedding is not a class of predictive models itself, but a means of pre-processing text so that it can be an input to a predictive model, or as an exploratory technique for data mining. It's a means by which we convert words and sentences into vectors of numbers, themselves called **word embeddings**. The document, or group of documents, that is used to train an embedding algorithm is called a **corpus**, and these provide our embedding algorithms with a **vocabulary** which they draw upon. As we've seen before, once we have these vectors of numbers, it's easy to do lots of computations on top of them.

There are basic techniques for doing this, notably the bag-of-words method, which focuses solely on **term frequency** (the amount of times a word appears in a document). Bag-of-words models output a term **frequency matrix**, which tracks how often words appear, and a single row of this matrix becomes the embedding for a single sentence:

	I	believe	that	cats	are	better	than	dogs
Doc 1	2	1	1	1	1		1	5
Doc 2	3	1				3		2
Doc 3	3				4		1	

This method is not very effective and should never be used in practice; it disregards grammar and word order, and results in incredibly large vectors. Imagine how large an embedding would be for a long sentence, or perhaps a paragraph?

The benefit of modern word embedding methods is that they give us compact vectors that decrease the computational load needed from the models that will use these vectors. These embeddings are low-dimensional vector representations of text that preserve the meaning and similarities of that text. For instance, take a look at the following diagram with a modern embedding model: man and woman should be the same distance apart as king is to queen, preserving the inherent linguistic relationships between the words. We can even do vector math with these embeddings, with the most popular example shown as follows:

king - man + woman = queen

Why is this important? It's because it shows that these modern embedding methods capture dimensions of meaning. A single digit in a word vector might embed the tense of the word, whether it's masculine or feminine, or other characters. This helps make sure that any predictive model that we use on top of word embeddings will easily be able to extract meaning from them.

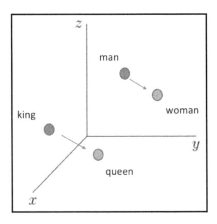

These methods are not just limited to the English language; word embedding techniques work for all spoken languages because of some of the inherent properties of natural language. Words naturally embed themselves into something called a **Lie group**, which has special properties in geometry.

There are two methods by means of which we can obtain word embeddings:

- **Dimensionality reduction**: Similar to PCA, we can condense sentences into a more compact representation that allows us to wrk with them in a simpler manner. This leads to more efficient representations.
- **Contextual similarity**: This method preserves information sepcifical to lead to greater analogous relationships, but is less efficient

These models can also be predictive, where they predict a word, sequence, or pair based on a trained predictive algorithm, or they can count based on where co-occurrence relationships help to determine word relationships.

In this chapter, we are going to take a look at the two most popular methods; a predictive method called **Word2vec**, and a count-based method called **GloVe**.

Word2vec

The Word2vec algorithm, invented by Tomas Mikolav while he was at Google in 2013, was one of the first modern embedding methods. It is a shallow, two-layer neural network that follows a similar intuition to the autoencoder in that network and is trained to perform a certain task without being actually used to perform that task. In the case of the Word2vec algorithm, that task is learning the representations of natural language. You can think of this algorithm as a context algorithm – everything that it knows is from learning the contexts of words within sentences. It works off something called the **distributional hypothesis**, which tells us that the context for each word is found from its neighboring words. For instance, think about a corpus vector with 500 dimensions. Each word in the corpus is represented by a distribution of weights across every single one of those elements. It's not a one-to-one mapping; the embedding of each word is dependent upon every other word in the corpus.

In its basic form, Word2vec has a structure similar to many of the feedforward neural networks that we've already seen – it has an **input layer**, a **hidden layer**, and an **output layer**, all parameterized by a matrix **W**. It iterates through an input corpus word by word and develops vectors for that word. The algorithm actually contains two distinct variations, the **CBOW** (**continuous bag of words**) model and the **skip-gram model,** which handle the creation of word vectors differently. Architecturally, the skip-gram model and the CBOW model are essentially reversed versions of one another.

The skip-gram model is shown in the following diagram:

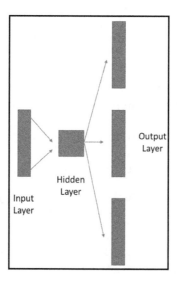

The mirror image of the skip-gram model is the CBOW model:

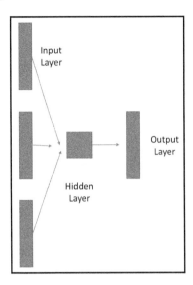

In the skip-gram model, the network looks at sequences of words and tries to predict the likelihood of a certain combination of words occurring. The skip-gram method predicts the context given a particular word. The model inputs a singular letter, w, and outputs a vector of words, $w_1, w_2... w_n$. Breaking down this process, the preceding model takes in a one-hot encoded representation of an input word during training. The matrix between the input layer and the hidden layer of the network represents the vocabulary that the network is building, the rows of which will become our vectors. Each row in the matrix corresponds to one word in the vocabulary. The matrix gets updated row by row with new embeddings as new data flows through the network. Again, recall how we are not actually interested in what comes out of the network; we are interested in the embeddings that are created in the matrix W. This method works well with small amounts of training data and is good at embedding rare words. In the CBOW method, the input to the model is $w_1, w_2 ... w_n$, the words surrounding the current word that the model is embedding. CBOW predicts the word given the context. The CBOW method is faster than the skip-gram method and is better at embedding frequent words, but it requires a great deal of data given that it relies on context as input.

To illustrate this further, take this simple sentence:

The dog jumped over the fence

The skip-gram model parses the sentence by focusing on a subject, breaking the subject into chunks called **grams**, each time skipping as follows:

{The dog jumped, The dog over, dog jumped over, dog jumped the .... and so on}

On the other hand, under the CBOW method, the grams would iteratively move through the context of the sentence as follows:

{The dog jumped, dog jumped over, jumped over the, over the fence}

Training Word2vec models

As Word2vec models are neural networks themselves, we train them just like a standard feedforward network with a loss function and stochastic gradient descent. During the training process, the algorithm scans over the input corpus and takes batches of it as input. After each batch, a loss is calculated. When optimizing, we want to minimize our loss as we would with a standard feedforward neural network.

Let's walk through how we would create and train a Word2vec model in TensorFlow:

1. First, let's start with our imports. We'll use our standard `tensorflow` and `numpy` imports and the Python library itertools, as well as two utility functions from the machine learning package `scikit-learn`. The following code block shows the same:

```
import numpy as np
import tensorflow as tf
from itertools import compress
from sklearn.base import BaseEstimator, TransformerMixin
from sklearn.metrics.pairwise import pairwise_distances
```

2. First things first, let's import our data. You can find the data file in the repo that corresponds to this chapter:

```
with open('/users/patricksmith/desktop/corpus.txt') as f:
    words = [word for line in f.readlines() for word in
line.split()]

words = words[:10000]
vocabulary_size = 500
```

3. Next, let's write a function to build our dataset. This will handle many of the necessary preparatory tasks that our model requires. We'll call this function `prepareData`. It takes two parameters, the corpus we will be feeding in words, and a vocabulary size, which is the maximum number of individual word tokens that we would produce in our vocabulary:

```python
from collections import Counter

def prepareData(words, vocabulary_size=50000):
    ## We are uses a token, UNK to replace rare words in the
corpus
    count = [['UNK', -1]]
count.extend(collections.Counter(words).most_common(vocabulary_size
 - 1))

    ## Initialize a dictionary to store the word counts in
    dictionary = dict()
    for word, _ in count:
        dictionary[word] = len(dictionary)
        data = list()
        unk_count = 0

 ## Add Words to the Vocabulary
 for word in words:
     if word in dictionary:
         index = dictionary[word]
     else:
         index = 0
         unk_count += 1
     data.append(index)

 count[0][1] = unk_count
 reverse_dictionary = dict(zip(dictionary.values(),
dictionary.keys()))

    ## Return the data, count of frequent words, and the dictionary
    return data, count, dictionary, reverse_dictionary
```

4. Next, let's work on building out our models; we're going to build out both the skip-gram model, and the CBOW model, and compare their workings.

5. Let's start with the skip-gram model; our inputs will be our raw data, the batch size for processing that data, and a window size, as can be seen in the following code block:

```python
def skipgram(data, batch_size, num_skips, skip_window):
    ## The Data Index Function will be available to both of our models
```

```
      global data_index
      ## Split the input data into batches
      batch = np.ndarray(shape=(batch_size), dtype=np.int32)
      labels = np.ndarray(shape=(batch_size, 1), dtype=np.int32)
      span = 2 * skip_window + 1 # [ skip_window target skip_window
]

      ## Collects the data within the window size
      buffer = collections.deque(maxlen=span)
      for _ in range(span):
          buffer.append(data[data_index])
          data_index = (data_index + 1) % len(data)
      ## Target at the center of the buffer
      for i in range(batch_size // num_skips):
          target = skip_window
          targets_to_avoid = [ skip_window ]
          for j in range(num_skips):
              while target in targets_to_avoid:
                  target = random.randint(0, span - 1)
              targets_to_avoid.append(target)
              batch[i * num_skips + j] = buffer[skip_window]
              labels[i * num_skips + j, 0] = buffer[target]
          buffer.append(data[data_index])
          data_index = (data_index + 1) % len(data)

  return batch, labels
```

6. Next, let's create our CBOW function; we'll give it the same parameters as the skip-gram function:

```
def cbow(data, batch_size, num_skips, skip_window):
  batch = np.ndarray(shape=(batch_size, num_skips), dtype=np.int32)
  labels = np.ndarray(shape=(batch_size, 1), dtype=np.int32)
  span = 2 * skip_window + 1
  buffer = collections.deque(maxlen=span)
    for _ in range(span):
      buffer.append(data[data_index])
      data_index = (data_index + 1) % len(data)
    for i in range(batch_size):
      mask = [1] * span
      mask[skip_window] = 0
      batch[i, :] = list(compress(buffer, mask))
      labels[i, 0] = buffer[skip_window]
      buffer.append(data[data_index])
      data_index = (data_index + 1) % len(data)
  return batch, labels
```

7. Now that we have our components, we can start creating our Word2vec model. We'll start by initializing all of the variables needed to run the model.

8. The parameters of the `BaseEstimator` and `TransformerMixin` classes are from sklearn's base package, and help with creating data pipelines:

```
class Word2Vec(BaseEstimator, TransformerMixin):

    ## These will be the default parameters of our network
    def __init__(self, batch_size=128, num_skips=2, skip_window=1,
        architecture='skip-gram', embedding_size=128,
    vocabulary_size=50000,
        loss_type='sampled_softmax_loss', n_neg_samples=64,
        optimize='Adagrad',
        learning_rate=1.0, n_steps=100001,
        valid_size=16, valid_window=100):

    ## As always, we must initialize all variables as placeholders in
    TensorFlow
        self.batch_size = batch_size
        self.num_skips = num_skips
        self.skip_window = skip_window
        self.architecture = architecture
        self.embedding_size = embedding_size
        self.vocabulary_size = vocabulary_size
        self.loss_type = loss_type
        self.n_neg_samples = n_neg_samples
        self.optimize = optimize
        self.learning_rate = learning_rate
        self.n_steps = n_steps
        self.valid_size = valid_size
        self.valid_window = valid_window
        self.chooseSamples()
        self.chooseGenerator()
        self._init_graph()
        self.sess = tf.Session(graph=self.graph)
```

9. Next, we'll create the two functions that we just initialized; `chooseSamples` and `chooseGenerator`. The first function, `chooseSamples`, makes sure that samples that our network draws are within the appropriate size as defined by our window and size parameters.

10. The other function, `chooseGenerator`, will simply allow us to toggle between the two different architectures that we have already built:

```
def chooseSamples(self):
    valid_examples =
    np.array(random.sample(range(self.valid_window), self.valid_size))
```

```
        self.valid_examples = valid_examples

    def chooseGenerator(self):
        if self.architecture == 'skip-gram':
            self.generate_batch = skipgram
        elif self.architecture == 'cbow':
            self.generate_batch = cbow
```

11. Next, we'll build a function to build a `dictionary` in order to map individual word tokens to their indices. This will help us to keep track of where each individual token was within a sentence:

```
    def TokenMapping(self, words):

        data, count, dictionary, reverse_dictionary =
    build_dataset(words, self.vocabulary_size)
        self.dictionary = dictionary
        self.reverse_dictionary = reverse_dictionary
        self.count = count

        return data
```

12. Now that we've set up our model and input functions, let's initiate all of our variables in the TensorFlow graph and wrap these operations in a function itself, which we will call `CreateGraph`:

```
    def CreateGraph(self):

        self.graph = tf.Graph()
        ## Tell the computer to use the CPU; change to GPU is you have
one
        with self.graph.as_default(), tf.device('/cpu:0')
            tf.set_random_seed(SEED)

            ## Set our input data based on the model selected
            if self.architecture == 'skip-gram':
              self.train_dataset = tf.placeholder(tf.int32,
shape=[self.batch_size])
            elif self.architecture == 'cbow':
              self.train_dataset = tf.placeholder(tf.int32,
shape=[self.batch_size, self.num_skips])

            ## Input our labels into the graph
            self.train_labels = tf.placeholder(tf.int32,
shape=[self.batch_size, 1])
            self.valid_dataset = tf.constant(self.valid_examples,
dtype=tf.int32)
```

```
        ## Set our embedding variables
        self.embeddings = tf.Variable(
          tf.random_uniform([self.vocabulary_size,
self.embedding_size], -1.0, 1.0))

        ## Set the weight variable based on the vocab and embedding
size
        self.weights = tf.Variable(
          tf.truncated_normal([self.vocabulary_size,
self.embedding_size],
            stddev=1.0 / math.sqrt(self.embedding_size)))

        ## Set the bias factor based on the embedding size
        self.biases = tf.Variable(tf.zeros([self.vocabulary_size]))
```

13. Under the initialization, we'll also set some operations to compute the loss at each step, calculate the similarity between the embedding structures, and optimize the loss function:

```
    if self.architecture == 'skip-gram':
        self.embed = tf.nn.embedding_lookup(self.embeddings,
self.train_dataset)
    elif self.architecture == 'cbow':
        embed = tf.zeros([self.batch_size, self.embedding_size])
        for j in range(self.num_skips):
          embed += tf.nn.embedding_lookup(self.embeddings,
self.train_dataset[:, j])
        self.embed = embed
    ## Compute the loss
    if self.loss_type == 'sampled_softmax_loss':
        loss = tf.nn.sampled_softmax_loss(weights=self.weights,
biases=self.biases, inputs=self.embed,
          labels=self.train_labels, num_sampled=self.n_neg_samples,
num_classes=self.vocabulary_size)
    elif self.loss_type == 'nce_loss':
        loss= tf.nn.nce_loss(weights=self.weights,
biases=self.biases, inputs=self.embed,
          labels=self.train_labels,
num_sampled=self.n_neg_samples,num_classes= self.vocabulary_size)
        self.loss = tf.reduce_mean(loss, name="loss")
    ## Optimizer for the loss function
    if self.optimize == 'Adagrad':
      self.optimizer =
tf.train.AdagradOptimizer(self.learning_rate).minimize(loss)
        ## Tell Word2Vec to optimize utilizing stochastic gradient
descent
    elif self.optimize == 'SGD':
      self.optimizer =
```

```
tf.train.GradientDescentOptimizer(self.learning_rate).minimize(loss
)
        ## Compute similarity distance metrics between the individual
embeddings
        norm = tf.sqrt(tf.reduce_sum(tf.square(self.embeddings), 1,
keep_dims=True))
        self.normalized_embeddings = self.embeddings / norm
        self.valid_embeddings = tf.nn.embedding_lookup(
          self.normalized_embeddings, self.valid_dataset)
        self.similarity = tf.matmul(self.valid_embeddings,
tf.transpose(self.normalized_embeddings))

        ## Lastly, Iniatialize all of the variables in the graph
        self.init_op = tf.global_variables_initializer()
```

14. Lastly, let's create a function to actually `fit` our Word2vec model to the data. We'll create this to work in a similar way to `scikit-learn` functions that you're already familiar with:

```
def fit(self, words):
    ## Our build dictionaries function for the data, which calls
open our original processing function
    data = self._build_dictionaries(words)

    ## Initialize a TensorFlow session
    session = self.sess

    ## Run the sessions
    session.run(self.init_op)

    average_loss = 0

    for step in range(self.n_steps):
        batch_data, batch_labels = self.generate_batch(data,
        self.batch_size, self.num_skips, self.skip_window)
        feed_dict = {self.train_dataset : batch_data,
self.train_labels : batch_labels}
        op, l = session.run([self.optimizer, self.loss],
feed_dict=feed_dict)
        average_loss += l
        if step % 2000 == 0:
            if step > 0:
                average_loss = average_loss / 2000
            print('Average loss at step %d: %f' % (step,
average_loss))
            average_loss = 0

    final_embeddings = session.run(self.normalized_embeddings)
```

```
    self.final_embeddings = final_embeddings

    return self
```

15. Now, the moment we've been waiting for; running the model! Let's initialize an instance of our newly created `word2vec` model; we'll use the CBOW architecture, and tell it to iterate for `10001` steps. All we have to do now is call `fit` on this initialized model, and away we go:

```
word2vec = Word2Vec(vocabulary_size=vocabulary_size,
architecture='cbow', n_steps=10001)
word2vec.fit(words)
```

You should see the result as follows:

```
Average loss at step 0: 5.470483
Average loss at step 2000: 4.858315
Average loss at step 4000: 1.993593
Average loss at step 6000: 1.808280
Average loss at step 8000: 1.732310
Average loss at step 10000: 1.690384
```

As mentioned earlier, Word2vec was built around the idea of preserving analogies (that is: *King - Man + Woman = Queen*). One of the downsides to this architectural approach, however, is that many of the latent statistical properties of the text get lost for the sake of preserving analogies. For example, the words *the* and *horse* might appear together often in a corpus, but the Word2vec algorithm would not be able to distinguish whether the word *the* was intrinsically linked to *horse*, or whether it is just a common word. To remedy this, in 2014, researchers developed another algorithm, GloVe, which would focus more on preserving key statistical information while still maintaining the analogous nature that made Word2vec so popular.

GloVe

Globalized Vectors (**GloVe**) was developed by the Stanford NLP group in 2014 as a probabilistic follow-up to Word2Vec. GloVe was designed to preserve the analogies framework used by Word2vec, but instead uses dimensionality reduction techniques that would preserve key statistical information about the words themselves. Unlike Word2vec, which learns by streaming sentences, GloVe learns embeddings by constructing a rich co-occurrence matrix. The co-occurrence matrix is a global store of semantic information, and is key to the GloVe algorithm. The creators of GloVe developed it on the principle that co-occurrence ratios between two words in a context are closely related to meaning.

So how does it work, and how is it different from Word2vec? GloVe creates a word embedding by means of the following:

1. Iterating over a sentence, word by word
2. For each word, the algorithm looks at its context
3. Given the word and its context, GloVe creates a new entry in the co-occurrence matrix
4. GloVe then reduces the dimensions of the co-occurrence matrix to create embeddings
5. After creating the embedding, GloVe calculates its new loss function based on the accuracy of that embedding

Let's walk through the GloVe algorithm alongside a Python implementation to see how it all pans out. We're going to be using the Cornell movie lines dataset, which contains over 200,000 fictional movie script lines. Later on, we'll use the embeddings we generated from this dataset in our intelligent agent. First, let's write a function to import the data:

```
import os
 def loadText(fileName, fields):
 ''' Function to Load the Movie Lines text '''
     lines = {}
     with open(fileName, 'r', encoding='iso-8859-1') as f:
     for line in f:
         values = line.split(" +++$+++ ")
         lineObj = {}
         for i, field in enumerate(fields):
             lineObj[field] = values[i]
         lines[lineObj['lineID']] = lineObj

     return lines
```

We can then use this function to actually load the movie lines:

```
lines = {}
movie_lines = ["lineID","characterID","movieID","character","text"]
lines = loadText("/users/patricksmith/desktop/glove/movie_lines.txt",
movie_lines)
```

Now, let's get back to GloVe. Unlike Word2vec, GloVe parses over a sentence word by word, focusing on local context by using a fixed context window size. In word embedding, the window size represents the extent to which and what an algorithm will focus on in order to provide context to a word's meaning. There are two forms of context window sizes in GloVe – symmetric and asymmetric. For example, take a look at the following sentence:

The horse ran fast across the finish line in the race.

With a symmetric window size, the algorithm would look at words on either side of the subject. If GloVe was looking at the word *finish* with a window size of 2 in the preceding example, the context would be *across the* and *line in*. Asymmetric windows look only at the preceding words, so the same window size of 2 would capture *across the*, but not *line in*.

Let's go ahead and initialize our GloVe class and variables:

```
class GloVeModel():
    def __init__(self, embedding_size, window_size, max_vocab_size=100000,
min_occurrences=1,
                 scaling_factor=3/4, cooccurrence_cap=100, batch_size=512,
learning_rate=0.05):
        self.embedding_size = embedding_size
        if isinstance(context_size, tuple):
            self.left_context, self.right_context = context_size
        elif isinstance(context_size, int):
            self.left_context = self.right_context = context_size
        self.max_vocab_size = max_vocab_size
        self.min_occurrences = min_occurrences
        self.scaling_factor = scaling_factor
        self.cooccurrence_cap = cooccurrence_cap
        self.batch_size = batch_size
        self.learning_rate = learning_rate
        self.__words = None
        self.__word_to_id = None
        self.__cooccurrence_matrix = None
        self.__embeddings = None

    def fit_to_corpus(self, corpus):
        self.__fit_to_corpus(corpus, self.max_vocab_size,
self.min_occurrences,
        self.left_context, self.right_context)
        self.__build_graph()

    def __fit_to_corpus(self, corpus, vocab_size, min_occurrences, left_size,
right_size):
        word_counts = Counter()
        cooccurrence_counts = defaultdict(float)
        for region in corpus:
            word_counts.update(region)
            for l_context, word, r_context in _context_windows(region,
left_size, right_size):
                for i, context_word in enumerate(l_context[::-1]):
                    cooccurrence_counts[(word, context_word)] += 1 / (i + 1)
                for i, context_word in enumerate(r_context):
                    cooccurrence_counts[(word, context_word)] += 1 / (i + 1)
        if len(cooccurrence_counts) == 0:
            raise ValueError("No coccurrences in corpus. Did you try to reuse
```

```
a generator?")
        self.__words = [word for word, count in
word_counts.most_common(vocab_size)
            if count >= min_occurrences]
    self.__word_to_id = {word: i for i, word in
enumerate(self.__words)}
        self.__cooccurrence_matrix = {
        (self.__word_to_id[words[0]], self.__word_to_id[words[1]]): count
            for words, count in cooccurrence_counts.items()
            if words[0] in self.__word_to_id and words[1] in
self.__word_to_id}
```

We end up with a co-occurrence matrix that can tell us how often certain words occur together given a certain window size:

	the	cat	sat	on	mat
the	2	1	2	1	1
cat	1	1	1	1	0
sat	2	1	1	1	0
on	1	1	1	1	1
mat	1	0	0	1	1

While this table looks simple, it contains global statistical properties about the co-occurrence of the words within. From it, we can calculate the probabilities of certain words occurring together:

Probability and Ratio	$k = solid$	$k = gas$	$k = water$	$k = fashion$
$P(k|ice)$	1.9×10^{-4}	6.6×10^{-5}	3.0×10^{-3}	1.7×10^{-5}
$P(k|steam)$	2.2×10^{-5}	7.8×10^{-4}	2.2×10^{-3}	1.8×10^{-5}
$P(k|ice)/P(k|steam)$	8.9	8.5×10^{-2}	1.36	0.96

As the co-occurrence matrix is combinatorial in size (it can become large very quickly), it leads to extremely large matrices of co-occurrence information. How do we remedy this? We can factorize the matrix to create a lower-dimensional matrix where each row contains a vector representation of a given word. This performs a form of dimensionality reduction on the co-occurrence matrix. We then pre-process the matrix by normalizing and log—smoothing the occurrence information. GloVe will learn vectors so that their differences predict occurrence ratios. All of this will maintain rich global statistical properties while still preserving the analogies that make Word2vec so desirable.

GloVe is trained by minimizing a reconstruction loss that helps the model find the lower-dimensional representations that can explain the highest amount of variance in the original data. It utilizes a least squares loss function that seeks to minimize the difference between the dot product of two embeddings of a word and the log of their co-occurrence count:

$$J = \sum_{i,j=1}^{V} f(X_{ij})(w_i^T \tilde{w}_j + b_i + \tilde{b}_j - \log(X_{ij}))^2$$

Let's break this down; w_i is a word vector and b_i is a bias factor for a specific word i, while w_j and b_j are the word vector and bias factor for the context vector. X_{ij} is the count from the co-occurrence matrix of how many times i and j occur together. f is a weighting function for both rare and frequent co-occurrences so that they do not skew the results. In all, this loss function looks at the weight co-occurrences of a word and its neighboring context words, and multiplies that by the right term, which computes a combination of the word, its contexts, biases, and co-occurrences.

Let's go ahead and initialize GloVe's graph in TensorFlow to proceed with the training process:

```
def __build_graph(self):
 self.__graph = tf.Graph()
 with self.__graph.as_default(), self.__graph.device(_device_for_node):
 count_max = tf.constant([self.cooccurrence_cap], dtype=tf.float32,
 name='max_cooccurrence_count')
 scaling_factor = tf.constant([self.scaling_factor], dtype=tf.float32,
 name="scaling_factor")

 self.__focal_input = tf.placeholder(tf.int32, shape=[self.batch_size],
 name="focal_words")
 self.__context_input = tf.placeholder(tf.int32, shape=[self.batch_size],
 name="context_words")
 self.__cooccurrence_count = tf.placeholder(tf.float32,
 shape=[self.batch_size],
 name="cooccurrence_count")
```

```
focal_embeddings = tf.Variable(
tf.random_uniform([self.vocab_size, self.embedding_size], 1.0, -1.0),
name="focal_embeddings")
context_embeddings = tf.Variable(
tf.random_uniform([self.vocab_size, self.embedding_size], 1.0, -1.0),
name="context_embeddings")

focal_biases = tf.Variable(tf.random_uniform([self.vocab_size], 1.0,
-1.0),
name='focal_biases')
context_biases = tf.Variable(tf.random_uniform([self.vocab_size], 1.0,
-1.0),
name="context_biases")

focal_embedding = tf.nn.embedding_lookup([focal_embeddings],
self.__focal_input)
context_embedding = tf.nn.embedding_lookup([context_embeddings],
self.__context_input)
focal_bias = tf.nn.embedding_lookup([focal_biases], self.__focal_input)
context_bias = tf.nn.embedding_lookup([context_biases],
self.__context_input)

weighting_factor = tf.minimum(
1.0,
tf.pow(
tf.div(self.__cooccurrence_count, count_max),
scaling_factor))

embedding_product = tf.reduce_sum(tf.multiply(focal_embedding,
context_embedding), 1)

log_cooccurrences = tf.log(tf.to_float(self.__cooccurrence_count))

distance_expr = tf.square(tf.add_n([
embedding_product,
focal_bias,
context_bias,
tf.negative(log_cooccurrences)]))

single_losses = tf.multiply(weighting_factor, distance_expr)
self.__total_loss = tf.reduce_sum(single_losses)
tf.summary.scalar("GloVe_loss", self.__total_loss)
self.__optimizer = tf.train.AdagradOptimizer(self.learning_rate).minimize(
self.__total_loss)
self.__summary = tf.summary.merge_all()

self.__combined_embeddings = tf.add(focal_embeddings, context_embeddings,
name="combined_embeddings")
```

Next, we'll write two functions to prepare the batches of data for the GloVe model, just as we did with Word2vec. Remember that all of this is still contained within our GloVe class:

```
def batchify(batch_size, *sequences):
    for i in range(0, len(sequences[0]), batch_size):
        yield tuple(sequence[i:i+batch_size] for sequence in sequences)

def MakeBatches(self):

    ''' Make Batches of Data to Feed The Model'''
    cooccurrences = [(word_ids[0], word_ids[1], count)
    for word_ids, count in self.__cooccurrence_matrix.items()]
        i_indices, j_indices, counts = zip(*cooccurrences)
        return list(batchify(self.batch_size, i_indices, j_indices,
counts))
```

Now, we're going to understand different properties. For those of you that have used Java before, you are familiar with the concept of getters and setters. These methods enable the changes that can happen to a variable to be controlled. The `@property` decorator is Python's response to these, as follows:

```
@property
def foo(self): return self._foo

## Is the same as

def foo(self):
    return self._foo

foo = property(foo)
```

Here, the `foo` function is replaced by a new function, `property(foo)`, which is an object with special properties called **descriptors**. Now, let's return to Word2vec:

```
@property
    def vocab_size(self):
        return len(self.__words)

    @property
    def words(self):
        if self.__words is None:
            raise NotFitToCorpusError("Need to fit model to corpus before
accessing words.")
            return self.__words

    @property
    def embeddings(self):
        if self.__embeddings is None:
```

```
        raise NotTrainedError("Need to train model before accessing
embeddings")
        return self.__embeddings

    def id_for_word(self, word):
        if self.__word_to_id is None:
            raise NotFitToCorpusError("Need to fit model to corpus before
looking up word ids.")
            return self.__word_to_id[word]
```

We'll also create a function for the `ContextWindow` that tells GloVe which words to focus on:

```
    def ContextWindow(region, left_size, right_size):
        for i, word in enumerate(region):
            start_index = i - left_size
            end_index = i + right_size
            left_context = _window(region, start_index, i - 1)
            right_context = _window(region, i + 1, end_index)
            yield (left_context, word, right_context)

## Function to Create the Window Itself
def window(region, start_index, end_index):
    last_index = len(region) + 1
    selected_tokens = region[max(start_index, 0):min(end_index,
last_index) + 1]
    return selected_tokens
```

Lastly, we'll write our function for training purposes:

```
    def train(self, num_epochs, log_dir=None, summary_batch_interval=1000):
        ## Initialize the total steps variable, which will be incrementally
adjusted in training
        total_steps = 0

        ## Start a TensorFlow session
        with tf.Session(graph=self.__graph) as session:
            if should_write_summaries:
                summary_writer = tf.summary.FileWriter(log_dir,
graph=session.graph)
                ## Initialize the variables in TensorFlow
                tf.global_variables_initializer().run()

            for epoch in range(num_epochs):
                shuffle(batches)

                for batch_index, batch in enumerate(batches):
                    i_s, j_s, counts = batch
```

```
if len(counts) != self.batch_size:
    continue
feed_dict = {
self.__focal_input: i_s,
self.__context_input: j_s,
self.__cooccurrence_count: counts}
session.run([self.__optimizer], feed_dict=feed_dict)
```

Finally, we can run our GloVe model with the following:

```
model = GloVeModel(embedding_size=300, context_size=1)
model.fit_to_corpus(corpus)
model.train(num_epochs=100)
```

GloVe's idea for dense matrices of co-occurrence information isn't new; it comes from a more traditional technique called **latent semantic analysis (LDA)** that learns embedding by decomposing bag-of-words term document matrices using a mathematical technique called **singular value decomposition (SVD)**.

Constructing a basic agent

The simplest way to construct an artificial assistant with TensorFlow is to use a **sequence-to-sequence (Seq2Seq)** model, which we learned in the chapter on RNNs.

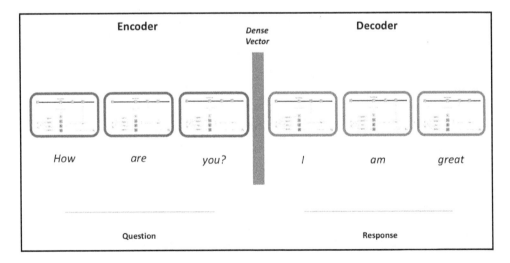

While originally developed for neural machine translation, we can adjust this model to act as an intelligent chatbot for our own purposes. We'll create the *brain* behind our assistant as a Python class called `IntelligentAssistant`. Then, we'll create the training and chatting functions for our assistant:

1. First, let's start with our standard imports and initialize our variables. Take special note of the `mask` variable here; `masks` are placeholders that allow us to handle variable-length inputs in our network:

```python
import numpy as np
import tensorflow as tf

class IntelligentAssistant:
 ''' The "Brain" behind our assistant '''

 def __init__(self, forwardPass, batch):
     self.fp = forwardPass
     self.batch = batch
     ## Here, we simple create a placeholder for the inputs to the
encoder portion of the sequence to sequence model
     self.encoder_inputs = [tf.placeholder(tf.int32, shape=[None],
name='encoder{}'.format(i)) for i in range(60)]
     ## Likewise, create a placeholder for the input to the decoder
portion of the model that will be passed from the output of the
encoder
     self.decoder_inputs = [tf.placeholder(tf.int32, shape=[None],
name='decoder{}'.format(i)) for i in range(64)]
     ## Mask for the decoder
     self.decoder_masks = [tf.placeholder(tf.float32, shape=[None],
name='mask{}'.format(i)) for i in range(64)]

     ## Placeholder for our target variables
     self.targets = self.decoder_inputs[1:]
```

2. Let's start by creating a loss function for our network. Here, we are codifying the forward pass of our network. We'll wrap this in a forward pass function, which will contain our sequence-to-sequence model and loss function:

```python
def ForwardPass(self):
    ''' The Forward Pass of Our ChatBot '''

    ## Create the Forward Pass of the Sequence to Sequence Model
    def _seq2seq_f(encoder_inputs, decoder_inputs, do_decode):
        ## Utilize a Gated Recurrent Unit as we learned about in
the previous chapter

        ## The setattr function sets our memory cells as a callable
```

```
function
        setattr(tf.contrib.rnn.GRUCell, '__deepcopy__', lambda
self, _: self)
        setattr(tf.contrib.rnn.MultiRNNCell, '__deepcopy__',
lambda self, _: self)
        return
        tf.contrib.legacy_seq2seq.embedding_attention_seq2seq(
        encoder_inputs, decoder_inputs, self.cell,
        num_encoder_symbols=EncVocabSize,
        num_decoder_symbols=DecVocabSize,
        ## Input Size for our embeddings
        embedding_size=256
        ## The output of our encoder model
        output_projection=self.output_projection,
        feed_previous=do_decode)

    if self.fw_only:
        self.outputs, self.losses =
tf.contrib.legacy_seq2seq.model_with_buckets(
        self.encoder_inputs,
        self.decoder_inputs,
        self.targets,
        self.decoder_masks,
        config.BUCKETS,
        lambda x, y: _seq2seq_f(x, y, True),
        softmax_loss_function=self.softmax_loss_function)

    ## Project the outputs for decoding
    if self.output_projection:
        for bucket in range(6):
            self.outputs[bucket] = [tf.matmul(output,
            self.output_projection[0]) + self.output_projection[1]
            for output in self.outputs[bucket]]
 else:
    self.outputs, self.losses =
tf.contrib.legacy_seq2seq.model_with_buckets(
    self.encoder_inputs,
    self.decoder_inputs,
    self.targets,
    self.decoder_masks,
    6,
    lambda x, y: _seq2seq_f(x, y, False),
    softmax_loss_function=self.softmax_loss_function)
```

3. Next, let's create the `Optimizer` for the network's loss function. We'll include everything within a TensorFlow scope:

```
def Optimizer(self):

    with tf.variable_scope('training') as scope:
        self.global_step = tf.Variable(0, dtype=tf.int32,
trainable=False, name='global_step')
        ## Tell our network to optimize if we are not doing a full
forward pass. Then, we'll set gradient descent as our optimizer.
        if not self.fp
            self.optimizer =
tf.train.GradientDescentOptimizer(config.LR)
            trainables = tf.trainable_variables()
            self.gradient_norms = []
            self.train_ops = []
            start = time.time()
            for bucket in range(6):
                ## Utilizing gradient clipping to stablize the
training
                clipped_grads, norm =
tf.clip_by_global_norm(tf.gradients(self.losses[bucket],
 trainables), 5.0)
                self.gradient_norms.append(norm)
self.train_ops.append(self.optimizer.apply_gradients(zip(clipped_gr
ads, trainables),
 global_step=self.global_step))
```

4. We can then create a small utility function to actually call the functions we just made at runtime:

```
def InitModel(self):
    self.ForwardPass()
    self.Optimizer()
```

5. Now, let's start to build out the part of the agent that will actually respond to users. This model will have three primary functions – the training state function, the production state function, and the main function – to handle the agent in its entirety:

- **The training state function**: Runs the forward pass that we just created, as well as the backward pass optimization procedure
- **The production state function**: The function that actually makes our agent chat with the world
- **The main function**: A top-level function to run the agent, training or production, in its entirety

6. Let's walk through these functions one by one:

```
def train():

    test_buckets, data_buckets, train_buckets_scale =
_get_buckets()
  IntelligentAssistant(False, 64).build_graph()

    ## Initialize The Training Session with a TensorFlow Session
    with tf.Session() as sess:
    ## Initialize all of the variables in the model
    sess.run(tf.global_variables_initializer())
    iteration = global_step.eval()
    ## Just as in the GloVe model, we need to start our loss at 0
    total_loss = 0

    while True:
        skip_step = _get_skip_step(iteration)
        bucket_id = _get_random_bucket(train_buckets_scale)
        encoder_inputs, decoder_inputs, decoder_masks =
data.get_batch(data_buckets[bucket_id],
 bucket_id, batch_size=64)

        _, step_loss, _ = run_step(sess, model, encoder_inputs,
decoder_inputs, decoder_masks, bucket_id, False)
        total_loss += step_loss
        iteration += 1

        if iteration % skip_step == 0:
            start = time.time()
            total_loss = 0
        if iteration % (10 * skip_step) == 0:
            evaluate(sess, model, test_buckets)
```

7. Next, let's look at the `production level` function:

```
def prod():
    """
    Production Level Chatting for our Intelligent Assistant
    """

    ## First, we load our vocab from the trained GloVe model
    _, enc_vocab = data.load_vocab('vocab.enc')
    inv_dec_vocab, _ = data.load_vocab('vocab.dec')

    ## Create an instance of our intelligent agent
     agent = IntelligentAgent(True, batch_size=1)
```

```
        ## Build the Tensorflow Graph
        agent.build_graph()

        ## Run the prod level chatting interface in a TensorFlow
session
        with tf.Session() as sess:
            sess.run(tf.global_variables_initializer())
            print('Hello! I am your virtual assistant)
            while True:
                line = _get_user_input() ## Retrieve the users'
responses
                if len(line) > 0 and line[-1] == '\n':
                    line = line[:-1]


    ## Tokenize the incoming sentence
    token_ids = sentence2id(enc_vocab, str(line))

    ## Assign the incoming sentence to a bucket
    bucket_id = _find_right_bucket(len(token_ids))


    encoder_inputs, decoder_inputs, decoder_masks =
    data.get_batch([(token_ids, [])],
    bucket_id,
    batch_size=1)

    _, _, output_logits = run_step(sess, model, encoder_inputs,
    decoder_inputs,
    decoder_masks, bucket_id, True)

    response = _construct_response(output_logits, inv_dec_vocab)

    ## Send the response to the user
    print(response)
```

8. Finally, the `main` function will run our agent for us:

```
def main():
''' Function to Run the Chatbot'''

## Parse the initization arguments from the command line
parser = argparse.ArgumentParser()
parser.add_argument('--mode', choices={'train', 'prod'})
args = parser.parse_args()

## Prepare the data
data.prepare_raw_data()
```

```
data.process_data()

## Train the Chatbot if train mode is selected
if args.mode == 'train':
train()

## Production Mode for the Chatbot
elif args.mode == 'prod':
prod()

if __name__ == '__main__':
main()
```

And that's it! To train the agent, run `python chabot.py --mode train` in your command-line interface. Training your agent may take a while due to the necessary load on the CPU/GPU. When it is finished training, you may run the agent by replacing the `train` flag with the `prod` flag.

Summary

In this section, we learned how to create novel, state-of-the-art intelligent assistants by using word embeddings and ANNs. Word embedding techniques are the cornerstone of AI applications for natural language. They allow us to encode natural language as mathematics that we can feed into downstream models and tasks.

Intelligent agents take these word embeddings and reason over them. They utilize two RNNs, an encoder and a decoder, in what is called a Seq2Seq model. If you cast your mind back to the chapter on recurrent neural networks, the first RNN in the Seq2Seq model encodes the input into a compressed representation, while the second network draws from that compressed representation to deliver sentences. In this way, an intelligent agent learns to respond to a user based on a representation of what it learned during the training process.

In the next chapter, we'll look into how we can create intelligent agents that can play board games.

10
Deep Learning for Game Playing

Over the past several years, one of the most notable applications of
Artificial Intelligence (**AI**) has been in the game-playing space. Especially with the recent
success of AlphaGo and AlphaGo Zero, game-playing AIs have been a topic of great public
interest. In this chapter, we'll implement two basic versions of game-playing AIs; one for a
video game and one for a board game. We'll primarily be utilizing reinforcement learning
methods as our workhorse. We'll also touch upon the methods behind some of the most
advanced game-playing AIs in existence at the moment.

In this chapter, the following topics will be covered:

- Game Trees and Fundamental Game Theory
- Constructing an AI agent to play tic-tac-toe
- Constructing an AI agent to play a simple Atari game

Technical requirements

In this chapter, we will be utilizing the following:

- TensorFlow
- OpenAI gym

It is recommend that you have access to a GPU for training the models in this chapter,
whether on your machine itself or via a cloud service platform.

Introduction

AI has been making a splash lately in the game-playing arena. DeepMind, the Google research group that created AlphaGo, have been proponents of utilizing reinforcement learning methods for game-playing applications. More and more video game companies are using deep learning methods for their AI players. So, where are we coming from, and where are we going with AI in the gaming space?

Traditionally, game-playing systems have been made up of a combination of hardcoded rules that have covered the range of behaviors that the AI is supposed to cover. Have you ever played an older adventure, first-person shooter, or strategy game where the AI players were clearly operating off a hardcoded strategy? More often than not, these AIs used a pathfinding algorithm such as Dijkstra's Algorithm to find the shortest distance between two points. IBM's Deep Blue, which won a game of chess against world champion Garry Kasparov, largely relied on more hardcoded, rule-based methods than we use now, along with an incredibly complex system of servers.

AI in the video gaming space really took off in 2015, when Google's DeepMind published their *Deep-Q learning* paper, in which they created a system to master the entire suite of classic Atari 2600 video games. By optimizing for long-term value in their networks by required them to focus on maximizing future cumulative reward, this system developed human-like strategies for game-playing that were previously unheard of. DeepMind also pushed boundaries by beating a human player in the most difficult board game known to man- Go.

 Creating AI applications with reinforcement learning is still in its infancy – it's readily apparent that these methods are poised to disrupt the entire industry. In this section, we'll discover how you can get up and running with the fundamentals of these methods to create powerful game-playing systems.

Networks for board games

When we talk about creating algorithms for game-playing, we are really talking about creating them for a specific type of game, known as a **finite two person zero-sum sequential game**. This is really just a fancy way of saying the following:

- An interactive situation between two independent actors (a game)
- There are a finite amount of ways in which the two actors can interact with each other at any point

- The game is zero-sum, meaning that the end state of the game results in a complete win for one of the actors
- The game is sequential, meaning that the actors make their moves in sequence, one after another

Classic examples of these types of games that we'll cover in this section are Tic Tac Toe, Chess, and the game of Go. Since creating and training an algorithm for a board game such as Go would be an immense task, for time and computation constraint, we'll be creating an agent to compete in a much more reasonable game with a finite amount of steps: chess. In this section, we'll introduce some of the fundamental concepts behind game-playing AIs, and walk through examples in Python for the different strategies.

Understanding game trees

If you're familiar with formal **game theory**, then you know that there is an entire branch of mathematics devoted to understanding and analyzing games. In the computer science world, we can analyze a game by simplifying it into a decision tree structure called a **game tree**. Game trees are a way of mapping out possible moves and states within a board game. Let's take the simple example of a game tree for Tic Tac Toe, as follows:

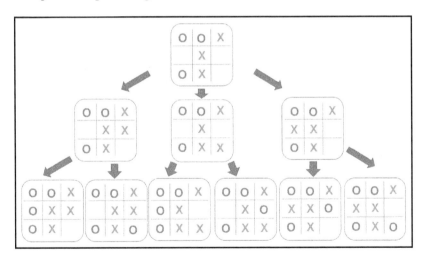

This tree gives us all of the possible combinations and outcomes for the game based on a certain starting point. Moving from one node to another represents a **move** in the game, and moves continue until a **terminal node** is reached, which represents a possible ending to the game. As you can imagine, the more complicated the game, the more combinations, and hence the larger the tree. Chess has a finite amount of states, and if you theoretically had enough computing power, you could create an artificial neural network to solve the entire game. The entire game has approximately 10^{43} positions that you could possibly play. In older systems such as IBM Deep Blue, you could use the **minimax function**, which we utilized in Chapter 7, *Generative Models*, to minimize the potential for making an erroneous move and maximize the potential for a positive move. In the context of these two-person games, the minimax function of the game becomes the following:

$$v_A(s_i) = \max_{a_i} v_B(M(s_i, a_i)) \qquad v_A(\hat{s}) = \text{eval}(\hat{s})$$

$$v_B(s_i) = \min_{a_i} v_A(M(s_i, a_i)) \qquad v_B(\hat{s}) = -\text{eval}(\hat{s})$$

Given a state s and an action a, our players want to maximize their own reward and minimize that of the other player. Let's break this down:

- $V_A()$ and $V_B()$ are functions that represent the reward a player gains from a certain move
- The $^{M()}$ function gives us the next state in the game, given the current state and an action taken (a move)
- The $^{eval()}$ functions represent the terminal states in the game

In this paradigm, however, computing power and network speed become a quick limitation. In IBM's case, they were only able to overcome the limitations with the pure power of the Watson Supercomputer. Now, take a game such as Go, which Google's Alpha Go famously mastered. The game of Go has roughly 10^{761} possible game combinations. When you compare this to the fact that there is estimated to be 10^{80} atoms in the entire universe, you can quickly see how complex the combinatorics become. The game tree for Go is incredibly, almost impossibly, large.

How do we solve this limitation? We can utilize a tool called the **Monte Carlo Tree Search (MCTS)** to help us. Remember when we discussed Monte Carlo simulations? We use the same approach here to search the game tree. Invented in 2006, MCTS takes a state, $^s0$, and , choosing the best move based on the results of that simulation. Using our Tic Tac Toe example, the algorithm would see something such as the following:

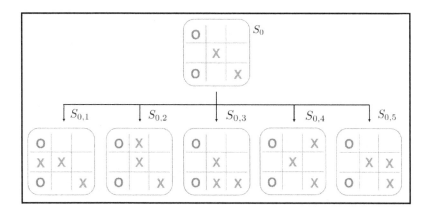

MCTS then uses a strategy called **rollout**, which randomly takes moves from a child state until an end state is reached (win, loss, or tie):

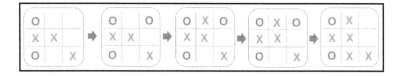

The wins are scored with +1, the losses with –1, and the ties with 0. If we conduct this strategy for all of the possibilities of S_0, we'd end up with the rewards for each rollout action:

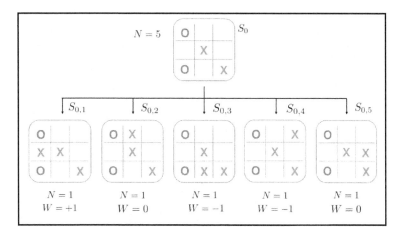

Rollout uses two statistics to keep track of each child strategy: the **simulation reward** and the **total number of visits**:

- **Simulation reward (R)** is the expected reward of an action played out during the simulation
- **Number of visits (N)** is something such as a weighting mechanism for nodes; it tells us how often a node had been used as part of the simulation, and therefore how much it contributed to the total reward

Commonly, you'll hear the reward referred to as the **exploitation** of the node, and the visits as the **exploration** of the node. These two statistics are computed for each of the nodes, and then backpropagated up the tree to the parent node.

At this point, you might be thinking to yourself, *doesn't this seem like a computationally expensive strategy?* This is where the Monte Carlo aspect of the simulation comes in. The algorithm chooses which nodes to expand based on something called the **upper confidence tree score**:

$$U_i = \frac{R_i}{N_i} + c\sqrt{\frac{2 \ln N_p}{N_i}}$$

Here, U_i is the upper confidence score for the ith tree.

MCTS faces a trade-off between explorations and exploitation strategies; the c parameter is a preset parameter that decides between exploitation (low c – choosing a winning action now) or exploration (high c – choosing to explore and develop a long strategy). During this whole process, the algorithm keeps track of which actor's turn it is in the game, and sums up the potential reward accordingly. This process continues for a defined amount of iterations.

There's one more aspect to MCTS that we have yet to discuss, and it's one that should be familiar to you from the reinforcement learning spaces policies. Like in Deep Q-learning or policy gradient networks, a policy π tells our network what to do and when. In the context of a game, it might be a policy that tells our algorithm what an expert player might do. We can adjust the preceding UTC formula to incorporate a policy:

$$U_i = \frac{R_i}{N_i} + c\pi_i\sqrt{\frac{2 \ln N_p}{1 + N_i}}$$

Now, the choice of exploitation versus exploration will be guided by whatever the policy thinks is most likely the best choice. As we've learned in previous chapters, choosing an appropriate policy can be difficult. In the next section, we'll see how Google's DeepMind chose policies for AlphaGo using deep learning methods. Before we go there, however, let's see how MCTS works in practice by developing the strategy in Python for a game of Tic Tac Toe.

We are going to design this program as a simple application that you can interact with terminal or command prompt. The game will face a human against an AI player that utilizes the MCTS method we just learned about. In this program, we'll be creating two files; one called `TicTacToe.py` that will control the gameplay, and one called `mcts.py` that will control the MCTS. Let's start with the `TicTacToe.py` file; we'll create a class called `TicTacToe` to contain our game-playing functions:

```
class TicTacToe:
  def __init__(self):
      self.board = list('_' * 9)
      self.result = 0
      self.player = 1
      self.win = [(0, 1, 2), (3, 4, 5), (6, 7, 8),
                      (0, 3, 6), (1, 4, 7), (2, 5, 8),
                      (0, 4, 8), (2, 4, 6)]
```

We're initializing a few variables here; `board` will represent the board itself, which will be a simple terminal picture of a board that is an array we are populating with blank underscores as placeholders. We'll be using this later to assign indexes to the game board, which will allow us to select certain spaces through terminal. `Result` will be an empty array that will keep track of the result of a move, `player` will be keep track of the player whose turn it is, and `win` will tell us the combinations that can win the game:

1. First, let's write a function to display the game board to the user. For simplicity's sake, let's print out the current state of the board at each turn. To give our users a way to choose a game board position to play, we'll index each position as a number between 0 and 8:

   ```
   def display_board(self):
       print('Game Board')
       boardDisplay = [f' {self.board[i]} ' if self.board[i] != '_'
   else f'({str(i)})' for i in range(9)]
       for i in range(3):
           print(' '.join(boardDisplay[3 * i:3 * (i + 1)]))
   ```

2. Next, let's make a function to handle user input from terminal. The function will take in raw input, and add the player's X to the spot on the board. If the spot is already taken, we'll send a message back to the user to let them know.

```
def player_input(self):
    input_msg = 'Please select your next position:'
    v = int(input(input_msg))
    if self.board[v] != '_':
        print("That space can been taken")
    self.board[v] = 'X
```

3. We'll also need to create a handler function for the AI player; this will take in input from the output of the MCTS formula we'll define later on, and put an O on the board for that choice:

```
def ai_input(self, v):
    self.board[v] = "O"
    print(f'AI chose {v}')
```

4. After each move, we'll check if there is a winning combination on the board:

```
def check_result(self):
    for w in self.win:
        if self.board[w[0]] != '_' and /
            self.board[w[0]] == self.board[w[1]]and /
            self.board[w[1]] == self.board[w[2]]:
                if self.board[w[0]] == 'X':
                    self.result = 1
                else:
                    self.result = 2
    if '_' not in self.board:
        self.result = 3
```

5. Now, let's create a function to control the gameplay; we'll call this function `switch_player`. We'll set this so if player 2 (the AI) is playing, we'll feed the input to the `ai_input` function that we created previously:

```
def switch_player(self, v):
    self.player = 3 - self.player
    if self.player == 2:
        self.ai_player(v)
    else:
        self.human_player()
```

We've created our gameplay and its control functions! Next, let's move on to the meat of the problem:

1. First, we'll create the `mcts.py` file and build out the MCTS itself. We'll start with our imports:

```
from TicTacToe import TicTacToe
from copy import deepcopy
from math import log, sqrt
from random import choice as rndchoice
import time
```

2. First things first, let's start by creating the game tree itself. This is what our MCTS will act on, and will hold all of the necessary information for parsing our various child trees. As such, there are variables that we'll have to initialize beforehand:

```
class GameTree:
    def __init__(self, s, par_node=None, pre_action=None):
        self.parent = par_node
        self.pre_action = pre_action
        self.child = []
        self.r = 0
        self.n = 0
        self.state = s
        self.utc = float('inf')
        self.player = MCTS.current_player(s)
        self.result = MCTS.is_terminal(s)
```

3. Great! Now, we'll create a list comprehension to parse through the tree. Note that we are using the `self.uct` variable here; we'll define the actual upper confidence tree function later on:

```
def __repr__(self):
    ratio = self.r / (self.n + 1)
    l = [str(e) for e in (self.pre_action, ''.join(self.state),
self.r, self.n, str(ratio)[:5], str(self.uct)[:5])]
    return ' '.join(l)
```

4. Lastly, we need to include an update function that will update the AI player's choice based on the output of the MCTS process. We're including this here instead of in the MCTS function itself so that we can operate on the *n* and *r* variables directly:

```
def update(self, v):
    self.n += 1
    if v == 3:
        self.r += 0.5
```

```
        elif v == 3 - self.player:
            self.r += 1
```

Thus far, we've built out the game of Tic Tac Toe itself, as well as the scaffolding for the game tree that we'll build upon. Now, let's build out the MCTS process that will inform the AI player of what moves to make in the game.

We'll contain all of our MCTS functions in a class which called MCTS:

1. To start building this class, we have to initialize a few variables; the variable root as the game tree itself and then a function that will expand the game tree from that root. We'll define that function, expand_node, in just a moment:

```
class MCTS:
    def __init__(self, s):
        self.root = GameTree(s)
        self.expand_node(self.root)
```

2. The next few functions that we'll create will be various functions that interpret the board for the MCTS algorithm. We'll define them as static methods, which will allow us to call them as part of the class later on. First, let's create one that tracks the current player:

```
@staticmethod
def current_player(s):
    n = s.count('_')
    if n % 2 == 1:
        return 1
    else:
        return 2
```

3. The function uses a modulo operator to check the remainder. Next, let's create a function that searches the board for available spots for MCTS to explore:

```
@staticmethod
 def available_move(s):
     l = []
     for i in range(9):
         if s[i] == '_': l.append(i)
     return l
```

4. The following function will keep track of actions and potential results for MCTS as it simulates scenarios:

```
@staticmethod
def action_result(s, a):
    p = MCTS.current_player(s)
```

```
new_s = deepcopy(s)
new_s[a] = 'X' if p == 1 else 'O'
return new_s
```

5. For the last of our static methods, we'll finally define the upper confidence tree formula:

```
@staticmethod
def uct(node):
    v = (node.r / (node.n + 1e-12)) + sqrt(log(node.parent.n + 1) /
(node.n + 1e-12))
    return v
```

You'll notice something here that is different from the formula that we previously defined:

$$U_i = \frac{R_i}{N_i} + c\sqrt{\frac{\ln N_p}{N_i}}$$

This UCT formula has no parameter, *c*, that decides between exploration and exploitation. We purposely left that parameter out for this game, since Tic Tac Toe is so simplistic. You'll also notice the 1e-12 in the code block (1^{-12}). This initializes a small value in the formula for its first iterations; the value is big enough to provide a starting place, but small enough not to affect the final calculations:

1. Before we get to the MCTS process, one last function will help the algorithm measure its progress by looking for terminal nodes in the games it is simulating:

```
@staticmethod
def terminal(s):
    for wc in TicTacToe().win:
        if s[wc[0]] != '_' and s[wc[0]] == s[wc[1]] and \
s[wc[1]] == s[wc[2]]:
            if s[wc[0]] == 'X':
                return 1
            else:
                return 2
        if '_' not in s:
            return 3
        else:
            return 0
```

2. Now, let's start building out the MCTS process with the node selection aspect:

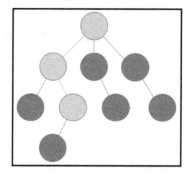

3. This is where MCTS decides which node children it will look at next:

```python
def node_selection(self, node):
    if node.child:
        imax, vmax = 0, 0
        for i, n in enumerate(node.child):
            n.uct = MCTS.uct(n)
            v = n.uct
            if v > vmax:
                imax, vmax = i, v
        selected = node.child[imax]
        return self.node_selection(selected)
    else:
        selected = node
        return selected
```

4. Next, we'll write the function to expand this node, where MCTS looks into the child nodes of the node it just selected:

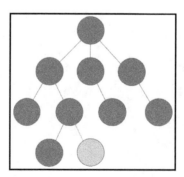

The function below, `expand_node`, does just that by first checking to see if the node is terminal, and if it isn't, taking a simulated action from that node.

```
def expand_node(self, node):
    if self.is_terminal(node.state) == 0:
        actions = self.available_move(node.state)
        for a in actions:
            state_after_action = self.action_result(node.state, a)
            node.child.append(GameTree(state_after_action, node,
a))
```

5. MCTS will now simulate the possible game combinations from that node:

```
def simulation(self, s):
    if self.is_terminal(s) == 0:
        actions = self.available_move(s)
        a = rndchoice(actions)
        s = self.action_result(s, a)
        return s
    else:
        return self.is_terminal(s)
```

6. And lastly, it will backpropagate its simulation results:

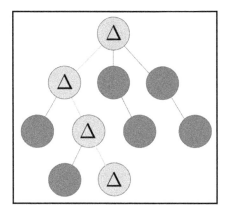

We'll do this by creating a backpropagation handler function and passing our parameters through the update function.

```
def backpropagation(self, node, v):
    node.update(v)
    if node.parent:
        self.backpropagation(node.parent, v)
```

Alright, now, let's create a function that chooses the best move for the AI player:

```
def ai_move(self):
    best_node, best_visits = None, 0
    for n in self.root.child:
        if n.n > best_visits: best_visits, best_node = n.n, n
    return best_node.pre_action
```

Great; we've created the MCTS process; we just need to finish up by creating two functions to run the process. The first of these we will call `mcts_loop`, which will use the functions we just created to select, expand, simulate, and backpropagate:

```
def mcts_loop(self):
    node = self.node_selection(self.root)
    self.expand_node(node)
    if node.child:
        selected_node = rndchoice(node.child)
    else:
        selected_node = node
    v = self.simulation(deepcopy(selected_node.state))
    self.backpropagation(selected_node, v)
```

And lastly, we'll tell the algorithm to run the MCTS based on time. Instead of giving an exploration versus exploitation criterion, we'll ask MCTS to search for two seconds to try to find the optimal next move:

```
def run_mcts(self, board):
    self.__init__(board)
    start_time = time.time()
    iii = 0
    while time.time() - start_time < 2:
        self.mcts_loop()
        iii += 1
```

All that's left to do now is create the functions to run the whole program! Let's assemble the pieces:

```
if __name__ == '__main__':
    game = TicTacToe()
    ai = MCTS(game.board)
    while game.result == 0:
        game.display_board()
        ai.run_mcts(board=game.board)
        game.switch_player(ai.ai_move())
        game.check_result()
    game.display_board()
    if game.result == 3:
        print('The game has ended in a draw')
```

```
    else:
        print(f'Player {game.result} has won
```

Here, we initialize a game of Tic Tac Toe, and initialize the MCTS process to guide the AI agent. We'll tell the program to display the board, let the AI player make a move, and then switch to a human player. It will then prompt us for input, and the game will continue until either a player wins or the game comes to a draw. If you run the `mcts.py` folder from your command line, it should look as follows:

```
Game Board
(0) (1) (2)
(3) (4) (5)
(6) (7) (8)
```

That's it! You've created a simple game-playing AI agent to play Tic Tac Toe. Now, let's dive into how these same MCTS methods can be used to create much more advanced systems.

AlphaGo and intelligent game-playing AIs

While MCTS has been a cornerstone of game-playing AI for a while, it was DeepMind's AlphaGo program that really took game-playing AIs into the modern age. AlphaGo and its derivatives (AlphaGo Zero and AlphaGo Master) are game-playing AI systems that utilize MCTS to play the notoriously difficult ancient Chinese game of Go. With 10^{761} possible game combinations, creating a system to play the game became something of a milestone in the AI world. It's even the subject of a much talked about documentary by the same name.

AlphaGo uses a combination of MCTS with deep learning methods that made the Alpha Go programs truly extraordinary. DeepMind trained deep neural networks, such as the ones that we have been learning about throughout this book, to learn the state of the game and effectively guide the MCTS in a more intelligent manner. This network looks at the current state of the board, along with the previous moves that have been made, and decides which move to play next. DeepMind's major innovation with AlphaGo was to use deep neural networks to understand the state of the game, and then use this understanding to intelligently guide the search of the MCTS. The system was architected in a way that AlphaGo would teach itself to learn the game, first by watching humans play the game, and secondly by playing the game against itself and correcting itself for its prior mistakes.

The architecture actually uses two different neural networks; a policy network and a value network:

- **Value network**: Reduces the depth of the MCTS search by approximating a value function.
- **Policy network**: Reduces the breadth of the MCTS search by simulating future actions. The policy network learns from actual human play of the game Go, and develops a policy accordingly:

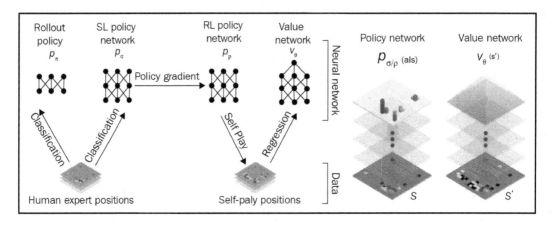

Let's dive into each of these to understand how the system works.

AlphaGo policy network

The goal of the policy network is to capture and understand the general actions of players on the board in order to aid the MCTS by guiding the algorithm toward promising actions during the search process; this reduces the **breadth of the search**. Architecturally, the policy network comes in two parts: a supervised learning policy network and a reinforcement learning policy network.

The first network, the supervised network, is a 13-layer **Convolutional Neural Network (CNN)**. It was trained by observing the moves that humans make while playing the game – 30 million, to be exact – and outputs a probability distribution for each action given a certain state. We call this type of supervised learning **behavior cloning**.

The second network, the reinforcement learning policy network, was architected to improve upon the first network through self-play. Utilizing the same CNN architecture and initializing with the weights of the first network, this network improved upon the results of the first network by playing against itself. You might be asking yourself – why? Well, DeepMind had a reason for this; by pitting the network against itself, both networks would be acting with the exact same policy. Therefore, the networks would be forced to adjust the policy toward winning games in the long run, rather than maximizing the predictive accuracy of the network.

AlphaGo value network

The value network was used to reduce the error in the system's play by guiding MCTS toward certain nodes. It helped reduce the **depth of the search**. The AlphaGo value network was trained by playing further games against itself in order to optimize the policy that it learned from the policy networks by estimating the value function, specifically the action value function. Recall from `Chapter 8`, *Reinforcement Learning*, that action value functions describe the value of taking a certain action while in a specific state. It measures the cumulative reward from a pair of states and actions; for a given state and action we take, how much will this increase our reward? It lets us postulate what would happen by taking a different action in the first time step than what they may want the agent to do, and then afterward following the policy. The action value function is also often called the **Q-function**, because of the Q that we use to represent it:

$$Q^\pi(s, a) = \mathbb{E}\left[\sum_{t \geq 0} \gamma^t r_t | s_0 = s, a_0 = a, \pi\right]$$

The network approximated the value function by utilizing a noisy version of the policy from the policy network and regressing the state of the board against the result of the game.

The network was trained using the reinforce algorithm that we learned about in `Chapter 8`, *Reinforcement Learning*. If you recall, Reinforce is a Monte Carlo policy gradient method that uses likelihood ratios to estimate the value of a policy at a given point. The Reinforce algorithm attempts to maximize the expected reward, so that the entire system has the dual goal of playing like a professional human player while attempting to win the game.

AlphaGo in action

We've gone over how AlphaGo helped select actions, so now let's get back to the core of any game-playing system: the game tree. While AlphaGo utilized game trees and MCTS, the authors created a variation of it called *asynchronous policy* and *value MCTS* (APV-MCTS). Unlike standard MCTS, which we discussed previously, APV-MCTS decides which node to expand and evaluate by two different metrics:

- The outcome of the value network
- The outcome of the Monte Carlo simulations

The results of these methods are combined with mixing parameters, λ. The algorithm then chooses an action according to the probabilities that were obtained during the initial supervised learning phase. While it may seem counter intuitive to use the probabilities from the first phase of learning, the authors had a strong reason for this architecture. The original policy from the supervised learning policy network was based on the raw human moves and plays in the game. Therefore, sampling from the original raw moves, during the tree search, and then optimizing according to the value function, ultimately gave the best results. In their update of AlphaGo to AlphaGo Zero, Google combined the Policy network and the Value network into a single network, allowing for more efficient training and performance.

Next, we're going to move into the realm of video game-playing AIs, creating algorithms that can play Atari video games just as well as a human can.

Networks for video games

Thus far, we've learned how we can use reinforcement learning methods to play board games utilizing UCT and MCTS; now, let's see what we can do with video games. In Chapter 8, *Reinforcement Learning*, we saw how we could use reinforcement learning methods to complete basic tasks such as the OpenAI cartpole challenge. In this section, we'll be focusing on a more difficult set of games: classic Atari video games, which have become standard benchmarks for deep learning tasks.

You might be thinking – *can't we extend the methods that we used in the cartpole environment to Atari games?* While we can, there's a lot more input that we have to handle. In Atari environments, and really any video game environment, the inputs to the network are individual pixels. Instead of the simple four control variables for cartpole, we are now dealing with 100,800 variables (210 * 160 * 3). As such, complexity and training times for these networks can be much higher. In this section, we'll try to make the network as simple as possible in order to make it easier to learn from and train.

We'll be using the OpenAI gym environment to simulate the Atari game Space Invaders:

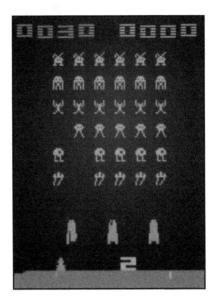

For those of you who aren't familiar with Space Invaders, the concept is simple – you (the green rocket at the bottom) must destroy a grouping of alien spaceships before they destroy you. The spaceships attempt to hit you with missiles, and vice versa. Google's DeepMind originally introduced Space Invaders as a benchmark task in their paper *Playing Atari with Deep Reinforcement Learning*, which really set off the concept of Atari games as benchmarks to beat with these intelligent agents.

We'll be constructing something called a **Deep Q-network**, which we touched upon in `Chapter 8`, *Reinforcement Learning*. In the next section, we expand upon many of the fundamental Q-learning subjects that we covered in that chapter. With that – let's dive in!

Constructing a Deep Q–network

Deep Q-networks were first introduced by DeepMind in their paper *Human-level control through deep reinforcement learning*, published in the British scientific journal *Nature*, and now commonly referred to as the *Nature Paper*. The goal of Deep Q-learning was to create an AI agent that could learn a policy from high-dimensional inputs such as video games. In our case, we'll want to construct a Deep Q-network that can advance through basic tasks and then towards harder tasks.

Deep Q-networks approximate Q-values instead of calculating them individually with Q tables, and they do this by using artificial neural networks as a value approximator. The input of the network will be a stack of preprocessed frames, and the output will be an estimate of the Q function that best represents a winning gameplay strategy. Recall that the Q function tries to maximize the reward of future actions:

$$Q(s, a) = r + \gamma max(Q(s', a'))$$

Here, r represents the reward gained from taking an action at a specific state, γ and (gamma) represents a **discount factor**. Recall that the discount factor can be any value between 0 and 1 that represents the relative importance between a current reward and a future reward. As the algorithm will play Space Invaders, it will save its initial state, reward, and subsequent state that it ended up with, based on each action that it takes.

The Deep-Q network takes in stacks of four preprocessed frames of game play at a time as a means to overcome the **temporal limitation** problem. A single frame isn't of too much use to an agent who wants to track movement. Therefore, we stack frames together in bundles of four to track subtle movements in the game. The network itself consists of a basic CNN with a fully connected layer to approximate Q-values that tell the game-playing agent what to do. Our network will have three convolutional layers and two fully connected layers shown as follows:

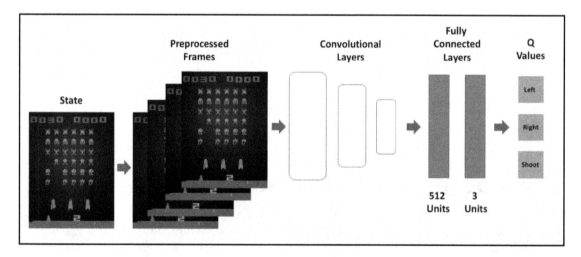

DeepMind trained this network on 50 million frames of play and achieved a score of 1,976, which in terms of AI play is quite good. If we tried to match these parameters, however, it would likely take your machine a week of full-time training to complete the training cycle. In our example, we are going to use much more reasonable parameters for a speedier training.

With that, let's go ahead and start building the network! We'll start out with our imports:

```
import tensorflow as tf
import numpy as np
import random
from collections import deque
```

We'll be calling our network DeepQ, and like our previous Tic Tac Toe—playing example, let's contain everything in a class called `deepQ`. First and foremost, when we initialize this network, we'll initialize some important variables with it. We'll assign the action variable, which contains the action input for the network. We'll initialize the value of epsilon, as well as the observe and explore rates. Lastly, you'll see the replay buffer, which we'll discuss in detail in this section later on:

```
class deepQ:
    def __init__(self, action):
        ## Initialize the network's variables
        self.action = action
        self.starting_ep = 1.0
        self.ending_ep = 0.1
        self.observe = 50000
        self.explore = 1000000
        self.replayBuffer = deque()
```

If you have the hardware and/or time and are willing to try to match DeepMind's performance, you can change the explore parameter. Let's create our architecture.

1. Next, let's create the layers themselves.
2. We'll be creating our architecture under a function that is aptly named `deepQarchitecture`.
3. Using the exact specifications from the DeepMind paper, we'll create the first convolutional layer with 32 units. Just as we did in previous sections, we'll use the higher-level `layers` functions from TensorFlow to make our jobs easier for us.

```
def deepQarchitecture(self):

    ## Network input layer
    input_layer = tf.placeholder("float",[None,84,84,4])
```

```
## Convolutional layers
    conv1 = tf.layers.conv2d(inputs = input_layer, filters = 32,
kernel_size=[8, 8],
        padding='same', kernel_initializer=initializer,
kernel_regularizer=regularizer,
            use_bias=True, bias_initializer=initializer,
bias_regularizer=regularizer,
            activation=tf.nn.relu
    )
```

4. Next, we'll go ahead and create the second and third convolutional layers in the same manner, but this time use 64 units per layer.

```
conv2 = tf.layers.conv2d(inputs = conv1, filters = 32,
kernel_size=[4, 4]
        padding='same', kernel_initializer=initializer,
kernel_regularizer=regularizer,
            use_bias=True, bias_initializer=initializer,
bias_regularizer=regularizer,
            activation=tf.nn.relu
    )

    conv3 = tf.layers.conv2d(inputs = conv2, filters = 64,
kernel_size=[3, 3]
        padding='same', kernel_initializer=initializer,
kernel_regularizer=regularizer,
            use_bias=True, bias_initializer=initializer,
bias_regularizer=regularizer,
            activation=tf.nn.relu
    )
```

5. We'll then create a dense layer with 512 units and set the last layer to be the same size as the action space. The input to the network is an 84 x 84 x 4 image of a current state of the game.

6. We'll then define three convolutional layers, each utilizing a ReLU activation function.

7. We'll feed the output of that into a fully connected layer, and lastly to a Q-value layer.

8. We'll be returning all of the variables from this section for use in later aspects of the network.

```
## Flatten the last convolutional layer
    conv3_shape = conv3.get_shape().as_list()
    conv3_flat = tf.reshape(conv3, [-1,3136])

    ## Fully Connected Layer
```

```
        fc = tf.layers.dense(inputs = conv3_flat, units = 512,
    kernel_initializer=initializer,
        kernel_regularizer=regularizer use_bias=True,
    bias_initializer=initializer,
        bias_regularizer=regularizer, activation=tf.nn.relu
        )

    ## Output Q Value
    QValue = tf.layers.dense(inputs = fc, units = self.action,
    kernel_initializer=initializer,
        kernel_regularizer=regularizer use_bias=True,
    bias_initializer=initializer,
        bias_regularizer=regularizer, activation = None)
```

Now that we have our basic network set, let's learn about how we can ensure a smooth training process with a **target network**.

Utilizing a target network

Let's look back at the Q- function optimization process:

$$Q(s, a) = r + \gamma max(Q(s', a'))$$

You might notice that this function has a unique property in that it's recursive; one set of Q-values depend on the value of the other set of Q-values. This becomes a problem in training; if we change one set of values, we'll end up changing the other set of values. To put it simply, as we get closer to the targeted Q-value, that Q-value moves even further away. It is continually moving the finish line when you are about to finish a race!

To remedy this, the Q-network creates a copy of itself every 10,000 iterations, called a **target network**, which will represent the targeted Q-value. We can do this in TensorFlow by creating a target network variable that we'll first initialize with the class, and later run in a TensorFlow session:

```
## def contained under  __init__(self, actions): ##

## Initialize the base network
self.inputVal, self.QValue = self.deepQarchitecture()

## Initialize the target network
self.inputValT, self.QValueT = self.deepQarchitecture()
```

As for the 10,000 iterations, we've already defined that as `self.update_time = 10000` when we started building out our DQN class.

Experience replay buffer

While we touched upon it briefly in `Chapter 8`, *Reinforcement Learning*, let's dive into the technical details of experience replay buffers. Experience replay is a biologically inspired tool that stores an agent's experience at each time step process. Specifically, it stores the [state, action, reward, next_state] pairs at each time step:

$$e_t = (s_t, a_t, r_t, s_{t+1})$$

Instead of running Q-learning on state-action pairs as they occur, experience replay stores these pairs as they are discovered. Experience replay buffers help with two things:

- Remember past experiences by storing and randomly sampling them
- Reduce the chance that experiences will be correlated with each other, thereby leading to stronger outcomes

Taking a look at some results from the paper *Human-level control through deep reinforcement learning*, we can see how experience replay buffers helped improve the scores that AIs achieved on a variety of Atari games:

Game	With replay	Without replay
Breakout	240.7	3.2
Enduro	831.4	29.1
River Raid	4102.8	1453.0
Seaquest	822.6	275.8
Space Invaders	826.3	302.0

One of the largest downsides to utilizing experience replay buffers in our networks is that they are memory hogs. If you conceptually think about the stored process in replay buffers, frames of a video game image are being processed and storage in the buffer, over and over and over with each game iteration. This ends up amounting to millions of frames that need to be stored, and a huge computational load on your machine.

The easiest way to utilize experience replay in Python is with the `deque` library, which helps manage list-like containers that have special properties that make referencing their data and appending to them fast and efficient. You already defined the basic replay memory bank when we initialized our variables at the beginning of this section:

```
self.replayMemory = deque()
```

We'll iterate on this in a bit when we write the code for training the network.

Choosing action

Thus far, we've told our network to follow random weights that we've initialized for it, without giving it direction on how to decide what actions to take to update those weights. In the case of policy methods such as the ones we used in Chapter 8, *Reinforcement Learning*, and preceding with Tic Tac Toe, Q-learning methods work toward approximating the value of the Q-function instead of learning a policy directly. So, what do we do?

Deep Q-networks use a tactic called **exploration** to determine what actions to take. If we didn't use a tactic, our network would probably be limited to the most basic levels of the game because it wouldn't have any idea what moves would allow it to improve!

To remedy this, we will utilize a strategy called **ϵ-greedy**. This strategy works by choosing actions to learn from based on two methods; first, choosing methods that give our model the highest reward (maximum Q-value), and second, choosing methods at random with the probability ϵ. In this strategy, we use a basic inequality:

$$n > \epsilon$$

We set the epsilon variable as 1, and draw random numbers from a distribution. If the number doesn't satisfy the inequality and is less than epsilon, our agent **explores** the space, meaning it seeks to figure out more information about where it is in order to start choosing state/action pairs so that we can calculate the Q-value. If the number is in fact larger than epsilon, we **exploit** the information that we already know to choose a Q-value to calculate. The algorithm starts with a high ϵ and reduces its value by a fixed amount as training continues. We call this process **annealing**. In the original DeepMind paper, the researchers used this strategy with an annealing from 1 to 0.1 over the first million frames, and then held at 0.1 afterward. Let's look back at the parameters we initialized in the beginning of the section:

```
self.starting_ep = 1.0
self.ending_ep = 0.1
```

You'll notice that we used these exact specifications. During the testing phase of the network, epsilon will be considerably lower, and hence be biased toward an exploitation strategy.

Let's implement this strategy in Python and take a closer look at the mechanics. We'll define a function, `getAction`, which sits within our `deepQ` class:

```python
def select(self):
    ## Select a Q Value from the Base Q Network
    QValue = self.QValue.eval(feed_dict =
{self.iputVal:[self.currentState]})[0]
    ## Initialize actions as zeros
    action = np.zeros(self.action)
    action_index = 0
    ## If this timestep is the first, start with a random action
    if self.timeStep % 1 == 0:
        ##
        if random.random() <= self.starting_ep:
            a_index = random.randrange(self.action)
            action[a_index] = 1
        else:
            action_index = np.argmax(QValue)
            action[action_index] = 1
    else:
        action[0] = 1
```

We'll also adjust our epsilon value:

```python
## Anneal the value of epsilon
    if self.starting_ep > self.ending_ep and self.timeStep > self.observe:
        self.starting_ep -= (self.starting_ep - self.ending_ep) /
self.explore
```

Now that we've defined the bulk of our network, let's move on to training.

Training methods

First, let's define our training method. We'll call this function `trainingPipeline`; it will take in an action input as well as a *y* input which represents the targeting Q-value, which we'll define here as placeholders, and calculate a Q-value for an action based on those action/state pairs:

$$Q = f(a, s)$$

We'll use a **Mean Squared Error** (**MSE**) loss function and calculate it, utilizing the predicted Q-value minus the actual Q-value. Lastly, you might notice that we are using an optimizer here that you might not be familiar with, RMSProp. It's an adaptive learning rate optimizer similar to Adam that was proposed by Geoffrey Hinton. We won't get into the details here, but you can find a good overview of it on Coursera. `https://www.coursera.org/lecture/deep-neural-network/rmsprop-BhJlm`:

```
def trainingPipeline(self):
    self.actionInput = tf.placeholder("float",[None,self.actions])
    self.yInput = tf.placeholder("float", [None])
    Q_Action = tf.reduce_sum(tf.multiply(self.QValue, self.actionInput),
reduction_indices = 1)
    self.cost = tf.reduce_mean(tf.square(self.yInput - Q_Action))
    self.trainStep =
tf.train.RMSPropOptimizer(0.00025,0.99,0.0,1e-6).minimize(self.cost)
```

The last variable that we define in this process, `trainStep`, will become the input to the training cycle that we'll define next.

Training the network

We'll give our training function a simple name: `train`. First, we'll feed it mini-batches of data from the replay memory:

```
def train(self):
    ''' Training procedure for the Q Network'''

    minibatch = random.sample(self.replayBuffer, 32)
    stateBatch = [data[0] for data in minibatch]
    actionBatch = [data[1] for data in minibatch]
    rewardBatch = [data[2] for data in minibatch]
    nextBatch = [data[3] for data in minibatch]
```

Next, we'll calculate the Q-value for each batch:

```
batch = []
    qBatch = self.QValueT.eval(feed_dict = {self.inputValT: nextBatch})
    for i in range(0, 32):
      terminal = minibatch[i][4]
      if terminal:
        batch.append(rewardBatch[i])
      else:
        batch.append(rewardBatch[i] + self.gamma * np.max(qBatch[i]))
```

Now, let's bind this all together with out training method. We'll take the `trainStep` variable that we defined and run the training cycle. We'll feed in three variables as input; the targeted Q-value, an action, and a state:

```
self.trainStep.run(feed_dict={
        self.yInput : batch,
        self.actionInput : actionBatch,
        self.inputVal : stateBatch
        })
```

We'll define a handler function to save network weights and states for us. While we didn't go over the definition of the saver explicitly in this chapter, you can find it in the fully assembled code in the GitHub repository:

```
## Save the network on specific iterations
    if self.timeStep % 10000 == 0:
        self.saver.save(self.session, './savedweights' + '-atari',
global_step = self.timeStep)
```

Lastly, let's define the cycle the appends to experience replay:

```
    def er_replay(self, nextObservation, action, reward, terminal):
        newState = np.append(nextObservation, self.currentState[:,:,1:], axis =
2)
        self.replayMemory.append((self.currentState, action, reward, newState,
terminal))
        if len(self.replayBuffer) > 40000:
          self.replayBuffer.popleft()
        if self.timeStep > self.explore:
          self.trainQNetwork()

        self.currentState = newState
        self.timeStep += 1
```

We've assembled our network, so now let's move on to running it!

Running the network

Now, let's get to the moment we've been waiting for! Let's import gym, NumPy, our deep-q network file, as well as a few handler functions:

```
import cv2
import sys
from deepQ import deepQ
import numpy as np
import gym
```

We'll define our agent class as `Atari`, and initialize the environment, network, and actions with the class:

```
class Atari:
    def __init__(self):
    self.env = gym.make('SpaceInvaders-v0')
    self.env.reset()
    self.actions = self.env.action_space.n
    self.deepQ = deepQ(self.actions)
    self.action0 = 0
```

Our Deep Q-network can't innately ingest the Atari games, so we have to write a bit of preprocessing code to handle the video input. We'll call this function `preprocess` and it will take in a single game observation:

```
def preprocess(self,observation):
    observation = cv2.cvtColor(cv2.resize(observation, (84, 110)),
cv2.COLOR_BGR2GRAY)
    observation = observation[26:110,:]
    ret, observation = cv2.threshold(observation,1,255,cv2.THRESH_BINARY)
    return np.reshape(observation,(84,84,1))
```

First, we'll downsample the observation to 110 x 84, just as specified in the original DeepMind paper. We'll also convert each frame to grayscale to reduce the amount of information we have to process. For playing a simple Atari game, we really don't care about what color the aliens are – just where they are!

Next, let's create a function that will actually run the gameplay for us. It will take in information from the Gym Atari environment, process it, and set a current observation as the state.

```
def run_atari(self):
        obs, rew, ter, info = self.env.step(self.action0)
        obs = self.preprocess(obs)
        self.deepQ.initialState(obs)
        self.deepQ.currentState = np.squeeze(self.deepQ.currentState)
```

The next chunk of code will continue to play the game for quite some time, choosing the best action at each state and adding actions to the experience replay buffer. After several hours of training, feel free to stop the prompt and check on the training process. The network will have saved its training weights, so you won't be losing anything!

```
while True:
    action = self.deepQ.select()
    action_max = np.argmax(np.array(action))
    nextObs, reward, terminal, info = self.env.step(action_max)
    if terminal:
```

```
nextObservation = self.env.reset()
nextObservation = self.preprocess(nextObs)
self.deepQ.er_replay(nextObs, action, reward, terminal)
```

Lastly, we just need to write a handler to run the `Atari` pipeline when we run the file:

```
if __name__ == '__main__':
  a = AtariGame()
  a.run_atari()
```

You may notice that your network takes a while to train; that's alright! Even if you do not get good results with your algorithm, understand that converging to the correct Q function is extremely difficult, which is of the reasons that reinforcement learning was abandoned back in the second wave of AI. Researchers were too tired of never converging!

Summary

We've learned a great deal in this chapter, from how to implement MCTS methods to play board games, to creating an advanced network to play an Atari game, and even the technology behind the famous AlphaGo system. Let's recap what we have learned.

Reinforcement learning methods have become the main tools to create AIs for playing games. Whether we are creating systems for real-life board games, or systems for video games, the fundamental concepts of policies, Q-learning, and more that we learned about in `Chapter 8`, *Reinforcement Learning*, form the basis for these complex AI systems. When we create AIs for board games, we rely on the building block of the game tree, and use MCTS to simulate various game outcomes from that game tree. For more advanced systems such as AlphaGo and chess-playing AIs, we utilize neural networks to help guide MCTS and make its simulations more effective.

When it comes to video game-playing AIs, we can utilize either policy gradient methods or Q-learning methods. In this chapter, we learned about utilizing a variant of the latter, deep Q-learning, to play the Atari game Space Invaders. Deep Q-learning makes advances on basic Q-learning by using techniques such as target networks and experience replay buffers to improve performance.

We'll look more into how reinforcement learning methods can create intelligent systems in one of our upcoming chapters on deep learning for robotics.

Deep Learning for Finance

11

Deep learning is one of the most exciting new technologies being used in the financial services industry, and when used correctly, can improve investment returns. While tasks such as computer vision and **natural language processing** (**NLP**) are well-researched areas, the use of **Artificial Intelligence** (**AI**) techniques in financial services is still growing. It's important to note that some of the most advanced, lucrative deep learning techniques in AI are not published, nor will they ever be. The lucrative nature of the financial services space necessitates guarding advanced algorithms and measures, and so in this chapter we will focus on principles.

The application of AI in the financial services industry is nuanced; it's being used in areas where it can perform faster and better than a human could, but still isn't being used ubiquitously. By far, the most ubiquitous use of deep learning in the financial services industry is in feature engineering.

An entire book could be written simply on the topic of deep learning in financial services. While we won't go into depth on financial topics, we will touch upon the definitions of terms and concepts that we introduce throughout this chapter. We'll be covering several basic AI-driven trading methods, as well as an event-based trading method that utilizes a new type of **Artificial Neural Network** (**ANN**) that we have yet to talk about—the Neural Tensor Network. Lastly, we'll look at how deep learning can aid us in developing optimal portfolios of stocks.

We will be looking at the following topics in this chapter:

- Introduction to deep learning in finance
- Deep learning in trading
- Deep learning in asset management

Requirements

As usual, we will be utilizing Python 3 for our analysis. Python is an excellent choice for quantitative trading applications that have a frequency that's greater than a few seconds. For high-frequency applications, it is recommended that you use a mid-level language such as Java or C++.

In this chapter, we will be using finance-specific Python libraries on top of our standard deep learning stack:

Zipline—An algorithmic trading library in Python. It is currently used as the backtesting package for the quantitative trading website Quantopian (https://www.quantopian.com).

Introduction to AI in finance

Despite being one of the most computationally intensive fields, financial services is full of heuristics. The application of advanced AI techniques is tenuous at best; many firms simply don't engage in strategies that allow for easy adoption of AI. Talent wars for top quantitative talent with Silicon Valley has also made the problem worse. You may be saying to yourself *don't I need to have a finance background to work with this data?* It's worth noting that two of the world's top hedge funds were founded by teams that participated in the famous Netflix Machine Learning challenge. While there is incredible benefit in studying the techniques of algorithmic trading, you can get started with your knowledge of ANNs and how to handle financial data appropriately with them.

Now, let's start setting up the landscape. In financial services, there are two general sides to the business:

- **Deal-based firms**: Investment banking, venture capital, and private equity
- **Public markets**: Hedge funds, trading departments at large banks, and various asset management firms

You may also hear the terms **buy-side** and **sell-side**, which attempt to divide the market into firms that generally buy large amounts of securities such as hedge funds, and those you sell large amounts of securities to, such as big banks. For our purposes, this isn't very useful as we are interested in exploring applications of AI for any public market, and hence we will be using the deals versus public markets definition.

Deep learning in trading

Trading is the buying and selling of items in the financial market; in financial parlance, we call these items **derivatives**. Trades can be short-term (inter-day), medium-term (several days), or long-term (several weeks or more). According to experts at JP Morgan Chase, one of the largest banks in the world, AI applications are proven to be better suited than humans at short and medium-term trading strategies. In this section, we'll explore some fundamental strategies for developing intelligent trading algorithms for short and medium-term trades. But first, let's cover some basic concepts.

Trading strategies seek to exploit market inefficiencies in order to make profit. One of the core policies in algorithmic training is called **alpha**, which is a measure of performance. Alpha measures the active return on a specific investment by matching a stock against an index. The difference between the performance of an individual investment and its matched index is the investment's alpha. In building networks for trading strategies, we want our networks to spot market inefficiencies that generate the most alpha for us.

We can generally break traditional stock analysis down into two categories:

- **Fundamental analysis** looks at the underlying factors that could influence a financial derivative, such as the general financial health of a company
- **Technical analysis** looks at the actual performance of the financial derivative in a more mathematical sense, attempting to predict price movements based on patterns in the asset's price movements

In both of these cases, analysis is typically done with human reasoning, whereas deep learning comes into the world of **quantitative analysis**, specifically in what is known as **algorithmic trading**. Broadly defined, algorithmic trading is just as it sounds: trading that is conducted by a coded algorithm and not a physical human. Algorithmic trading strategies are validated by a process called **backtesting**, which runs the algorithm on historical data to determine whether it will perform well in the market.

Algorithmic trading is used in several different types of areas:

- **Buy-side firms**: Firms utilize algorithmic trading to manage their mid-to long-term portfolio investments
- **Sell-side firms**: Firms use high-frequency algorithmic trading to take advantage of market opportunities and move markets themselves
- **Systematic traders**: These individuals and firms try to match a long-term investment with a short-term investment of highly correlated financial derivatives

What's shared among all three of these market entities is that algorithmic trading provides a more stable and systematic approach to active investing, which is something that a human instinct could not provide.

Another strategy relies on technical indicators, which are mathematical calculations based on the historical analysis of data. Most trading algorithms are used in what is known as **high-frequency trading** (**HFT**), which attempts to exploit market inefficiencies by conducting large numbers of extremely fast trades across markets. Unless you have access to some seriously fast computer hardware, it's unlikely for an individual to compete in this arena. Instead, we're going to build some fundamental algorithms in TensorFlow for non-HFT algorithmic trading.

Building a trading platform

Before we dive into any particular strategies, let's get started with building the basis for our trading platform. In this section, we'll build out the code that will handle data ingestion and trading, and then we'll dive into two specific strategies.

Basic trading functions

Let's start with the fundamental actions our platform could take on the market; we need it to be able to buy, sell, or hold stock:

1. First, let's start with some imports:

```
import math
from time import time
from enum import Enum
```

2. To make things easier on us down the road, we're going to wrap these functions inside a single class that we'll call TradingPosition:

```
class TradingPosition(object):
    ''' Class that manages the trading position of our platform'''

    def __init__(self, code, buy_price, amount, next_price):
        self.code = code ## Status code for what action our
algorithm is taking
        self.amount = amount ## The amount of the trade
        self.buy_price = buy_price ## The purchase price of a trade
        self.current_price = buy_price ## Buy price of the trade
        self.current_value = self.current_price * self.amount
        self.pro_value = next_price * self.amount
```

3. Let's break the input variables down. The first variable that we are initializing is code, which we'll be using later as a status code for the action we are taking to buy, sell, or hold. We then create the variables for the price of the security, the amount of the security (that is, how much stock), and the current value of the security.

4. Now that we have our variables, we can start coding our trading actions. We'll want to create a status function, which tracks the movement of prices in the market. For simplicity, we'll call this function TradeStatus:

```
def TradeStatus(self, current_price, next_price, amount):
        ''' Manages the status of a trade that is in action '''
        self.current_price = current_price ## updates the current
price variable that is maintained within the class
        self.current_value = self.current_price * amount
        pro_value = next_price * amount
```

5. Next, let's create a function to buy a stock:

```
def BuyStock(self, buy_price, amount, next_price):
    ''' Function to buy a stock '''
        self.buy_price = ((self.amount * self.buy_price) + (amount *
buy_price)) / (self.amount + amount)
    self.amount += amount
        self.TradeStatus(buy_price, next_price)
```

6. Here, our function takes a buy price, the amount, and the next price in the series. We calculate the buy price, update our trading volume, and return a trade status. Next, let's move on to sell a stock:

```
def SellStock(self, sell_price, amount, next_price):
    ''' Function to sell a stock '''
        self.current_price = sell_price
        self.amount -= amount
        self.TradeStatus(sell_price, next_price)
```

7. In terms of the buy function, we feed in the sell price and the volume, update the class's internal variables, and return a status. Lastly, we'll just create a simple function to hold a stock, which more or less gives us a status of what the current price of that stock is:

```
def HoldStock(self, current_price, next_price):
    ''' Function to hold a stock '''
        self.TradeStatus(current_price, next_price)
```

8. Now, let's move on to creating a class that will represent our artificial trader.

Creating an artificial trader

While utilizing algorithms to inform trading decisions is the definition of algorithmic trading, this is not necessarily automated trading. For that, we need to create an artificial trading agent that will execute our strategies for us:

1. We'll call this class `Trader` and initialize all of the variables that we'll need for the trader algorithm:

```
class Trader(object):
    ''' An Artificial Trading Agent '''

    def __init__(self, market, cash=100000000.0):
        ## Initialize all the variables we need for our trader
        self.cash = cash ## Our Cash Variable
        self.market = market ##
        self.codes = market.codes
        self.reward = 0
        self.positions = []
        self.action_times = 0
        self.initial_cash = cash
        self.max_cash = cash * 3
        self.total_rewards = 0
        self.cur_action_code = None
        self.cur_action_status = None
        self.episode_time = 0
        self.history_profits = []
        self.history_baselines = []
        self.action_dic = {ActionCode.Buy: self.buy,
ActionCode.Hold: self.hold, ActionCode.Sell: self.sell}
```

2. Next, let's create some global properties that will help direct our agent's actions:

```
## CountCode will keep track of how many action codes to handle
@property
def CountCodes(self):
    return len(self.codes)

@property
def ActionSpace(self):
    return self.CountCodes * 3

## Define what our total profits are
@property
def TotalProfits(self):
    return self.cash + self.holdings_value - self.initial_cash
```

```
## Define the total value of all currently held assets
@property
def HoldingsValue(self):
    holdings_value = 0
    for position in self.positions:
        ## Define holdings value as the total value of all current
positions
        holdings_value += position.current_value
    return holdings_value
```

3. Now, we'll want to create a function that purchases `stock` if it is available:

```
def BuyAction(self, code, stock, amount, stock_next):
        ## Check if there is enough cash in the account
        amount = amount if self.cash > stock.close * amount else
int(math.floor(self.cash / stock.close))
        if amount > 0:
            ## Check if we already hold a certain security
            if not self._exist_position(code):
                ## If we do not own the security, feed the
information needed to purchase it to our TradingPosition Class
                position = TradingPosition(code, stock.close,
amount, stock_next.close)
                self.positions.append(position) ## Add the new
security to our list of securities owned
            else:
                # Get position and update if possible.
                position = self._position(code)
                position.BuyStock(stock.close, amount,
stock_next.close)
            ## Udate our current cash on hand
            self.cash -= amount * stock.close
            self._update_reward(ActionCode.Buy,
ActionStatus.Success, position)
```

4. Within the same function, we'll create a condition that handles exceptions; say that our account level is too low:

```
else:
    self.market.logger.info("Code: {}, insufficient cash
reserves.".format(code))
    if self._exist_position(code):
        position = self._position(code)
        position.update_status(stock.close, stock_next.close)
        self._update_reward(ActionCode.Buy, ActionStatus.Failed,
position)
```

5. Next, let's create our `sell action`. This function will take the stock in question as input, and the desired amount of stock to be sold. It will then check if the stock exists, and if so, sell the stock:

```
def SellAction(self, code, stock, amount, stock_next):
 ## First, check to see if we own the secutiry in questions, if
not, return an error
    if not self._exist_position(code):
        self.market.logger.info("Code: {}, does not exits in your
account".format(code))
        return self._update_reward(ActionCode.Sell,
ActionStatus.Failed, None)
 ## Otherwise, attempt to sell the stock
 position = self._position(code)
 amount = amount if amount < position.amount else position.amount
 position.sub(stock.close, amount, stock_next.close)

 ## Lastly, update the amount of cash we now have on hand
 self.cash += amount * stock.close
 self._update_reward(ActionCode.Sell, ActionStatus.Success,
position)
```

6. Lastly, we need to give our automated trader an action for when we simply want to hold the stock:

```
def HoldAction(self, code, stock, _, stock_next):
    if not self._exist_position(code):
        self.market.logger.info("Code: {}, you do not own this
stock".format(code))
        return self._update_reward(ActionCode.Hold,
ActionStatus.Failed, None)
    position = self._position(code)
    position.update_status(stock.close, stock_next.close)
    self._update_reward(ActionCode.Hold, ActionStatus.Success,
position)
```

Now that we have our automated trader, we need to create one more class, this time for handling the market itself.

Managing market data

As with any machine learning algorithm, selecting features for market prediction algorithms is critical, and can lead to the success or failure of the algorithm's strategy. To reduce price curve data into its most fundamental parts, we can use a dimensionality reduction algorithm such as PCA, or even embed stock information to try to capture the most salient latent features. As we have learned, deep learning can help us overcome some of these selection issues, as ANNs implicitly conduct feature selection during the training process:

1. We'll call our new class `MarketHandler` and initialize all of the parameters and data that will be needed to handle our different trading strategies:

```
class MarketHandler(object):
    ''' Class for handling our platform's interaction with market
data'''
    Running = 0
    Done = -1

    def __init__(self, codes, start_date="2008-01-01",
end_date="2018-05-31", **options):
        self.codes = codes
        self.index_codes = []
        self.state_codes = []
        self.dates = []
        self.t_dates = []
        self.e_dates = []
        self.origin_frames = dict()
        self.scaled_frames = dict()
        self.data_x = None
        self.data_y = None
        self.seq_data_x = None
        self.seq_data_y = None
        self.next_date = None
        self.iter_dates = None
        self.current_date = None

        ## Initialize the stock data that will be fed in
        self._init_data(start_date, end_date)

        self.state_codes = self.codes + self.index_codes
        self.scaler = [scaler() for _ in self.state_codes]
        self.trader = Trader(self, cash=self.init_cash)
        self.doc_class = Stock if self.m_type == 'stock' else
Future
```

2. We'll also need to initialize a great deal of data handling processes to correctly manipulate our data for analysis:

```
def _init_data_frames(self, start_date, end_date):
    self._validate_codes()
    columns, dates_set = ['open', 'high', 'low', 'close',
'volume'], set()
    ## Load the actual data
    for index, code in enumerate(self.state_codes):
        instrument_docs = self.doc_class.get_k_data(code,
start_date, end_date)
        instrument_dicts = [instrument.to_dic() for instrument in
instrument_docs]
        dates = [instrument[1] for instrument in instrument_dicts]
        instruments = [instrument[2:] for instrument in
instrument_dicts]
        dates_set = dates_set.union(dates)
        scaler = self.scaler[index]
        scaler.fit(instruments)
        instruments_scaled = scaler.transform(instruments)
        origin_frame = pd.DataFrame(data=instruments, index=dates,
columns=columns)
        scaled_frame = pd.DataFrame(data=instruments_scaled,
index=dates, columns=columns)
        self.origin_frames[code] = origin_frame
    self.scaled_frames[code] = scaled_frame
        self.dates = sorted(list(dates_set))
    for code in self.state_codes:
        origin_frame = self.origin_frames[code]
        scaled_frame = self.scaled_frames[code]
        self.origin_frames[code] =
origin_frame.reindex(self.dates, method='bfill')
        self.scaled_frames[code] =
scaled_frame.reindex(self.dates, method='bfill')
```

3. Now we initialize the `env_data()` method and call the `self` class:

```
def _init_env_data(self):
    if not self.use_sequence:
        self._init_series_data()
    else:
        self._init_sequence_data()
```

4. Lastly, let's initialize the data handling function that we just created:

```
self._init_data_frames(start_date, end_date)
```

Next, let's dive into building the models for our platform.

Price prediction utilizing LSTMs

Let's start by walking through a supervised learning example utilizing an LSTM to predict where the price of a given stock is going, based on its past performance. As we learned in previous chapters, LSTMs and **Recurrent Neural Networks** (**RNN**) in general are superior at modeling and prediction for series data. This model will utilize the trading platform structure that we created previously:

1. Let's start with our imports:

```
import tensorflow as tf
from sklearn.preprocessing import MinMaxScaler
import logging
import os
```

2. Let's create a class that will contain all of the code needed to run the RNN, which we'll call `TradingRNN`. We'll also initialize the necessary variables:

```
class TradingRNN():
    ''' An RNN Model for Derivatives Training '''
    def __init__(self, session, env, seq_length, x_space, y_space,
**options):

        self.seq_length, self.x_space, self.y_space = seq_length,
x_space, y_space

        try:
            self.hidden_size = options['hidden_size']
        except KeyError:
            self.hidden_size = 1

        self.x = tf.placeholder(tf.float32, [None, self.seq_length,
self.x_space])
        self.label = tf.placeholder(tf.float32, [None, self.y_space])
```

For the rest of our network, we'll contain everything in scope; for the main layers of the network, we'll define a scope called `'network_body'` and add a dynamic RNN layer with a fully connected layer for aggregation, and a dense layer for output:

```
with tf.variable_scope('network_body'):
    self.rnn = self.add_rnn(1, self.hidden_size)
    self.rnn_output, _ = tf.nn.dynamic_rnn(self.rnn, self.x,
dtype=tf.float32)
    self.rnn_output = self.rnn_output[:, -1]
    self.rnn_output_dense = self.add_fc(self.rnn_output, 16)
    self.y = self.add_fc(self.rnn_output_dense, self.y_space)
```

3. Next, we'll define our optimization procedure. Since we are predicting continuous values, we'll use the mean squared error as our `loss` function:

```
with tf.variable_scope('loss'):
    self.loss = tf.losses.mean_squared_error(self.y, self.label)
    with tf.variable_scope('train'):
        self.global_step = tf.Variable(0, trainable=False)
        self.optimizer = tf.train.RMSPropOptimizer(self.learning_rate)
        self.train_op = self.optimizer.minimize(self.loss)
        self.session.run(tf.global_variables_initializer())
```

4. We then need to define our training procedure, which is similar to the procedures that you've seen before:

```
def train(self):
    for step in range(self.train_steps):
        batch_x, batch_y =
self.env.get_batch_data(self.batch_size)
        _, loss = self.session.run([self.train_op, self.loss],
feed_dict={self.x: batch_x, self.label: batch_y})
        if (step + 1) % 1000 == 0:
            logging.warning("Step: {0} | Loss: {1:.7f}".format(step +
1, loss))
        if step > 0 and (step + 1) % self.save_step == 0:
            if self.enable_saver:
                self.save(step)
```

5. Lastly, we'll give our network a predict function so that we call a `predict` method, just like you would in many Python-based machine learning frameworks:

```
def predict(self, x):
    return self.session.run(self.y, feed_dict={self.x: x})
```

Outside of the `network` class, let's create a `main` function to run our entire program:

```
def main(args):
    mode = 'test'
    codes = ["600036", "601998"]
    market = args.market
    train_steps = 20000
    training_data_ratio = 0.98

    env = Market(codes, start_date="2008-01-01",
end_date="2018-01-01", **{
        "market": market,
```

```
        "use_sequence": True,
        "scaler": MinMaxScaler,
        "mix_index_state": True,
        "training_data_ratio": training_data_ratio,
        })

    model_name = os.path.basename(__file__).split('.')[0]

    RNN = TradingRNN(tf.Session(config=config), env,
env.seq_length, env.data_dim, env.code_count, **{
        "mode": mode,
        "hidden_size": 5,
        "enable_saver": True,
        "train_steps": train_steps,
        "enable_summary_writer": True,
        "save_path": os.path.join(CHECKPOINTS_DIR, "SL",
model_name, market, "model"),
     "summary_path": os.path.join(CHECKPOINTS_DIR, "SL", model_name,
market, "summary"),
     })

    RNN.run()
    RNN.eval_and_plot()
```

6. Last but not least, we'll just create a `main handler` function to run the model when prompted:

```
if __name__ == '__main__':
    main(model_launcher_parser.parse_args())
```

Backtesting your algorithm

Backtesting is the process of testing your trading algorithm on bits of historical data in order to simulate its performance. While it's no guarantee that the algorithm will perform well in the wild, it gives us a good idea of how it will perform.

In Python, we can backtest our algorithms using a library called **Zipline**. Zipline was created by the online trading algorithms platform Quantopian as their backtesting platform, and it's been open sourced to the public on GitHub. It provides ten years of historical stock data and a realistic trading environment in which you can test algorithms, including transaction costs, order delays, and slippage. Slippage is the price difference that can occur between the expected price at which a trade happens and the actual price it's executed at. To get started with Zipline in Python, we simply need to run `pip install zipline` on the command line.

Any time we use Zipline, we must define two functions:

- `initialize(context)`: This is called by Zipline before it starts running your algorithm. The context variable contains all of the global variables needed in your algorithm. Initialize is very similar to how we initialize variables in TensorFlow before running them through a session.
- `handle_data(context, data)`: This function does exactly what it says: it passes the open, high, low, and close stock market data to your algorithm, along with the necessary context variables.

Event-driven trading platforms

Event-driven investing is an investing strategy that focuses on socioeconomic factors that might influence the stock market's movements, particularly right before a financial event such as an earnings call or merger. This strategy is typically used by larger funds, as they frequently have access to information not entirely open to the public and because it requires a large amount of expertise in analyzing these events correctly.

To do this, we'll extract events from raw text into tuples that describe the event. For instance, if we said that *Google* buys *Facebook*, the tuple would be (*Actor = Google, Action = buys, Object = Facebook, Time = January 1 2018*). These tuples can help us boil down events into their most fundamental parts. Next, we'll embed the words utilizing GloVe. From there, we'll embed entire events that represent the tuple actions, as we described previously. Lastly, we'll use a **Convolutional Neural Network** (**CNN**) to learn the relationships among events. This process is based on the one that was outlined by Ding, et al. in their 2015 paper *Deep Learning for Event-Driven Stock Prediction*.

As always, let's start with our imports:

```
import tensorflow as tf
import params
import ntn_input
import random
```

Gathering stock price data

The majority of real-time market data comes though paid services; think Bloomberg terminals or a brokerage firm's website. Currently, the only non-paid real-time data API for financial markets is Alpha Vantage, which is maintained by a conglomerate of business and academic interests. You can install it by running `pip install alpha_vantage` on your command line. You can sign up for a free API key on Alpha Vantage's website.

Once you have your key, you can easily query the `api` with the following:

```
ts = TimeSeries(key='YOUR_API_KEY', output_format='pandas')
data, meta_data = ts.get_intraday(symbol='TICKER',interval='1min',
outputsize='full')
```

Generating word embeddings

For our embedding scheme, we are going to be using the implementation of GloVe from the previous chapter:

```
from collections import Counter, defaultdict
import os
from random import shuffle
import tensorflow as tf
import nltk

class GloVeModel():
 def __init__(self, embedding_size, window_size, max_vocab_size=100000,
min_occurrences=1,
 scaling_factor=3/4, cooccurrence_cap=100, batch_size=512,
learning_rate=0.05):
 self.embedding_size = embedding_size
#First we define the hyper-parameters of our model
 if isinstance(context_size, tuple):
 self.left_context, self.right_context = context_size
 elif isinstance(context_size, int):
 self.left_context = self.right_context = context_size


 self.max_vocab_size = max_vocab_size
 self.min_occurrences = min_occurrences
 self.scaling_factor = scaling_factor
 self.cooccurrence_cap = cooccurrence_cap
 self.batch_size = batch_size
 self.learning_rate = learning_rate
 self.__words = None
 self.__word_to_id = None
 self.__cooccurrence_matrix = None
 self.__embeddings = None

#Next we define a method that collects the concurrency #statistics to be
used in the training process, and that builds #graph.
 def fit_to_corpus(self, corpus):
 self.__fit_to_corpus(corpus, self.max_vocab_size, self.min_occurrences,
 self.left_context, self.right_context)
 self.__build_graph()
```

```
# Fit corpus creates a global word-word co-occurrence matrix
 def __fit_to_corpus(self, corpus, vocab_size, min_occurrences, left_size,
right_size):
 word_counts = Counter()
 cooccurrence_counts = defaultdict(float)
 for region in corpus:
 word_counts.update(region)
 for l_context, word, r_context in _context_windows(region, left_size,
right_size):
 for i, context_word in enumerate(l_context[::-1]):
 # add (1 / distance from focal word) for this pair
 cooccurrence_counts[(word, context_word)] += 1 / (i + 1)
 for i, context_word in enumerate(r_context):
 cooccurrence_counts[(word, context_word)] += 1 / (i + 1)
 if len(cooccurrence_counts) == 0:
 raise ValueError("No coccurrences in corpus. Did you try to reuse a
generator?")
 self.__words = [word for word, count in
word_counts.most_common(vocab_size)
 if count >= min_occurrences]
 self.__word_to_id = {word: i for i, word in enumerate(self.__words)}
 self.__cooccurrence_matrix = {
 (self.__word_to_id[words[0]], self.__word_to_id[words[1]]): count
 for words, count in cooccurrence_counts.items()
 if words[0] in self.__word_to_id and words[1] in self.__word_to_id}


#Build graph specifies the computational graph to be used for #training the
GloVe embeddings
 def __build_graph(self):
 self.__graph = tf.Graph()
 with self.__graph.as_default(),
 self.__graph.device(_device_for_node):


#Specify placeholder variables and parameters that will be fed #into the
computation graph
 count_max = tf.constant([self.cooccurrence_cap], dtype=tf.float32,
 name='max_cooccurrence_count')
 scaling_factor = tf.constant([self.scaling_factor], dtype=tf.float32,
 name="scaling_factor")

 self.__focal_input = tf.placeholder(tf.int32, shape=[self.batch_size],
 name="focal_words")
 self.__context_input = tf.placeholder(tf.int32, shape=[self.batch_size],
 name="context_words")
 self.__cooccurrence_count = tf.placeholder(tf.float32,
shape=[self.batch_size],
 name="cooccurrence_count")
```

```
#Define the embedding variables
focal_embeddings = tf.Variable(
 tf.random_uniform([self.vocab_size, self.embedding_size], 1.0, -1.0),
 name="focal_embeddings")
 context_embeddings = tf.Variable(
 tf.random_uniform([self.vocab_size, self.embedding_size], 1.0, -1.0),
 name="context_embeddings")

 focal_biases = tf.Variable(tf.random_uniform([self.vocab_size], 1.0,
-1.0),
 name='focal_biases')
 context_biases = tf.Variable(tf.random_uniform([self.vocab_size], 1.0,
-1.0),
 name="context_biases")

 focal_embedding = tf.nn.embedding_lookup([focal_embeddings],
self.__focal_input)
 context_embedding = tf.nn.embedding_lookup([context_embeddings],
self.__context_input)
 focal_bias = tf.nn.embedding_lookup([focal_biases], self.__focal_input)
 context_bias = tf.nn.embedding_lookup([context_biases],
self.__context_input)

 #Specify the forward propagation operations
 weighting_factor = tf.minimum(
 1.0,
 tf.pow(
 tf.div(self.__cooccurrence_count, count_max),
 scaling_factor))

 embedding_product = tf.reduce_sum(tf.multiply(focal_embedding,
context_embedding), 1)

 log_cooccurrences = tf.log(tf.to_float(self.__cooccurrence_count))

 #Specify the loss computing and optimization operations
 distance_expr = tf.square(tf.add_n([
 embedding_product,
 focal_bias,
 context_bias,
 tf.negative(log_cooccurrences)]))

 single_losses = tf.multiply(weighting_factor, distance_expr)
 self.__total_loss = tf.reduce_sum(single_losses)
 tf.summary.scalar("GloVe_loss", self.__total_loss)
 self.__optimizer = tf.train.AdagradOptimizer(self.learning_rate).minimize(
 self.__total_loss)
 self.__summary = tf.summary.merge_all()
```

```
self.__combined_embeddings = tf.add(focal_embeddings, context_embeddings,
name="combined_embeddings")

#Next we train the GloVe model
def train(self, num_epochs, log_dir=None, summary_batch_interval=1000,
tsne_epoch_interval=None):
should_write_summaries = log_dir is not None and summary_batch_interval
should_generate_tsne = log_dir is not None and tsne_epoch_interval
batches = self.__prepare_batches()
total_steps = 0


#Initialize session that encapsulates operations
with tf.Session(graph=self.__graph) as session:
if should_write_summaries:
print("Writing TensorBoard summaries to {}".format(log_dir))
summary_writer = tf.summary.FileWriter(log_dir, graph=session.graph)

#Initialize variables
tf.global_variables_initializer().run()
for epoch in range(num_epochs):
shuffle(batches)
for batch_index, batch in enumerate(batches):
i_s, j_s, counts = batch
if len(counts) != self.batch_size:
continue

#Specify which variables to pass into the computation graph
feed_dict = {
self.__focal_input: i_s,
self.__context_input: j_s,
self.__cooccurrence_count: counts}

#Perform a learning step
session.run([self.__optimizer], feed_dict=feed_dict)
if should_write_summaries and (total_steps + 1) %

#collect summary of the training process
summary_batch_interval == 0:
summary_str = session.run(self.__summary, feed_dict=feed_dict)
summary_writer.add_summary(summary_str, total_steps)
total_steps += 1
if should_generate_tsne and (epoch + 1) % tsne_epoch_interval == 0:
current_embeddings = self.__combined_embeddings.eval()
output_path = os.path.join(log_dir, "epoch{:03d}.png".format(epoch + 1))
self.generate_tsne(output_path, embeddings=current_embeddings)
self.__embeddings = self.__combined_embeddings.eval()
if should_write_summaries:
```

```
summary_writer.close()

#Method to retrieve the embedding for a single word
def embedding_for(self, word_str_or_id):
if isinstance(word_str_or_id, str):
return self.embeddings[self.__word_to_id[word_str_or_id]]
elif isinstance(word_str_or_id, int):
return self.embeddings[word_str_or_id]

#Method to prepare batches of data that will be fed into the #computation
graph
def __prepare_batches(self):
if self.__cooccurrence_matrix is None:
raise NotFitToCorpusError(
"Need to fit model to corpus before preparing training batches.")
cooccurrences = [(word_ids[0], word_ids[1], count)
for word_ids, count in self.__cooccurrence_matrix.items()]
i_indices, j_indices, counts = zip(*cooccurrences)
return list(_batchify(self.batch_size, i_indices, j_indices, counts))

#Define class properties
@property
def vocab_size(self):
return len(self.__words)

@property
def words(self):
if self.__words is None:
raise NotFitToCorpusError("Need to fit model to corpus before accessing
words.")
return self.__words

@property
def embeddings(self):
if self.__embeddings is None:
raise NotTrainedError("Need to train model before accessing embeddings")
return self.__embeddings

#Method that returns the id for a specific word
def id_for_word(self, word):
if self.__word_to_id is None:
raise NotFitToCorpusError("Need to fit model to corpus before looking up
word ids.")
return self.__word_to_id[word]
```

We'll fit the `GloVeModel` to our `corpus` with the following:

```
model = GloVeModel(embedding_size=300, context_size=1)
model.fit_to_corpus(corpus)
model.train(num_epochs=100)
```

Once we have our trained model with embeddings, we'll need to start reasoning to create relationships between entities. For this task, we'll need to represent events in the financial market in mathematical space. For that, we will use a type of ANN that we haven't seen before—the **Neural Tensor Network**, or **NTN**.

Neural Tensor Networks for event embeddings

A **Neural Tensor Network** (**NTN**) is a new form of neural network that works like a standard feed-forward network, only it contains something known as a **tensor layer** instead of standard hidden layers. The network was originally developed as a means of completing knowledge bases by connecting unconnected entities. For instance, if we had the entities Google and YouTube, the network would help connect the two entities so that Google -> Owns -> YouTube. It passes different relationship pairs through the network instead of through a singular vector, and it does this by passing them as a tensor. Each slice of that tensor represents a different variation of a relationship that two entities can have.

In the realm of event-driven trading, we're interested in NTNs because of their ability to relate entities to each other. For us, that means learning the entity event pairs that we created in the first part of this section:

1. Let's start by building our NTN with our core network, which we'll contain in a function called `NTN`:

```
def NTN(batch_placeholders, corrupt_placeholder, init_word_embeds, 
entity_to_wordvec,\
 num_entities, num_relations, slice_size, batch_size, is_eval,
label_placeholders):
    d = 100
    k = slice_size
    ten_k = tf.constant([k])
    num_words = len(init_word_embeds)
    E = tf.Variable(init_word_embeds)
    W = [tf.Variable(tf.truncated_normal([d,d,k])) for r in
range(num_relations)]
    V = [tf.Variable(tf.zeros([k, 2*d])) for r in
range(num_relations)]
    b = [tf.Variable(tf.zeros([k, 1])) for r in
range(num_relations)]
```

```
    U = [tf.Variable(tf.ones([1, k])) for r in
range(num_relations)]

    ent2word = [tf.constant(entity_i)-1 for entity_i in
entity_to_wordvec]
    entEmbed = tf.pack([tf.reduce_mean(tf.gather(E, entword), 0)
for entword in ent2word])
```

2. Still within the NTN function, we'll loop over our embeddings and start to generate relationship embeddings from them:

```
predictions = list()
for r in range(num_relations):
    e1, e2, e3 = tf.split(1, 3, tf.cast(batch_placeholders[r],
tf.int32)) #TODO: should the split dimension be 0 or 1?
    e1v = tf.transpose(tf.squeeze(tf.gather(entEmbed, e1,
name='e1v'+str(r)),[1]))
    e2v = tf.transpose(tf.squeeze(tf.gather(entEmbed, e2,
name='e2v'+str(r)),[1]))
    e3v = tf.transpose(tf.squeeze(tf.gather(entEmbed, e3,
name='e3v'+str(r)),[1]))
    e1v_pos = e1v
    e2v_pos = e2v
    e1v_neg = e1v
    e2v_neg = e3v
    num_rel_r = tf.expand_dims(tf.shape(e1v_pos)[1], 0)
    preactivation_pos = list()
    preactivation_neg = list()
```

3. Lastly, we'll run the relationship through a nonlinearity and output them:

```
for slice in range(k):
preactivation_pos.append(tf.reduce_sum(e1v_pos*tf.matmul(W[r][:,:,s
lice], e2v_pos), 0))
    preactivation_neg.append(tf.reduce_sum(e1v_neg*tf.matmul(
W[r][:,:,slice], e2v_neg), 0))

preactivation_pos = tf.pack(preactivation_pos)
preactivation_neg = tf.pack(preactivation_neg)

temp2_pos = tf.matmul(V[r], tf.concat(0, [e1v_pos, e2v_pos]))
temp2_neg = tf.matmul(V[r], tf.concat(0, [e1v_neg, e2v_neg]))

preactivation_pos = preactivation_pos+temp2_pos+b[r]
preactivation_neg = preactivation_neg+temp2_neg+b[r]

activation_pos = tf.tanh(preactivation_pos)
activation_neg = tf.tanh(preactivation_neg)
```

```
score_pos = tf.reshape(tf.matmul(U[r], activation_pos), num_rel_r)
score_neg = tf.reshape(tf.matmul(U[r], activation_neg), num_rel_r)
if not is_eval:
    predictions.append(tf.pack([score_pos, score_neg]))
else:
    predictions.append(tf.pack([score_pos,
tf.reshape(label_placeholders[r], num_rel_r)]))
```

4. Lastly, let's return all of our relationships that are embedding `predictions`:

```
predictions = tf.concat(1, predictions)

return predictions
```

5. Next, let's define our `loss` function for the network. We'll manually build out our `loss` function from TensorFlow's native operations:

```
def loss(predictions, regularization):
    temp1 = tf.maximum(tf.sub(predictions[1, :], predictions[0,
:]) + 1, 0)
    temp1 = tf.reduce_sum(temp1)
    temp2 = tf.sqrt(sum([tf.reduce_sum(tf.square(var)) for var in
tf.trainable_variables()]))
    temp = temp1 + (regularization * temp2)
    return temp
```

6. We'll define a training algorithm that simply returns the minimized `loss` function utilizing TensorFlow's built-in functions:

```
def training(loss, learningRate):
    return tf.train.AdagradOptimizer(learningRate).minimize(loss)
```

7. Finally, we'll create a short function to evaluate the performance of the network:

```
def eval(predictions):
    print("predictions "+str(predictions.get_shape()))
    inference, labels = tf.split(0, 2, predictions)
    return inference, labels
```

Next, we'll finish up our model by predicting price movements with a CNN.

Predicting events with a convolutional neural network

Now that we have our embedding structure, it's time to predict off of that structure with a CNN. When you typically think of a CNN, and the work that we have completed on them, you're probably thinking of computer vision tasks such as recognizing an object in an image. Although this is what they were designed for, CNNs can also be great at detecting features in text.

When we use CNNs in NLP, we replace the standard input of pixels with word embeddings. While in typical computer vision tasks you utilize the CNNs filters over small patches of the image, for NLP tasks, we use the same sliding window over the rows of a matrix of embeddings. The width of the sliding window, therefore, becomes the width of the input matrix. Typically, this window will look at the embeddings of between around two and five words (or action pairs, in our case) at a time. Because of their condensing nature, this is much more efficient than if we tried the same task with an RNN.

With that being said, let's get started with building our CNN. The input will be our embedded relations, and the output will be a binary classifier; will a stock price go up or down? Let's start by setting up our imports and the CNN itself, which we will contain a Python class named `StockCNN`:

```
import tensorflow as tf
import numpy as np

class StockCNN(object):
    """ CNN for Event Driven Stock Price Prediction"""

    def __init__(
      self, sequence_length, num_classes, vocab_size,
      embedding_size, filter_sizes, num_filters, l2_reg_lambda=0.0):

        ## Tensorflow placeholder for the input variables, as well
        self.input_x = tf.placeholder(tf.int32, [None, sequence_length],
name="input_x")

        self.input_y = tf.placeholder(tf.float32, [None, num_classes],
name="input_y")

        self.dropout_keep_prob = tf.placeholder(tf.float32, name="dropout")
```

Here, we are initializing the variables for the sequence length of the input, the number of classes, our vocabulary and embedding sizes, and the filter parameters for the CNN, just as we did in `Chapter 5`, *Convolutional Neural Network*.

After that, we'll initialize placeholders in the TensorFlow graph for the input variables, as well as our `dropout` variable for the convolutional layers.

1. Next, we'll create an input layer to handle the embeddings:

```
## Placeholder for keeping track of the loss function
l2_loss = tf.constant(0.0)

## The embedding layer for the network
with tf.device('/cpu:0'), tf.name_scope("embedding"):
    self.W = tf.Variable(
        tf.random_uniform([vocab_size, embedding_size], -1.0, 1.0),
name="W")

    self.embedded_chars = tf.nn.embedding_lookup(self.W,
self.input_x)

    self.embedded_chars_expanded =
tf.expand_dims(self.embedded_chars, -1)
```

2. Now, we'll get to the meat of things. Let's create our `convolutional layer`, as well as the `max-pooling layer`:

```
pooled_outputs = []
for i, filter_size in enumerate(filter_sizes):
    with tf.name_scope("conv-maxpool-%s" % filter_size):
        ## Define the Convolutional Layer
        filter_shape = [filter_size, embedding_size, 1, num_filters]
        ## Weights and Bias Factors
        W = tf.Variable(tf.truncated_normal(filter_shape, stddev=0.1),
name="W")
        b = tf.Variable(tf.constant(0.1, shape=[num_filters]),
name="b")
        ## Define a 2d TF Conv Layer and pass in the parameters
        conv = tf.nn.conv2d(
            self.embedded_chars_expanded,
            W,
            strides=[1, 1, 1, 1],
            padding="VALID",
            name="conv")

        ## Add the Non-Linearity
        h = tf.nn.relu(tf.nn.bias_add(conv, b), name="relu")
```

```
## Add the Max-Pooling Layer
pooled = tf.nn.max_pool(
    h,
    ksize=[1, sequence_length - filter_size + 1, 1, 1],
    strides=[1, 1, 1, 1],
    padding='VALID',
    name="pooling-layer")

pooled_outputs.append(pooled)
```

3. We'll then combine all of our features from the pooling layers:

```
num_filters_total = num_filters * len(filter_sizes)
self.h_pool = tf.concat(pooled_outputs, 3)
self.h_pool_flat = tf.reshape(self.h_pool, [-1, num_filters_total])
```

4. Next, we'll have to add dropout to our network with TensorFlow's dropout function:

```
with tf.name_scope("dropout"):
    self.h_drop = tf.nn.dropout(self.h_pool_flat,
self.dropout_keep_prob)
```

5. Lastly, we'll calculate the final scores and predictions. We'll wrap these functions in a TensorFlow scope, and perform final output calculations using the xw_plus_b function from TensorFlow, which computes the matrix multiplication of the input, *x* times the weights, plus bias:

```
with tf.name_scope("output"):
    W = tf.get_variable(
    "W",
    shape=[num_filters_total, num_classes],
    initializer=tf.contrib.layers.xavier_initializer())
    b = tf.Variable(tf.constant(0.1, shape=[num_classes]), name="b")
    l2_loss += tf.nn.l2_loss(W)
    l2_loss += tf.nn.l2_loss(b)
    self.scores = tf.nn.xw_plus_b(self.h_drop, W, b, name="scores")
    self.predictions = tf.argmax(self.scores, 1, name="predictions")
```

6. Lastly, we'll set up two scopes to calculate the `loss` of the network and the accuracy of its predictions:

```
with tf.name_scope("loss"):
    losses =
tf.nn.softmax_cross_entropy_with_logits(logits=self.scores,labels=s
elf.input_y)
    self.loss = tf.reduce_mean(losses) + l2_reg_lambda * l2_loss
with tf.name_scope("accuracy"):
    correct_predictions = tf.equal(self.predictions,
tf.argmax(self.input_y, 1))
    self.accuracy = tf.reduce_mean(tf.cast(correct_predictions,
"float"), name="accuracy")
```

7. Now that we have our network set up, we need to write a few final functions for the training process:

```
def train(x_train, y_train, vocab_processor, x_dev, y_dev):

    with tf.Graph().as_default():
    session_conf = tf.ConfigProto(
    allow_soft_placement=FLAGS.allow_soft_placement,
    log_device_placement=FLAGS.log_device_placement)
    sess = tf.Session(config=session_conf)
    with sess.as_default():
    cnn = StockCNN(
    sequence_length=x_train.shape[1],
    num_classes=y_train.shape[1],
    vocab_size=len(vocab_processor.vocabulary_),
    embedding_size=FLAGS.embedding_dim,
    filter_sizes=list(map(int, FLAGS.filter_sizes.split(","))),
    num_filters=FLAGS.num_filters,
    l2_reg_lambda=FLAGS.l2_reg_lambda)
```

8. Next, let's define the `optimizers` for our training procedure. We'll use the standard `Adam Optimizer`, `call compute`, and apply the gradient descent procedure:

```
## Define the optimizers for training
global_step = tf.Variable(0, name="global_step", trainable=False)
optimizer = tf.train.AdamOptimizer(1e-3)
grads_and_vars = optimizer.compute_gradients(cnn.loss)
train_op = optimizer.apply_gradients(grads_and_vars,
global_step=global_step)
```

9. We'll also need to track our gradient descent progress:

```
## Keep track of the gradients through training
grad_summaries = []
for g, v in grads_and_vars:
if g is not None:
grad_hist_summary =
tf.summary.histogram("{}/grad/hist".format(v.name), g)
sparsity_summary =
tf.summary.scalar("{}/grad/sparsity".format(v.name),
tf.nn.zero_fraction(g))
grad_summaries.append(grad_hist_summary)
grad_summaries.append(sparsity_summary)
grad_summaries_merged = tf.summary.merge(grad_summaries)
```

10. We'll save the model outputs:

```
## Save the model outputs
timestamp = str(int(time.time()))
out_dir = os.path.abspath(os.path.join(os.path.curdir, "runs",
timestamp))
print("Writing to {}\n".format(out_dir))
```

11. We'll also print out the summaries for the model:

```
## Summaries for the loss and accuracy of the model
loss_summary = tf.summary.scalar("loss", cnn.loss)
acc_summary = tf.summary.scalar("accuracy", cnn.accuracy)

## Summary of the training process
train_summary_op = tf.summary.merge([loss_summary, acc_summary,
grad_summaries_merged])
train_summary_dir = os.path.join(out_dir, "summaries", "train")
train_summary_writer = tf.summary.FileWriter(train_summary_dir,
sess.graph)
```

12. TensorFlow automatically expects there to be a directory to save the model checkpoints to, so we need to ensure that the correct path is present:

```
## Create a directory for model checkpoints
checkpoint_dir = os.path.abspath(os.path.join(out_dir,
"checkpoints"))
checkpoint_prefix = os.path.join(checkpoint_dir, "model")
if not os.path.exists(checkpoint_dir):
os.makedirs(checkpoint_dir)
saver = tf.train.Saver(tf.global_variables(),
max_to_keep=FLAGS.num_checkpoints)
```

13. Finally, we'll initialize the variables and start the training steps:

```
ocab_processor.save(os.path.join(out_dir, "vocab"))

# Initialize all variables
sess.run(tf.global_variables_initializer())

def train_step(x_batch, y_batch):
    feed_dict = {
    cnn.input_x: x_batch,
    cnn.input_y: y_batch,
    cnn.dropout_keep_prob: FLAGS.dropout_keep_prob
}
    _, step, summaries, loss, accuracy = sess.run(
    [train_op, global_step, train_summary_op, cnn.loss, cnn.accuracy],
     feed_dict)
    time_str = datetime.datetime.now().isoformat()
    print("{}: step {}, loss {:g}, acc {:g}".format(time_str,
step, loss, accuracy))
    train_summary_writer.add_summary(summaries, step)
```

14. Next we define a method to compute a validation step (forward-prop only) that will be used to track the model's performance on the validation dataset.

```
def dev_step(x_batch, y_batch, writer=None):
    feed_dict = {
cnn.input_x: x_batch,
cnn.input_y: y_batch,
cnn.dropout_keep_prob: 1.0
}

step, summaries, loss, accuracy = sess.run(
[global_step, dev_summary_op, cnn.loss, cnn.accuracy],
feed_dict)
time_str = datetime.datetime.now().isoformat()
print("{}: step {}, loss {:g}, acc {:g}".format(time_str, step,
loss, accuracy))
if writer:
writer.add_summary(summaries, step)
```

15. And last but not least, we'll generate the `batches` for training from our input data:

```
batches = data_helpers.batch_iter(
list(zip(x_train, y_train)), FLAGS.batch_size, FLAGS.num_epochs)
for batch in batches:
x_batch, y_batch = zip(*batch)
train_step(x_batch, y_batch)
```

```
current_step = tf.train.global_step(sess, global_step)
if current_step % FLAGS.evaluate_every == 0:
print("\nEvaluation:")
dev_step(x_dev, y_dev, writer=dev_summary_writer)
print("")
if current_step % FLAGS.checkpoint_every == 0:
path = saver.save(sess, checkpoint_prefix,
global_step=current_step)
print("Saved model checkpoint to {}\n".format(path))
```

Deep learning in asset management

In financial services, a portfolio is a range of investments that are held by a person or organization. To achieve the best return possible (as anyone would want to!), portfolios are optimized by deciding how much capital should be invested into certain financial assets. In portfolio optimization theory, the objective is to have an allocation of assets that minimize risk and maximize reward. We would therefore need to create an algorithm that predicts the expected risks and rewards for each asset so that we may find the best optimization. Traditionally, this work is done by a financial advisor, however, AI has been shown to outperform many traditional advisor-built portfolios.

Lately, there have been several attempts to develop deep learning models for asset allocations. Giving credence to the fact that many of these techniques are not published publicly, we are going to take a look at some fundamental methods that we as AI scientists may use for accomplishing this task.

Our goal will be to train a model on an index of stocks, and see if we can outperform that index by at least 1%. We are going to effectively build an autoencoder to encode latent market information, and then use the decoder to construct an optimal portfolio. As we are dealing with series information, we'll use an RNN for both our encoder and decoder. Once we have an autoencoder trained on the data, we'll use it as the input for a simple feed-forward network that will predict our optimal portfolio allocations.

Let's walk through how we would do this in TensorFlow.

1. As usual, let's start with our imports:

   ```
   import numpy as np
   import tensorflow as tf from tensorflow.contrib.rnn import LSTMCell
   ```

2. Let's load up our stock data:

```
ibb = defaultdict(defaultdict)
ibb_full = pd.read_csv('data/ibb.csv',
index_col=0).astype('float32')

ibb_lp = ibb_full.iloc[:,0]
ibb['calibrate']['lp'] = ibb_lp[0:104]
ibb['validate']['lp'] = ibb_lp[104:]

ibb_net = ibb_full.iloc[:,1]
ibb['calibrate']['net'] = ibb_net[0:104]
ibb['validate']['net'] = ibb_net[104:]

ibb_percentage = ibb_full.iloc[:,2]
ibb['calibrate']['percentage'] = ibb_percentage[0:104]
ibb['validate']['percentage'] = ibb_percentage[104:]
```

3. Let's begin our modeling process by creating our `AutoEncoder`, which we will contain in an `AutoEncoder` class. We'll start by initializing the primary network variables, like we did previously:

```
class AutoEncoder():
    ''' AutoEncoder for Data Drive Portfolio Allocation '''
    def __init__(self, config):
        """First, let's set up our hyperparameters"""
        num_layers = tf.placeholder('int')
        hidden_size = tf.placeholder('int')
        max_grad_norm = tf.placeholder('int')
        batch_size = tf.placeholder('int')
        crd = tf.placeholder('int')
        num_l = tf.placeholder('int')
        learning_rate = tf.placeholder('float')
        self.batch_size = batch_size
        ## sl will represent the length of an input sequence, which
we would like to eb dynamic based on the data
        sl = tf.placeholder("int")
        self.sl = sl
```

4. Next, we'll create the `placeholders` for the input data, *x*:

```
self.x = tf.placeholder("float", shape=[batch_size, sl],
name='Input_data')
self.x_exp = tf.expand_dims(self.x, 1)
self.keep_prob = tf.placeholder("float")
```

5. Next, let's create our encoder. We'll create a series of LSTM cells to encode the series data, but we will do it in a way we haven't seen yet: by using a handy function from TensorFlow called `MultiRNNCell`. This function acts as a larger placeholder of RNNs that we can iterate inside of so that we may dynamically create the amount of layers based on whatever we decide the `num_layers` parameter is:

```
## Create the Encoder as a TensorFlow Scope
with tf.variable_scope("Encoder") as scope:
    ## For the encoder, we will use an LSTM cell with Dropout
    EncoderCell =
tf.contrib.rnn.MultiRNNCell([LSTMCell(hidden_size) for _ in
range(num_layers)])
    EncoderCell = tf.contrib.rnn.DropoutWrapper(EncoderCell,
output_keep_prob=self.keep_prob)

    ## Set the initial hidden state of the encoder
    EncInitialState = EncoderCell.zero_state(batch_size,
tf.float32)

    ## Weights Factor
    W_mu = tf.get_variable('W_mu', [hidden_size, num_l])

    ## Outputs of the Encoder Layer
    outputs_enc, _ = tf.contrib.rnn.static_rnn(cell_enc,
    inputs=tf.unstack(self.x_exp, axis=2),
    initial_state=initial_state_enc)
    cell_output = outputs_enc[-1]

    ## Bias Factor
    b_mu = tf.get_variable('b_mu', [num_l])

    ## Mean of the latent space variables
    self.z_mu = tf.nn.xw_plus_b(cell_output, W_mu, b_mu,
name='z_mu')

    lat_mean, lat_var = tf.nn.moments(self.z_mu, axes=[1])
    self.loss_lat_batch = tf.reduce_mean(tf.square(lat_mean) +
lat_var - tf.log(lat_var) - 1)
```

6. Next, we'll create a layer to handle the hidden states that are generated by the encoder:

```
## Layer to Generate the Initial Hidden State from the Encoder
 with tf.name_scope("Initial_State") as scope:
 ## Weights Parameter State
 W_state = tf.get_variable('W_state', [num_l, hidden_size])
```

```
## Bias Paramter State
b_state = tf.get_variable('b_state', [hidden_size])

## Hidden State
z_state = tf.nn.xw_plus_b(self.z_mu, W_state, b_state,
name='hidden_state')
```

7. We can then create the `decoder` layer in the same fashion that we did with the encoder layer:

```
## Decoder Layer
with tf.variable_scope("Decoder") as scope:

    DecoderCell =
tf.contrib.rnn.MultiRNNCell([LSTMCell(hidden_size) for _ in
range(num_layers)])

    ## Set an initial state for the decoder layer
    DecState = tuple([(z_state, z_state)] * num_layers)
    dec_inputs = [tf.zeros([batch_size, 1])] * sl

    ## Run the decoder layer
    outputs_dec, _ = tf.contrib.rnn.static_rnn(cell_dec,
inputs=dec_inputs, initial_state=DecState)
```

8. Lastly, we'll create the output layer for the network:

```
## Output Layer
with tf.name_scope("Output") as scope:
    params_o = 2 * crd
    W_o = tf.get_variable('W_o', [hidden_size, params_o])
    b_o = tf.get_variable('b_o', [params_o])
    outputs = tf.concat(outputs_dec, axis=0)
    h_out = tf.nn.xw_plus_b(outputs, W_o, b_o)
    h_mu, h_sigma_log = tf.unstack(tf.reshape(h_out, [sl,
batch_size, params_o]), axis=2)
    h_sigma = tf.exp(h_sigma_log)
    dist = tf.contrib.distributions.Normal(h_mu, h_sigma)
    px = dist.log_prob(tf.transpose(self.x))
loss_seq = -px
self.loss_seq = tf.reduce_mean(loss_seq)
```

9. Now that we have the actual model constructed, we can go ahead and set up the training process. We'll use exponential decay for the learning rate, which helps stabilize the training process by slowly decreasing the value of the learning rate:

```
## Train the AutoEncoder
with tf.name_scope("Training") as scope:
```

```
## Global Step Function for Training
global_step = tf.Variable(0, trainable=False)

## Exponential Decay for the larning rate
lr = tf.train.exponential_decay(learning_rate, global_step,
1000, 0.1, staircase=False)

## Loss Function for the Network
self.loss = self.loss_seq + self.loss_lat_batch

## Utilize gradient clipping to prevent exploding gradients
grads = tf.gradients(self.loss, tvars)
grads, _ = tf.clip_by_global_norm(grads, max_grad_norm)
self.numel = tf.constant([[0]])

## Lastly, apply the optimization process
optimizer = tf.train.AdamOptimizer(lr)
gradients = zip(grads, tvars)
self.train_step = optimizer.apply_gradients(gradients,
global_step=global_step)
self.numel = tf.constant([[0]])
```

10. Now, we can run the training process:

```
if True:
    sess.run(model.init_op)
    writer = tf.summary.FileWriter(LOG_DIR, sess.graph) # writer
for Tensorboard

 step = 0 # Step is a counter for filling the numpy array
perf_collect
 for i in range(max_iterations):
     batch_ind = np.random.choice(N, batch_size, replace=False)
     result = sess.run([model.loss, model.loss_seq,
model.loss_lat_batch, model.train_step],
 feed_dict={model.x: X_train[batch_ind], model.keep_prob: dropout})

 if i % plot_every == 0:
     perf_collect[0, step] = loss_train = result[0]
     loss_train_seq, lost_train_lat = result[1], result[2]

 batch_ind_val = np.random.choice(Nval, batch_size, replace=False)

 result = sess.run([model.loss, model.loss_seq,
model.loss_lat_batch, model.merged],
 feed_dict={model.x: X_val[batch_ind_val], model.keep_prob: 1.0})
 perf_collect[1, step] = loss_val = result[0]
 loss_val_seq, lost_val_lat = result[1], result[2]
```

```
summary_str = result[3]
writer.add_summary(summary_str, i)
writer.flush()

print("At %6s / %6s train (%5.3f, %5.3f, %5.3f), val (%5.3f,
%5.3f,%5.3f) in order (total, seq, lat)" % (
i, max_iterations, loss_train, loss_train_seq, lost_train_lat,
loss_val, loss_val_seq, lost_val_lat))
step += 1
if False:

start = 0
label = [] # The label to save to visualize the latent space
z_run = []

while start + batch_size < Nval:
run_ind = range(start, start + batch_size)
z_mu_fetch = sess.run(model.z_mu, feed_dict={model.x:
X_val[run_ind], model.keep_prob: 1.0})
z_run.append(z_mu_fetch)
start += batch_size

z_run = np.concatenate(z_run, axis=0)
label = y_val[:start]

plot_z_run(z_run, label)

saver = tf.train.Saver()
saver.save(sess, os.path.join(LOG_DIR, "model.ckpt"), step)
config = projector.ProjectorConfig()

embedding = config.embeddings.add()
embedding.tensor_name = model.z_mu.name
```

After we autoencode our stock index, we'll look at the difference between each different stock and its corresponding autoencoder version. We'll then rank the stocks by how well they have been autoencoded. As the algorithm learns the most important information about each of the stocks, the proximity of a stock to its version that has been run through the autoencoder provides a measure for that stock against the entire potential portfolio.

As there is no benefit in having multiple stocks contributing to the latent information, we will limit the selected stocks to the top ten of these stocks that are close to their autoencoded version:

```
communal_information = []

for i in range(0,83):
    diff = np.linalg.norm((data.iloc[:,i] - reconstruct[:,i])) # 2 norm
difference
    communal_information.append(float(diff))

print("stock #, 2-norm, stock name")
ranking = np.array(communal_information).argsort()
for stock_index in ranking:
    print(stock_index, communal_information[stock_index],
stock['calibrate']['net'].iloc[:,stock_index].name) # print stock name from
lowest different to highest
```

We can take a look at how the autoencoder is working as follows:

```
which_stock = 1

stock_autoencoder = copy.deepcopy(reconstruct[:, which_stock])
stock_autoencoder[0] = 0
stock_autoencoder = stock_autoencoder.cumsum()
stock_autoencoder += (stock['calibrate']['lp'].iloc[0, which_stock])

pd.Series(stock['calibrate']['lp'].iloc[:, which_stock].as_matrix(),
index=pd.date_range(start='01/06/2012', periods=104,
freq='W')).plot(label='stock original', legend=True)
pd.Series(stock_autoencoder, index=pd.date_range(start='01/06/2012',
periods = 104,freq='W')).plot(label='stock autoencoded', legend=True)
```

While we still have to choose between the available stock, our picking decisions are now based on the out of sample performance of these stocks, making our market autoencoder a novel, data-driven approach.

Summary

In this chapter, we learned how to apply our deep learning knowledge to the financial services sector. We learned the principles of trading systems, and then designed a trading system of our own in TensorFlow. We then looked at how we can create a different type of trading system, one that utilizes events surrounding a company to predict its stock prices. Lastly, we explored a novel technique for embedding the stock market and utilizing those embeddings to predict price movement.

Financial markets can be tricky to model due to their properties, but the techniques that we have covered in this chapter will give you the basis to build further models. Remember to always backtest your algorithm before deploying it in a real-time environment!

In the next chapter, we're going to move on to what many people in the general public imagine **Artificial Intelligence** (**AI**) to be: self-learning robots.

12
Deep Learning for Robotics

So far, we've learned how to build an intelligent chatbot, which can play board games just as a human does, and glean insights from stock market data. In this chapter, we're going to move on to what many people in the general public imagine **Artificial Intelligence** (**AI**) to be: self-learning robots. In `Chapter 8`, *Reinforcement Learning*, you learned all about reinforcement learning and how to use those methods for basic tasks. In this chapter, we'll learn how to apply those methods to robotic motion.

In this chapter, we'll be using GPUs to help train these powerful algorithms. If you don't have a GPU- enabled computer, it's recommended that you use either AWS or Google Cloud to give you some more computing power.

The following topics will be covered in this chapter:

1. Setting up your environment
2. Setting u a deep deterministic policy gradients model
3. The actor-critic network
4. DDPG and its implementation

Technical requirements

In this chapter, we'll be working with TensorFlow and the OpenAI gym environment, so you'll need the following programs installed on your computer:

- TensorFlow
- OpenAI gym

Introduction

Traditional robotics, known as **Robotics Process Automation**, is the process of automating physical tasks that would normally be done by a human. Much like the term **machine learning** covers a variety of methods and approaches, including deep learning approaches; robotics covers a wide variety of techniques and methods. In general, we can break these approaches down into two categories: **traditional approaches** and **AI approaches**.

Traditional robotic control programming takes a few steps:

1. **Measurement**: The robot receives data from its sensors regarding actions to take for a given task.
2. **Inference**: The orientation of the robot is relative to its environment from the data received in the sensors.
3. **Modeling**: Models what the robot must do at each state of action to complete an action.
4. **Control**: Codes the low-level controls, such as the steering mechanism, that the model will use to control the robot's movement.
5. **Deployment of the model**: Checks how the model works in the actual surroundings for which it has been created.

In traditional robotic development, these methods are hardcoded. With deep learning, however, we can create algorithms that learn actions from end to end, thereby eliminating step 2 through 4 in this process, and significantly cutting down on the time it takes to develop a successful robot. What's even more important is the ability of deep learning techniques to generalize; instead of having to program motions for variations of a given task, we can teach our algorithms to learn a general response to that task. In recent years, this AI approach to robotics has made breakthroughs in the field and allowed for significantly more advanced robots.

Due to a lack of consistency of parts and control systems in the robotics market, designing and creating a physical robot can be a difficult task. In February 2018, OpenAI added virtual simulated robotic arms to its training environments, which opened the door for a myriad of new applications and development. These virtual environments use a physical environment simulator to allow us to immediately begin testing our robot control algorithms without the need to procure expensive and disparate parts.

Setting up your environment

We'll be utilizing the gym environment from OpenAI that we learned about in Chapter 8, *Reinforcement Learning*, to create an intelligent robotic arm. OpenAI created a virtual environment based on Fetch Robotic Arms, which created the first fully virtualized test space for robotics algorithms:

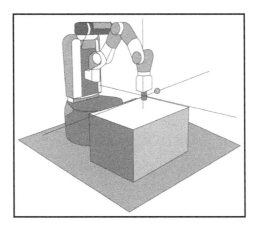

You should have these environments already installed on your computer from when we installed gym in Chapter 11, *Deep Learning for Finance*. We'll just need to add two more packages to get this robotics environment up and running:

```
brew install cmake openmpi
```

Both cmake and openmpi are designed to help with the computational efficiency of our program. We'll cover their usage in a more in-depth manner as we work through the code.

MuJoCo physics engine

MuJoCo is a virtual environment that simulates real physical environments for testing intelligent algorithms. It's the environment that the leading AI researchers at Google DeepMind, OpenAI, and others use to teach virtual robots tasks, virtual humans, and spiders to run, among other tasks. Google in particular made quite a splash in the news in 2017 when they published a video of a virtual human that taught itself to run and jump based on reinforcement learning techniques:

MuJoCo is a paid licensed program, but they allow for 30-day free trials which we will use to complete our tasks. If you are a student, you can obtain a perpetual license of MuJoCo for free for your own personal projects. There are a few steps to go through to obtain MuJoCo and set up your environment for AI applications:

1. Download the MuJoCo binary files from their website
2. Sign up for a free trial of MuJoCo
3. Place your license key in the `~|.mujoco|mjkey.txt` folder
4. Install the Python package for MuJoCo

This may seem a bit cumbersome, but it does give us access to the most cutting-edge simulator that is used in the AI world. If you're having issues with any of these steps, we'll be keeping an up-to-date help document on the GitHub repository for this book. With that, let's walk through these steps.

Downloading the MuJoCo binary files

First things first, let's download the MuJoCo program itself. Navigate to `https://www.roboti.us/index.html` and download the `mjpro150` file that corresponds to your operating system. You can also do this through the command line with the following code:

```
cd ~
mkdir .mujoco
cd .mujoco
curl https://www.roboti.us/download/mjpro150_osx.zip
```

Signing up for a free trial of MuJoCo

Go through the following steps to sign-up for a free trial of MuJoCo:

1. Once you've downloaded the binary files for MuJoCo, navigate to `https://www.roboti.us/license.html` to sign up for a free trial. You should see the following prompt box for signing up for MuJoCo:

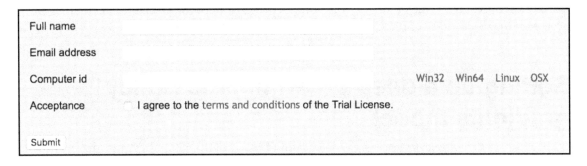

2. See those blue links to the right of the computer ID box? You'll need to download the one that corresponds to your operating system. This will generate a key for MuJoCo to keep track of your computer and its trial. If you are using macOS, you can download and get the key with the following code:

```
curl https://www.roboti.us/getid/getid_osx
sudo ./getid_osx
```

3. If you are on a Linux machine, you can download your MuJoCo key with the following code:

```
wget https://www.roboti.us/getid/getid_linux
sudo ./getid_linux
```

Once you have your key, place it in the prompt box. You should receive an email with a license that will enable you to use MuJoCo.

Configuring your MuJoCo files

Next, you'll need to configure your access files. You should receive your license key from MuJoCo in an email. Once you do, place it in the following folder so the program can access it:

```
~/.mujoco/mjkey.txt
```

Installing the MuJoCo Python package

Lastly, we need to install the MuJoCo Python package that will allow Python to speak to the program. We can do that easily with a `pip install`:

```
pip install mujoco-py
```

You should now have access to the most powerful virtualized environment for robotics testing. If you've had issues with any part of this process, remember that you can always access an up-to-date issues page from this book's GitHub repository.

Setting up a deep deterministic policy gradients model

In `Chapter 8`, *Reinforcement Learning*, we learned about how to use policy optimization methods for continuous action spaces. Policy optimization methods learn directly by optimizing a policy from actions taken in their environment, as explained in the following diagram:

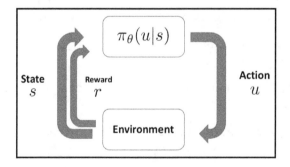

Remember, policy gradient methods are **off-policy**, meaning that their behavior in a certain moment is not necessarily reflective of the policy they are abiding by. These policy gradient algorithms utilize **policy iteration**, where they evaluate the given policy and follow the policy gradient in order to learn an optimal policy.

Before we get started, let's quickly review the Markov process that is in reinforcement learning algorithms. The entity (our algorithm) that navigates a Markov Decision process is called an **agent**. In this case, the agent would be the stock market itself. We can remember the parameters of the Markov process by using SAP:

- **Set of possible states** (**S**): The possible states of beings that an agent can be in at any given time. When we talk about states in reinforcement learning, this is what we are referring to.
- **Set of possible actions** (**A**): All of the possible actions that an agent can take in its environment. These are the lines between the states; what actions can happen between two states?
- **Transition Probability** (**P**): The probability of moving to any of the new given states.

The goal of any reinforcement learning agent is to solve a given Markov Decision process by maximizing the **reward** it receives from taking specific actions. There are a few global parameters that we should take note of that we'll use throughout the network:

- **BufferSize**: The size of the replay buffer, measured in the amount of transition states that we take
- **TimeHorizon**: The length of time for each episode

Our model and code will be based upon the one released by OpenAI; if you're having trouble with some of the code, you can refer to some of the reference links that are included in the GitHub repository.

Experience replay buffer

Next, let's create the experience replay buffer as we did in `Chapter 11`, *Deep Learning for Finance*, when we looked at creating deep learning models for game playing.

Hindsight experience replay

To improve on robotic movement, OpenAI researchers released a paper on a technique known as **Hindsight experience replay** (**HER**) in 2018 to attempt to overcome issues that arise when training reinforcement learning algorithms in **sparse environments**. Recall `Chapter 8`, *Reinforcement Learning*, choosing an appropriate reward for an agent can make or break the performance of that agent. Anecdotes such as the following often appear as the result of bad reward functions:

> *A friend is training a simulated robot arm to reach toward a point above a table. It turns out the point was defined with respect to the table, and the table wasn't anchored to anything. The policy learned to slam the table really hard, making the table fall over, which moved the target point, too. The target point just so happened to fall next to the end of the arm.*

HER helps deal with the issues that arise from spare reward spaces. Typical reinforcement learning algorithms have **sparse reward spaces**, meaning that a reward is binary (0 or 1). Using these reward functions, a robotic arm will not learn from bad behavior—it would simply keep repeating actions until it finds a good action to emulate.

If you were trying to complete a task, let's say, catching a ball, and on your first few tries you didn't catch that ball, would you say that you've failed and learn nothing from the endeavor? Or, would you at least learn how not to catch a ball? The latter is how HER learns – it learns that it did complete some task, albeit the wrong task, and receives a reward for doing something. Instead of not trying to learn how to catch a ball at all, it's like receiving a participation award for showing up. You're trying! With the idea that practice makes perfect, if you show up enough and attempt to catch the ball, you are going to eventually learn how to catch that ball.

HER uses experience replay, just like we learned about with Deep Q learning and **deep deterministic policy gradients** (**DDPG**). Instead of choosing actions based on the optimal reward at the moment, the HER method's goals are chosen prior to training ever beginning. Hence, it's replaying experience from hindsight, with a particular end goal in mind (that is, catching the ball). This may sound as basic as a human, but that's part of the point—we want to make these systems more human-like.

If we try to solve this problem with standard reinforcement learning techniques, we could edit the reward function to be more in line with the actual environment—we call this process **shaping the reward**. Let's say we're trying to successfully complete the preceding example with a robotic arm; we could add weights to the various actions it takes to catch the ball to ensure that the agent is learning from its environment, and update those weights in training with a parameter:

$$Reward = w1 \times catchGoal + distance \times w_{2...}$$

We'd need to account for all of the possible states that could affect our agent's ability to catch the ball; distance, angles, maybe even wind? Can you see how crafting an appropriate reward function becomes immensely complicated quite quickly? While some problems can be solved with this method, many become too complex, too fast. This is why we use HER as a viable alternative.

Recall standard experience replay—it stores the [state, action, reward, next_state] pairs at each time step. Instead of running the algorithm on state-action pairs as they occur, experience replay stores these pairs as they are discovered:

$$e_t = (s_t, a_t, r_t, s_{t+1})$$

1. Let's start by creating a function that needs work:

$$replay = 1 + \frac{1}{1 + replayRatio}$$

```
import numpy as np

def createHERsample(replay_ratio):
        return future_prob = 1 - (1. / (1 + replay_ratio))
```

The replay ratio is proportional to how many HER experience replays we would like as opposed to regular experience replays. So, if `replay_ratio` were set to 6 here, we would have six times as many HER experience replays as regular experience replays. Remember; HER experience replays reward our agent for acting, so it is a good idea to have several times more HER replays than regular replays for sparse tasks such as our robotic movement task. OpenAI found that 4 and 8 were the optimal ratio numbers.

2. Next, let's create the function that samples back from the experience replay buffer. We'll call this function `HERsampler`:

```
def HERsampler(episode_batch, batch_size, reward_function,
future_prob):
    TimeHorizon = episode_batch['u'].shape[1]
    rollout_batch_size = episode_batch['u'].shape[0]
```

`HERsampler` will take in a batch of episodes, or experiences, along with the size of that batch, the reward function for successfully completing an action, and the probabilities for conducting future actions that we defined previously.

3. Next, we'll write a few lines of code that tell the `HER` function which episodes and time steps to use for its experience replay:

```
episodes = np.random.randint(0, rollout_batch_size, batch_size)
timed_samples = np.random.randint(TimeHorizon, size=batch_size)
transitions = {key: episode_batch[key][episodes,
timed_samples].copy() for key in episode_batch.keys()}
```

4. The transitions that HER will select are stored in a dictionary called **transitions**. The keys of the dictionary will be the episode batches, and the values will be the indexes of the episodes and their time samples:

```
her_indexes = np.where(np.random.uniform(size=batch_size) <
future_p)
future_offset = np.random.uniform(size=batch_size) * (T -
t_samples)
future_offset = future_offset.astype(int)
future_t = (t_samples + 1 + future_offset)[her_indexes]
```

5. Next, we'll replace the goal with the achieved goal for the HER replay instances so that we are adding the HER actions to the experience replay buffer:

```
futureAchGoal = episode_batch['ag'][episodes[her_indexes],
future_time]
transitions['g'][her_indexes] = futureAchGoal
```

6. Next, we'll compute the reward signal that comes from one of the HER actions. This is where we will tell the algorithm, good job!, for completing an action:

```
info = {}
 for key, value in transitions.items():
     if key.startswith('info_'):
         info[key.replace('info_', '')] = value
```

```
reward = {k: transitions[k] for k in ['ag_2', 'g']}
reward['info'] = info
transitions['r'] = reward_function(**reward)
transitions = {k: transitions[k].reshape(batch_size,
*transitions[k].shape[1:]) for k in transitions.keys()}
```

Note the use of `*` and `**` here; these are Python magic variables that allow us to pass a variable amount of arguments to the function. In this case, we don't necessarily know the reward value that will be passed into the `reward` function, so we will use the `**` variable to allow for variation.

7. Lastly, to close out our original function, we'll simply return the `transitions` dictionary:

```
return transitions
```

As a future strategy, replay with k random states which come from the same episode as the transition being replayed and were observed after it.

The actor–critic network

DDPG models rely on actor-critic frameworks, which are used to learn policies without having to calculate the value function again and again.

Actor-critic models are essential frameworks in reinforcement learning. They are the basis and inspiration for **Generative Adversarial Networks** (**GANs**), which we learned about in `Chapter 7`, *Generative Models*.

As you may have guessed,these actor-critic models consist of two parts:

- **The actor**: Estimates the policy function
- **The critic**: Estimates the value function

The process works exactly as it sounds; the actor model tries to emulate an action, and the critic model criticizes the actor model to help it improve its performance. Let's take our robotics use case; the goal of robotic motion is to create a robot that simulates human ability. In this case, the actor would want to observe human actions to emulate this, and the critic would help guide the robotic actor to be more human. With actor-critic models, we simply take this paradigm and translate it into mathematical formulas. Altogether, the actor-critic process looks as follows:

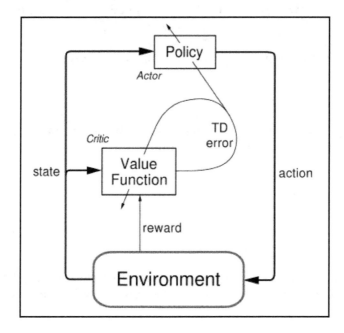

Each of these networks has its own loss function.

The actor

The actor network is also called the **target policy network**. The actor is trained by utilizing gradient descent that has been mini-batched. Its loss is defined with the following function:

$$La = -EsQ(s, \pi(s))$$

Here, s represents a state that has been sampled from the replay buffer.

The critic

The output of the critic is the estimate of the action-value function Q $^{(s,a)}$, and as such you might see the critic network sometimes called the **action-value function approximator**. Its job is to help the actor appropriately approximate the action-value function.

The critic model works very similarly to the Q-function approximator that we saw in `Chapter 10`, *Deep Learning for Game Playing*. The critic produces a **temporal-difference** (**TD**) error, which it uses to update its gradients. The TD error helps the algorithm reduce the variance that occurs from trying to make predictions off of highly correlated data. DDPG utilizes a target network, just as the Deep Q-network did in `Chapter 10`, *Deep Learning for Game Playing*, only the targets are computed by utilizing the outputs of the actor:

$$y_i = r_i + \gamma Q'(s_{i+1}, \mu'(s_{i+1}|\theta^{\mu'})|\theta^{Q'})$$

This target network generates targets for the TD error calculations, and acts as a regularizer. Let's break this down:

- y_i represents our TD error.
- r^i represent the reward received from a certain action.
- $\gamma Q'(s_{i+1}, \mu'(s_{i+1}|\theta^{\mu'})|\theta^{Q'})$ collectively represents the target Q' for the actor and critic models. Recall that γ (gamma) represents a **discount factor**. Recall that the discount factor can be any value between 0 and 1 that represents the relative importance between a current reward and a future reward. So, our target then becomes the output of the actor/critic models multiplied by the mixing parameter.
- $\mu'(s_{i+1}|\theta^{\mu'})$ represents the target of the actor network; it's saying that the target μ' is a function of state s, given a particular policy $\theta^{\mu'}$.
- Likewise, we then say that the output of the actor network is dependent on the critic network by representing that critic network by its weights $\theta^{Q'}$.

The critic tries to minimize its own loss function:

$$L = \frac{1}{N} \sum_i (y_i - Q(s_i, a_i|\theta^Q)^2)$$

Deep Deterministic Policy Gradients

There is a natural extension of **Deep Deterministic Policy Gradients** (DDPG) by replacing the feedforward neural networks used for approximating the actor and the critic with recurrent neural networks. This extension is called the **recurrent deterministic policy gradient** algorithm (**RDPG**) and is discussed in the f paper N. Heess, J. J. Hunt, T. P. Lillicrap and D. Silver. *Memory-based control with recurrent neural networks*. 2015.

The recurrent critic and actor are trained using **backpropagation through time** (BPTT). For readers who are interested in it, the paper can be downloaded from https://arxiv.org/abs/1512.04455.

Implementation of DDPG

This section will show you how to implement the actor-critic architecture using TensorFlow. The code structure is almost the same as the DQN implementation that was shown in the previous chapter.

The ActorNetwork is a simple MLP that takes the observation state as its input:

```
class ActorNetwork:
    def __init__(self, input_state, output_dim, hidden_layers,
activation=tf.nn.relu):
        self.x = input_state
        self.output_dim = output_dim
        self.hidden_layers = hidden_layers
        self.activation = activation
        with tf.variable_scope('actor_network'):
            self.output = self._build()
            self.vars = tf.get_collection(tf.GraphKeys.TRAINABLE_VARIABLES,
                                          tf.get_variable_scope().name)
    def _build(self):
        layer = self.x
        init_b = tf.constant_initializer(0.01)
        for i, num_unit in enumerate(self.hidden_layers):
            layer = dense(layer, num_unit, init_b=init_b,
name='hidden_layer_{}'.format(i))
        output = dense(layer, self.output_dim, activation=self.activation,
init_b=init_b, name='output')
        return output
```

The constructor requires four arguments: `input_state`, `output_dim`, `hidden_layers`, and `activation`. `input_state` is a tensor for the observation state. `output_dim` is the dimension of the action space. `hidden_layers` specifies the number of the hidden layers and the number of units for each layer. `activation` indicates the activation function for the output layer.

The `CriticNetwork` is also a MLP, which is enough for the classic control tasks:

```
class CriticNetwork:
    def __init__(self, input_state, input_action, hidden_layers):
        assert len(hidden_layers) >= 2
        self.input_state = input_state
        self.input_action = input_action
        self.hidden_layers = hidden_layers
        with tf.variable_scope('critic_network'):
            self.output = self._build()
            self.vars = tf.get_collection(tf.GraphKeys.TRAINABLE_VARIABLES,
                                          tf.get_variable_scope().name)
    def _build(self):
        layer = self.input_state
        init_b = tf.constant_initializer(0.01)
        for i, num_unit in enumerate(self.hidden_layers):
            if i != 1:
                layer = dense(layer, num_unit, init_b=init_b,
name='hidden_layer_{}'.format(i))
            else:
                layer = tf.concat([layer, self.input_action], axis=1,
name='concat_action')
                layer = dense(layer, num_unit, init_b=init_b,
name='hidden_layer_{}'.format(i))
        output = dense(layer, 1, activation=None, init_b=init_b,
name='output')
        return tf.reshape(output, shape=(-1,))
```

The network takes the state and the action as its inputs. It first maps the state into a hidden feature representation and then concatenates this representation with the action, followed by several hidden layers. The output layer generates the Q-value that corresponds to the inputs.

The actor-critic network combines the actor network and the critic network together:

```
class ActorCriticNet:
    def __init__(self, input_dim, action_dim,
                 critic_layers, actor_layers, actor_activation,
                 scope='ac_network'):
        self.input_dim = input_dim
        self.action_dim = action_dim
```

```
        self.scope = scope
        self.x = tf.placeholder(shape=(None, input_dim), dtype=tf.float32,
    name='x')
        self.y = tf.placeholder(shape=(None,), dtype=tf.float32, name='y')
        with tf.variable_scope(scope):
            self.actor_network = ActorNetwork(self.x, action_dim,
                                              hidden_layers=actor_layers,
                                              activation=actor_activation)
            self.critic_network = CriticNetwork(self.x,
    self.actor_network.get_output_layer(),
    hidden_layers=critic_layers)
            self.vars = tf.get_collection(tf.GraphKeys.TRAINABLE_VARIABLES,
                                          tf.get_variable_scope().name)
        self._build()
    def _build(self):
        value = self.critic_network.get_output_layer()
        actor_loss = -tf.reduce_mean(value)
        self.actor_vars = self.actor_network.get_params()
        self.actor_grad = tf.gradients(actor_loss, self.actor_vars)
        tf.summary.scalar("actor_loss", actor_loss, collections=['actor'])
        self.actor_summary = tf.summary.merge_all('actor')
        critic_loss = 0.5 * tf.reduce_mean(tf.square((value - self.y)))
        self.critic_vars = self.critic_network.get_params()
        self.critic_grad = tf.gradients(critic_loss, self.critic_vars)
        tf.summary.scalar("critic_loss", critic_loss,
    collections=['critic'])
        self.critic_summary = tf.summary.merge_all('critic')
```

The constructor requires six arguments, as follows: `input_dim` and `action_dim` are the dimensions of the state space and the action space, respectively. `critic_layers` and `actor_layers` specify the hidden layers of the critic network and the actor network. `actor_activation` indicates the activation function for the output layer of the actor network. `scope` is the scope name used for the `scope` TensorFlow variable.

The constructor first creates an instance of the `self.actor_network` actor network with an input of `self.x`, where `self.x` represents the current state. It then creates an instance of the critic network using the following as the inputs: `self.actor_network.get_output_layer()` as the output of the actor network and `self.x` as the current state. Given these two networks, the constructor calls `self._build()` to build the loss functions for the actor and critic that we discussed previously. The actor loss is `-tf.reduce_mean(value)`, where `value` is the Q-value computed by the critic network. The critic loss is `0.5 * tf.reduce_mean(tf.square((value - self.y)))`, where `self.y` is a tensor for the predicted target value computed by the target network.

The class `ActorCriticNet` provides the functions for calculating the action and the Q-value given the current state, that is, `get_action` and `get_value`. It also provides `get_action_value`, which computes the `state-action value` function given the current state and the action taken by the agent:

```
class ActorCriticNet:
    def get_action(self, sess, state):
        return self.actor_network.get_action(sess, state)
    def get_value(self, sess, state):
        return self.critic_network.get_value(sess, state)
    def get_action_value(self, sess, state, action):
        return self.critic_network.get_action_value(sess, state, action)
    def get_actor_feed_dict(self, state):
        return {self.x: state}
    def get_critic_feed_dict(self, state, action, target):
        return {self.x: state, self.y: target,
                self.critic_network.input_action: action}
    def get_clone_op(self, network, tau=0.9):
        update_ops = []
        new_vars = {v.name.replace(network.scope, ''): v for v in
network.vars}
        for v in self.vars:
            u = (1 - tau) * v + tau * new_vars[v.name.replace(self.scope,
'')]
            update_ops.append(tf.assign(v, u))
        return update_ops
```

Because DPG has almost the same architecture as DQN, the implementations of the replay memory and the optimizer are not shown in this chapter. For more details, you can refer to the previous chapter or visit our GitHub repository (`https://github.com/PacktPublishing/Python-Reinforcement-Learning-Projects`). By combining these modules together, we can implement the DPG class for the deterministic policy gradient algorithm:

```
class DPG:
    def __init__(self, config, task, directory, callback=None,
summary_writer=None):
        self.task = task
        self.directory = directory
        self.callback = callback
        self.summary_writer = summary_writer
        self.config = config
        self.batch_size = config['batch_size']
        self.n_episode = config['num_episode']
        self.capacity = config['capacity']
        self.history_len = config['history_len']
        self.epsilon_decay = config['epsilon_decay']
```

```
        self.epsilon_min = config['epsilon_min']
        self.time_between_two_copies = config['time_between_two_copies']
        self.update_interval = config['update_interval']
        self.tau = config['tau']
        self.action_dim = task.get_action_dim()
        self.state_dim = task.get_state_dim() * self.history_len
        self.critic_layers = [50, 50]
        self.actor_layers = [50, 50]
        self.actor_activation = task.get_activation_fn()
        self._init_modules()
```

Here, `config` includes all the parameters of DPG, for example, batch size and learning rate for training. The `task` is an instance of a certain classic control task. In the constructor, the replay memory, Q-network, target network, and optimizer are initialized by calling the `_init_modules` function:

```
    def _init_modules(self):
        # Replay memory
        self.replay_memory = ReplayMemory(history_len=self.history_len,
                                          capacity=self.capacity)
        # Actor critic network
        self.ac_network = ActorCriticNet(input_dim=self.state_dim,
                                         action_dim=self.action_dim,
                                         critic_layers=self.critic_layers,
                                         actor_layers=self.actor_layers,
        actor_activation=self.actor_activation,
                                         scope='ac_network')
        # Target network
        self.target_network = ActorCriticNet(input_dim=self.state_dim,
                                             action_dim=self.action_dim,
        critic_layers=self.critic_layers,
        actor_layers=self.actor_layers,
        actor_activation=self.actor_activation,
                                              scope='target_network')
        # Optimizer
        self.optimizer = Optimizer(config=self.config,
                                   ac_network=self.ac_network,
                                   target_network=self.target_network,
                                   replay_memory=self.replay_memory)
        # Ops for updating target network
        self.clone_op = self.target_network.get_clone_op(self.ac_network,
        tau=self.tau)
        # For tensorboard
        self.t_score = tf.placeholder(dtype=tf.float32, shape=[],
        name='new_score')
        tf.summary.scalar("score", self.t_score, collections=['dpg'])
        self.summary_op = tf.summary.merge_all('dpg')
    def choose_action(self, sess, state, epsilon=0.1):
```

```
        x = numpy.asarray(numpy.expand_dims(state, axis=0),
dtype=numpy.float32)
        action = self.ac_network.get_action(sess, x)[0]
        return action + epsilon * numpy.random.randn(len(action))
    def play(self, action):
        r, new_state, termination = self.task.play_action(action)
        return r, new_state, termination

    def update_target_network(self, sess):
        sess.run(self.clone_op)
```

The `choose_action` function selects an action based on the current estimate of the actor-critic network and the observed state.

Note that a Gaussian noise controlled by `epsilon` is added for exploration.

The `play` function submits an action into the simulator and returns the feedback from the simulator. The `update_target_network` function updates the target network from the current actor-critic network.

To begin the training process, the following function can be called:

```
    def train(self, sess, saver=None):
        num_of_trials = -1
        for episode in range(self.n_episode):
            frame = self.task.reset()
            for _ in range(self.history_len+1):
                self.replay_memory.add(frame, 0, 0, 0)
            for _ in range(self.config['T']):
                num_of_trials += 1
                epsilon = self.epsilon_min + \
                        max(self.epsilon_decay - num_of_trials, 0) / \
                        self.epsilon_decay * (1 - self.epsilon_min)
                if num_of_trials % self.update_interval == 0:
                    self.optimizer.train_one_step(sess, num_of_trials,
self.batch_size)
                state = self.replay_memory.phi(frame)
                action = self.choose_action(sess, state, epsilon)
                r, new_frame, termination = self.play(action)
                self.replay_memory.add(frame, action, r, termination)
                frame = new_frame
                if num_of_trials % self.time_between_two_copies == 0:
                    self.update_target_network(sess)
                    self.save(sess, saver)
```

```
                    if self.callback:
                        self.callback()
                    if termination:
                        score = self.task.get_total_reward()
                        summary_str = sess.run(self.summary_op,
    feed_dict={self.t_score: score})
                        self.summary_writer.add_summary(summary_str,
    num_of_trials)
                        self.summary_writer.flush()
                        break
```

In each episode, it calls `replay_memory.phi` to get the current state and calls
the `choose_action` function to select an action based on the current state. This action is
submitted into the simulator by calling the `play` function, which returns the corresponding
reward, next state, and termination signal. Then, the `(current state, action,
reward, termination)` transition is stored into the replay memory. For
every `update_interval` step (`update_interval = 1`, by default), the actor-critic
network is trained with a batch of transitions that are randomly sampled from the replay
memory. For every `time_between_two_copies` step, the target network is updated and
the weights of the Q-network are saved to the hard disk.

After the training step, the following function can be called for evaluating the performance
of our trained agent:

```
        def evaluate(self, sess):
            for episode in range(self.n_episode):
                frame = self.task.reset()
                for _ in range(self.history_len+1):
                    self.replay_memory.add(frame, 0, 0, 0)
                for _ in range(self.config['T']):
                    print("episode {}, total reward {}".format(episode,
    self.task.get_total_reward()))
                        state = self.replay_memory.phi(frame)
                        action = self.choose_action(sess, state, self.epsilon_min)
                        r, new_frame, termination = self.play(action)
                        self.replay_memory.add(frame, action, r, termination)
                        frame = new_frame

                    if self.callback:
                        self.callback()
                    if termination:
                        break
```

Summary

In this chapter, we expanded upon the knowledge that we obtained about in Chapter 8, *Reinforcement Learning*, to learn about DDPG, HER, and how to combine these methods to create a reinforcement learning algorithm that independently controls a robotic arm.

The Deep Q network that we used to solve game challenges worked in discrete spaces; when building algorithms for more fluid motion tasks such as robots or self-driving cards, we need a class of algorithms that can handle continuous action spaces. For this, use policy gradient methods, which learn a policy from a set of actions directly. We can improve this learning by using an experience replay buffer, which stores positive past experiences so that they may be sampled during training time so that the algorithm knows how to act.

Sometimes, our algorithms can fail to learn due to them not being able to find positive actions toward their goal. Even with standard experience replay buffers, sparse information on past experiences can make learning hard. HER remedies this by tricking the algorithm into thinking it did something good, when it really just did something. This adds action to the replay buffer, and helps reward the network for action, not inaction.

References

Python Reinforcement Learning Projects, Sean Saito, Yang Wenzhuo, and Rajalingappaa Shanmugamani, https://www.packtpub.com/big-data-and-business-intelligence/python-reinforcement-learning-projects.

13
Deploying and Maintaining AI Applications

Throughout this book, we've learned all about how to create **Artificial Intelligence** (**AI**) applications to perform a variety of tasks. While writing these applications has been a considerable feat in itself, it's often only a small portion of what it takes to turn your model into a serviceable production system. For many practitioners, the workflow for deep learning models often ends at the validation stage. You've created a network that performs extremely well; We're done, right?

It's becoming increasingly common for data scientists and machine learning engineers to handle their applications from the discovery to deployment stages. According to Google, more than 60-70% of the time it takes to build an AI application is spent on the deployment architecture of that application. Given that this book is designed to help you build AI applications from start to finish, this section will give you the essentials that you need to be full-stack.

At the moment, there are no industry best practices on what a good deep learning deployment architecture looks like. Many cloud providers, such as **Amazon Web Services** (**AWS**) and **Google Cloud Platform** (**GCP**), have attempted to fill this gap with their own deployment frameworks. Google in particular has created a very clean end-to-end system that capitalizes on the fact that they maintain TensorFlow. We'll learn how to do these processes both manually, and with platforms such as Google Cloud, so that you can take your deep learning models into a live state as easily as possible.

In this chapter, we will cover:

- Deploying AI applications
- Scaling AI Applications
- Testing AI Applications

Technical requirements

While this chapter will contain some materials that are typically part of the job of a DevOps engineer, we'll touch on these tools and topics on a need-to-know basis, and refer to other resources and tools that can help you learn about the topics in more depth. In this chapter, we'll be utilizing the following:

- TensorFlow
- PyTorch
- Docker, a containerization service for deploying our models
- Amazon Web Services or Google Cloud Platform as a cloud provider
- Introductory knowledge of Kubernetes

Introduction

The deployment and maintenance of AI applications is more than just a single action; it's a process. In this section, we will work through creating sustainable applications in the cloud by creating a **deep learning deployment architecture**. These architectures will help us create end-to-end systems: **deep learning systems**.

In many machine learning/AI applications, the typical project pipeline and workflow might look something like the following:

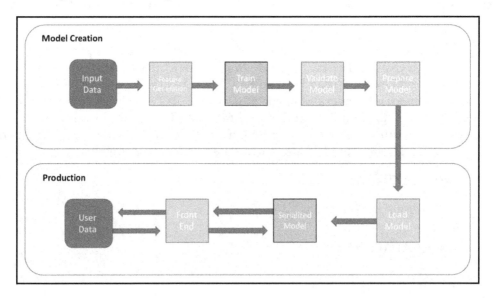

The training processes are strictly offline, and serialized models are pushed to the cloud and interact with a user through an API. These processes often leave us with several different languages/packages/tools talking to each other in a way that slows down our processes. Often, the model creation part of this process becomes the domain of data scientists, while the deployment and maintenance part becomes that of an engineering team. In an effort to become a bit more full-stack, we'll be learning how to manage this architecture more efficiently by maintaining the training, evaluation, monitoring, and serving within the TensorFlow ecosystem. This will help us not only decrease switching between different languages and systems, but will help streamline the deployment process. Our system architecture can be broken down into four major components:

- **Data storage and Ingest**: Where our training data is stored, as well as the scripts to ingest data.
- **Training architecture**: Where and how will the model be trained?
- **Serving**: Making your model accessible to outside sources. This is what is traditionally thought of as deployment.
- **Evaluation and Monitoring**: The continued monitoring of performance, usage, and updates.

All together, our architecture will look as follows:

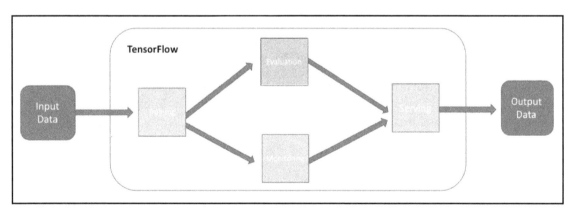

To practice building these full-stack systems, we are going to use a basic feedforward neural network in TensorFlow. Before we begin, let's set up that basic model; we are going to be deploying a simple feed forward network that classifies fraudulent credit card transactions. For this example, we'll be utilizing the credit card fraud detection dataset from Kaggle, which you may also find in the GitHub repository that corresponds with this chapter.

The data contains a set of features that have been masked through principal component analysis that describe a user and the transaction, and two obfuscated features—the amount of the transactions, and whether the transaction was considered fraud.

V8	V9	...	V21	V22	V23	V24	V25	V26	V27	V28	Amount	Class
0.098698	0.363787	...	-0.018307	0.277838	-0.110474	0.066928	0.128539	-0.189115	0.133558	-0.021053	149.62	0
0.085102	-0.255425	...	-0.225775	-0.638672	0.101288	-0.339846	0.167170	0.125895	-0.008983	0.014724	2.69	0
0.247676	-1.514654	...	0.247998	0.771679	0.909412	-0.689281	-0.327642	-0.139097	-0.055353	-0.059752	378.66	0
0.377436	-1.387024	...	-0.108300	0.005274	-0.190321	-1.175575	0.647376	-0.221929	0.062723	0.061458	123.50	0
-0.270533	0.817739	...	-0.009431	0.798278	-0.137458	0.141267	-0.206010	0.502292	0.219422	0.215153	69.99	0

We won't go too much into the details of the model but let's briefly go over it's structure. First, let's start with our standard imports:

```
import tensorflow as tf
import numpy as np
import pandas as pd
import os
```

We'll also import some specific packages that will help us handle our data:

```
from tensorflow.python.lib.io import file_io
from sklearn.preprocessing import StandardScaler
from sklearn.cross_validation import train_test_split
```

You may not be familiar with the TensorFlow `file_io` library; this will help our algorithm handle imports in production. Let's start by defining our classifier as a Python class called `simple_classifier`. With this, we'll initialize some training parameters, as well as placeholders for the features *x* and labels *y*.

```
class simple_classifier:
    ''' A simple feed-forward classifier in TensorFlow'''
    def __init__(self):
        self.num_epochs = 50
        self.batch_size = 100
        self.display = 1
        self.test_ratio = 0.25
        self.x = tf.placeholder("float", [None, 18], name='features')
        self.y = tf.placeholder("float", shape=(None,2), name='target')
```

Next, let's preprocess the data; we'll scale the unscaled columns, and we'll also need to drop some columns. The distributions of these columns are far to similar for the fraudulent and non-fraudulent transactions, and they may create unnecessary noise for our model:

```
def preprocess_data(self):
        with file_io.FileIO('creditcard.csv', mode ='r') as f:
            fraud_data = pd.read_csv(f)
        fraud_data['normAmount'] =
StandardScaler().fit_transform(fraud_data['Amount'].values.reshape(-1, 1))
        fraud_data =
fraud_data.drop(['Time','Amount','V28','V27','V26','V25','V24','V23','V22',
'V20','V15','V13','V8'], axis =1)
        x_data = pd.concat([fraud_data.iloc[:,0:17],
fraud_data.iloc[:,18]], axis=1)
        y_data = fraud_data.iloc[:,17]
        x_train, x_test, y_train, y_test = train_test_split(x_data, y_data,
test_size=self.test_ratio, random_state=42)
        return x_train, x_test, y_train, y_test
```

We'll then create a feed forward neural network that will classify our data as fraud or not fraud. For simplicity's sake, we'll make it two layers, with a softmax layer for prediction:

```
def mlp(self, x):
    initializer = tf.contrib.layers.xavier_initializer()
    h0 = tf.layers.dense(x, x.shape[1], tf.nn.relu,
kernel_initializer=initializer)
    h1 = tf.layers.dense(h0, 2, activation=None)
    logits = tf.nn.softmax(h1)
    return logits
```

Next, we need to prepare for training! We'll prepare our data, loss function, and optimizer, as well as set up a saver for our model parameters:

```
def train_model(self, job_dir):
        ## Gather the data
        x_train, x_test, y_train, y_test = self.preprocess_data()
        ## The model requires needs a column for each class as input
        y_train = np.array([y_train, -(y_train-1)]).T
        ## Prepare the Network
        logits = self.mlp(self.x)
        loss =
tf.reduce_mean(tf.nn.softmax_cross_entropy_with_logits(labels=self.y,
logits=logits))
        training_operation = tf.train.AdamOptimizer(2e-4).minimize(loss)
        ## Initialize the variables
        init = tf.global_variables_initializer()
        total_batch = int(len(x_train)/self.batch_size)
        ## Create the batches
```

```
        X_batches = np.array_split(x_train, total_batch)
        Y_batches = np.array_split(y_train, total_batch)
        ## Initialize the model saver
        save_model = os.path.join(job_dir, 'saved_classifier.ckpt')
        saver = tf.train.Saver()
```

Lastly, let's write out the training operation itself:

```
## Start the training session
 with tf.Session() as sess:
 sess.run(init)
 for epoch in range(self.num_epochs):
     for i in range(total_batch):
         batch_x, batch_y = X_batches[i], Y_batches[i]
         _, c = sess.run([training_operation, loss], feed_dict={self.x:
batch_x, self.y: batch_y})
     if epoch % self.display == 0:
         print("Epoch:", '%04d' % (epoch+1),
         "cost=", "{:.9f}".format(c))

## Save the model checkpoints
saver.save(sess, saver_path)
```

Before we get started, go ahead and run this model. You can either run in manually in a notebook by initializing it and passing it a save directory:

```
c = simple_classifier()
c.train_model("./")
```

or by running it as a Python script. Both are available to you in the corresponding repo. You should now have this super-simple model, and a set of saved training checkpoints from the model. In the next sections, we'll be using this model as a base to learn about deployment and maintenance.

Deploying your applications

So, what does it mean to deploy a model? Deployment is an all-encompassing term that covers the process of taking a tested and validated model from your local computer, and setting it up in a sustainable environment where it's accessible. Deployment can be handled in a myriad of ways; in this chapter, we'll focus on the knowledge and best practices that you should know about to get your models up into production.

Your choice of deployment architecture depends on a few things:

- Is your model being trained in one environment and productionalized in another?
- How many times are you expecting your model to be called predictions to be made from it?
- Is your data changing over time or is it static? Will you need to handle large inflows of data?

Each of these questions can be answered by breaking down our model selection options into two buckets. We can break down our models by the location from which they are served, as well as the way in which they are trained. The following figure shows these options in a matrix, as well as the costs and benefits of each method:

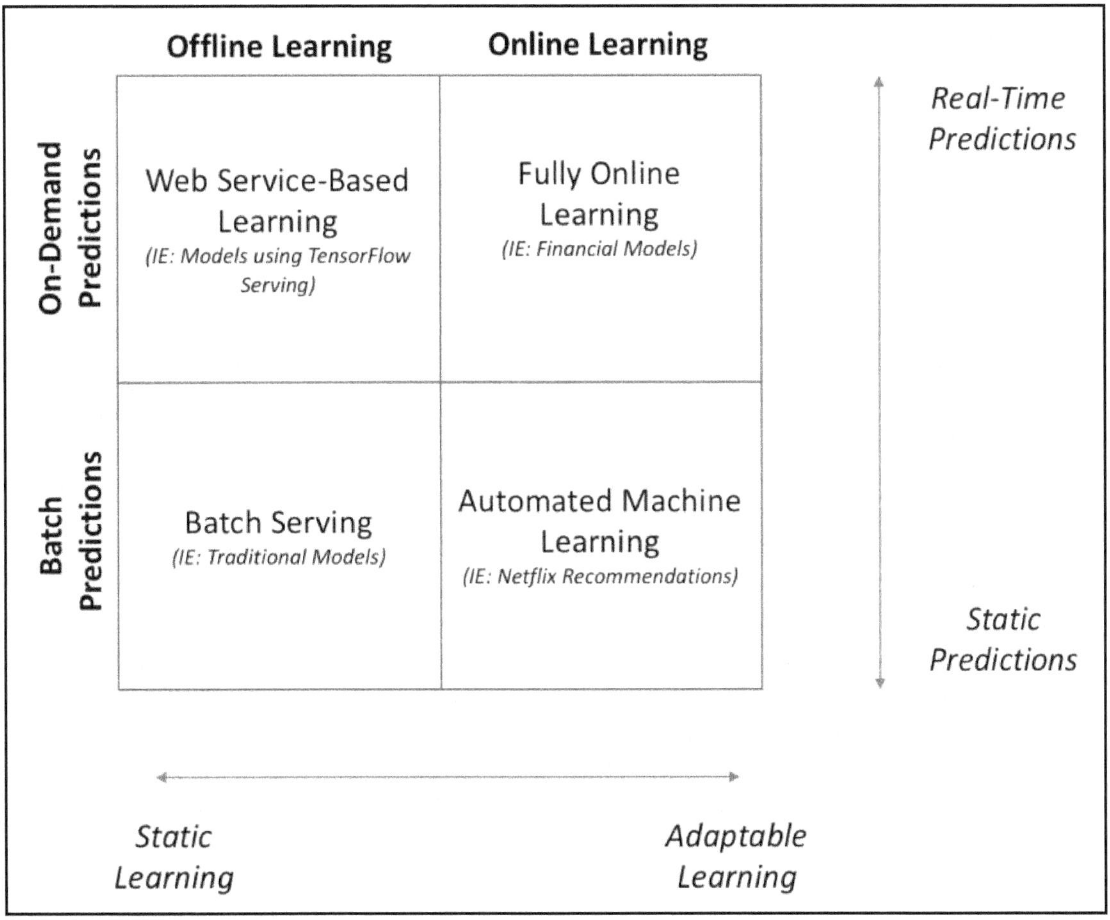

Models that are trained on a specific piece of data, in a separate environment from where they are deployed, are called **offline models**, whereas models that actively learn from new data in their deployment environment are called **online models**.

The simplest form of serving for offline models is called **batch serving**. If you are a data scientist or come from academia, you're probably very familiar with this model. Batch serving involves simply taking a static dataset, feeding it to your model, and receiving predictions back. Typically, you'll probably do this on your local machine, perhaps with a Jupyter Notebook or simply by running a script from your terminal or Command Prompt. In the majority of cases, we want our models to be accessible to larger groups of users so that we encase them in a **web service**.

Online models are more difficult to manage due to the complications that can arise from the handling of data flows and potentially bad input data. Microsoft's fated Tay Twitter bot was an example of a Fully online learning model which took tweets as input, and quickly became racist and crude. Managing these models can become complicated because of the open training process, and many safeguards must be put in place to ensure that your model does not deviate too far from its desired output.

Automated machine learning models, on the other hand, are becoming increasingly popular. They have controlled input, but are actively retraining to consider new data. Think about Netflix's recommendation system – it actively responds to your behavior by training on the data you generate based on your browsing and viewing activity.

Now that we have a grasp of our ecosystem, let's get started by learning how to set up a common web service deployment architecture with TensorFlow. If you are not interested in learning about manual deployment processes, and only wish to use deployment service, please feel free to skip the next section.

Deploying models with TensorFlow Serving

In general, when deploying models, we want the inner machinations of the model to be isolated from the public behind an HTTP interface. With a traditional machine learning model, we would wrap this serialized model in a deployment framework such as Flask to create an API, and serve our model from there. This could lead us to a myriad of issues with dependencies, versioning, and performance, so instead, we are going to use a tool provided to us by the TensorFlow authors called **TensorFlow Serving**. This spins up a small server that runs a TensorFlow model and provides access to it.

TensorFlow Serving implements a specific type of remote procedure call known as **GPRC**. In computer science, remote procedure calls allow code to be executed from a remote computer, just as if it were running locally. This allows the model to communicate with the outside world with the help of a **client**, thereby mitigating potentially malicious requests against your model. It's also a much simpler interface than REST. To utilize GPRC with Python, we'll have to install it:

```
pip install grpcio grpcio-tools
```

Now, before we can use TensorFlow Serving, we have to save our model in an appropriate format that Serving can understand. For this, we use a process called **serialization**, which is a computer science term for the process of translating a model into a format that is appropriate for transmission and storage. You may have experience of using Python's `pickle` library, which is one form of serialization. TensorFlow has its own form of model saving, called a **SavedModel**, which saves the variables, graph, and metadata of a model in a language neutral-format. This is what we need in order to deploy our model.

There are three forms of models that TensorFlow can export:

- **Predict**: A general saved format that can be used for any type of problem; it accepts tensors as input and outputs tensors
- **Classify**: Specific to classification problems; it produces classes and scores as output
- **Regress**: Specific to regression problems

If you are using the general predict method, saving a model for production is simple with the `simple_save` function. The function takes in:

- A TensorFlow session object
- A path to where you'd like to model to be saved
- The model's input data
- The model's output

All together, it's just a few lines of code:

```
simple_save(sess,
  'path/to/saved/directory',
  inputs={"x": x, "y": y},
  outputs={"z": z})
```

TensorFlow freezes and saves the computational graph that runs behind your program. TensorFlow stores models as a **Protocol buffer**, or **Protobuf**, which **serializes** the model. Let's see how we can create a SavedModel from our classification network above. To save the model, we'll replace the standard checkpoint saver `saver.save(sess, save_model)` with the script as follows:

```
predicted_indicies = tf.argmax(logits, 1)

## Model Serving Inputs
inputs={"x": self.x}

## Model Serving Outputs
outputs={
        "probs": logits,
        "pred_indicies": predicted_indicies
        }
saved = os.path.join(job_dir, 'binaries')

tf.saved_model.simple_save(sess, saved, inputs, outputs)
print('Model Saved')
```

Let's walk through what's happening here step-by-step; keep in mind that we aren't actually performing any operations here, we're simply laying out a roadmap to tell a compressed, saved version of the model what to do when faced with a new prediction.

The first function that we encounter here is using `argmax` on the output of our softmax function, `logits`:

```
predicted_indicies = tf.argmax(logits, 1)
```

The `argmax` function in TensorFlow returns the index of the tensor with the largest value. In other words, it tells us which label, fraud of not fraud, it most likely. Next, we're passing the model the placeholders for input and output. It's using the inherited `self.x` placeholder that we initialized with the classifier previously, and using it as a placeholder for the SavedModel's input. As output, we'll send both the probabilities (`logits`), as well as the predicted index of the most likely label:

```
## Model Serving Inputs
inputs={"x": self.x}

## Model Serving Outputs
outputs={
        "probs": logits,
        "pred_indicies": predicted_indicies
        }
```

Lastly, we simply define the directory to saved the model in, and pass all of the parameters to the model saver function:

```
saved = os.path.join(job_dir, 'binaries')
tf.saved_model.simple_save(sess, saved, inputs, outputs)
```

If you now run the model with these lines of code added, you should see a message like the one below. Keep in mind that the no assets to write message simply means that the model does not have any external dependencies:

```
INFO:tensorflow:Assets added to graph.
INFO:tensorflow:No assets to write.
INFO:tensorflow:SavedModel written to: b'./checkpoint/binaries/saved_model.pb'
Done
```

If you have a more complex model, or your model does not return prediction predictions, you can also save a model in TensorFlow with the `SavedModelBuilder` module, which is a more customizable version of the `simple_save` method.

Now that we have a SavedModel, we can work on deploying it! Next, we'll go over three different ways you can deploy this model: first, by setting up the deployment architecture yourself and deploying the model on AWS, second by utilizing AWS Lambda for a streamlined deployment, and third by using the GCP's Cloud ML service. In this section, we'll cover the manual deployment process.

Utilizing docker

Since we'll be deploying our model to the cloud, we'll need some type of mechanism to run the model itself. While we could spin up a virtual machine on AWS, it's a bit overkill for what we need and there are many simpler (and cheaper) processes that can help us.

Instead, we will utilize a tool known as a **container**. Containers are a lightweight virtualization technique that contain all of the necessary runtime packages and methods for running an application. The most popular container service is called **Docker**.

While we won't cover the Docker installation process here, you can install Docker by following the official installation guidelines:

1. Create a **Docker image**
2. Create a **container from** the Docker image
3. Build TensorFlow Serving on the container

The configuration of a Docker image is defined in something called a **Docker file**. TensorFlow Serving gives these files to us, one for utilizing CPUs and one for utilizing GPUs.

Google's TensorFlow team maintains a Docker image that is ready to use for TensorFlow Serving:

1. Once you have Docker installed, you can grab it easily with the `docker pull` command in your terminal or command prompt:

   `docker pull tensorflow/serving`

   You should see a series of messages that look something as follows:

   ```
   Using default tag: latest
   latest: Pulling from tensorflow/serving
   3b37166ec614: Pull complete
   504facff238f: Pull complete
   ebbcacd28e10: Pull complete
   c7fb3351ecad: Pull complete
   2e3debadcbf7: Pull complete
   663c9c41af87: Pull complete
   d6e28cd78fff: Pull complete
   27ac5da5d75a: Pull complete
   f272a0508079: Pull complete
   Digest: sha256:3cd54a904eecbd91a2ca3483fb2edece1727f088261090ab2ae94ac87751ed16
   Status: Downloaded newer image for tensorflow/serving:latest
   ```

2. Once you've downloaded the Docker image, you can move on to creating a container on the image. We can easily do that by running the build command:

   ```
   ## Builds a docker container from the image
   docker build --pull -t $USER/tensorflow-serving-devel -f
   tensorflow_serving/tools/docker/Dockerfile.devel .
   ```

   Building the docker container can take a while—don't worry, this is normal.

3. Once the container is built, go ahead and run the container:

   ```
   ## Run the container; we'll name it nn_container
   docker run --name=nn_container -it $USER/tensorflow-serving-devel
   ```

4. You should now have shell access to your Docker container. Next, we'll download the actual TensorFlow serving files into the container:

```
git clone -b r1.6 https://github.com/tensorflow/serving
cd serving
```

5. Lastly, we'll need to install the TensorFlow modelserver on the container. Modelserver will be doing the actual serving for our model:

```
bazel build -c opt
tensorflow_serving/model_servers:tensorflow_model_server
```

Once we have a container, our environment is configured. The next thing to do is place our saved model inside the docker container.

 When you exit the shell of a Docker container, the container shuts down. If you'd like to start the container again, you can do so by running `docker start -i nn_container` in the container's directory.

Let's create a directory to place our model in. While you are still in the command line for the container, create a new directory with:

```
mkdir model_serving
```

Next, we'll upload our saved model to this directory. From wherever you saved the classifier from previously, run the following commend. You'll replace `output_directory` with whatever the sub-folder is that the TensorFlow SavedModel binaries are saved in.

```
docker cp ./output_directory nn_container:/model_serving
```

Let's try serving our model. Run the following command inside the docker container:

```
tensorflow_model_server --port=9000 --model_name=nn --
model_base_path=/model_serving/binaries &> nn_log &
```

Your model should now be running locally with TensorFlow serving. We're not done, however, as we need to create a way that the model can interact with requests once it is deployed in the cloud. For that, we'll need to create something called a **client**, which is a small program that acts as a gatekeeper for the model to talk with the outside world.

Building a TensorFlow client

Lastly, we need to build a client to interact with our TensorFlow model. Building a custom client to interact with your model is a bit beyond the scope of this book, so we've provided this in the corresponding GitHub repository:

1. Go ahead and download it with the following code:

```
pip install git+ssh://git@github.com/PacktPublishing/hands-On-
Artificial-Intelligence-for-Beginners/tf-client.git
```

2. Let's try using the client to send a request to the model:

```
from predict_client.prod_client import ProdClient

client = ProdClient('localhost:9000', 'simple', 1)
req_data = [{'in_tensor_name': 'a', 'in_tensor_dtype': 'DT_INT32',
'data': 2}]
client.predict(req_data)
```

What's happening here?

- The first line imports the client itself, `TfClient`, which sends requests to our model
- In constructing the request, send the web-address, the name of the model, and the version of the model
- In the actual request, we'll want to construct a tensor to send to the model, and it will send back an output tensor. We'll feed it the name of the input tensor that we defined in the preceding section, a datatype, and the data we want to predict off

If you found this a little tedious—you're not alone. AWS and Google Cloud have created much simpler ways to handle the entire process with platform as a service offerings that take care of a lot of these manual deployment processes for us.

Training and deploying with the Google Cloud Platform

For a much simpler deployment procedure, we can deploy a TensorFlow SavedModel to production with the **Google Cloud Platform** (**GCP**). In this section, we'll cover the basics of how to both train and deploy a model using GCP.

The GCP currently provides one of the most straightforward and easy interfaces for training and deploying models. If you are interested in getting your model up to production as quickly as possible, GCP is often your answer. Specifically, we'll be using the Cloud ML service, which is a compliment to AWS SageMaker that we just learned previously. Cloud ML is enabled currently enabled to run TensorFlow, Scikit-learn, and XGBoost right out of the box, although you can add your own packages manually. Compared to SageMaker, Cloud ML receives updates automatic updates to TensorFlow much at a rapid speed due to the library's Google integration, and hence it is recommended to use it for TensorFlow-based applications.

Before we get started, let's set up a new Google Cloud Storage Bucket that will be the basis for our application. Go ahead and log onto your GCP account, look for Cloud Storage, and click **Create bucket**. You should see a screen that looks like the one as follows:

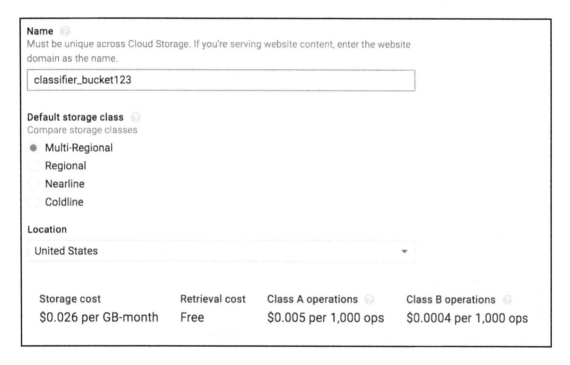

This bucket will act as the staging ground for our data, model, training checkpoints, and model binaries. Go ahead and upload the `creditcard.csv` file that we've been using to the bucket , we'll be using it soon!

Next, let's make our model ready for training on GCP, we'll have to give it a couple lines of code so that it can run from the command line. In a script that contains the model code from previously, we'll add this to the bottom:

```python
if __name__ == '__main__':
    parser = argparse.ArgumentParser()
    parser.add_argument(
        '--job-dir',
        help='GCS location to write checkpoints and export models'
    )
    parser.add_argument(
        '--train-file',
        help='GCS or local paths to training data'
    )
    args, unknown = parser.parse_known_args()
    c = SimpleClassifier()
    c.train_model(**args.__dict__)
```

This script will enable us to pass in the only parameter for the model, `job_dir`, from the command line. For the full GCP-ready code, check out the `simple_classifier.py` script in this chapter's GitHub. Once you have your Cloud Storage and script set up, we're ready to start our training and deployment!

Training on GCP

Google has made the entire deep learning training / deployment process streamlined and simple by allowing us to train models, store them, and deploy them with minimal code. Before we start training in the cloud, let's train our model locally to ensure that everything is working as intended. First, we need to set some environment variables. First and foremost, we'll have to put our files in a particular structure to train with Cloud ML. Look for the training folder in the chapter GitHub folder, and you will find the correct file structure. The __init__.py file that you see there will simply tell GCP that our file is an executable Python program.

First we'll define a job directory, which should be the folder where your `simple_classifier.py` model is stored, and a path to the data which the model will be using:

```
JOB_DIR="model_folder"
TRAIN_DATA="/path/to/data"
```

Now, all we have to do now is issue a `gcloud` command to tell our model to train:

```
gcloud ml-engine local train --job-dir $JOB_DIR --module-name trainer.task
--package-path trainer/ -- --train-file $TRAIN_DATA
```

If your model has successfully trained locally, then we're ready to move to the cloud. For cloud training, we need to define a few more environment variables that are required from Cloud ML. First and foremost, training on Cloud ML is issued as a job; the platform takes care of the environment setup, training, and clean-up for us instead of having to develop it all manually as we did above in the TensorFlow serving section. Each job needs a unique name - we'll call our `classifier_model`. Instead of the local job directory that we defined earlier, we'll point GCP to create a folder for our training job in the bucket that we created precedingly. We'll also define a service region to run the model in. Within in the United States, choose the location that is closest to you:

- us-west1
- us-central1
- us-east1

```
JOB_NAME="classifier_model"
JOB_DIR="gs://classifier_bucket123/$JOB_NAME"
PACKAGE_STAGING_PATH="gs://classifier_bucket123"
MAIN_TRAINER_MODULE="trainer.simple_classifier"
REGION="us-east1"
TRAIN_DATA="gs://classifier_bucket123/creditcard.csv"
```

Now we're ready to train! Go ahead and submit the command below to kick off training:

```
gcloud ml-engine jobs submit training $JOB_NAME --staging-bucket
$PACKAGE_STAGING_PATH --job-dir $JOB_DIR --package-path /trainer --module-
name $MAIN_TRAINER_MODULE --runtime-version 1.8 --region $REGION -- --
train-file $TRAIN_DATA
```

The argument `--runtime-version` should correspond to whatever version of TensorFlow that you have running locally on your machine. If you are not sure what version you are running, you can run `python -c 'import tensorflow as tf; print(tf.__version__)'` in your command line.

After you submit the training job, you should see a prompt returned to you confirming that the job has been kicked off:

```
$ gcloud ml-engine jobs stream-logs classifier_model
jobId: classifier_model
state: QUEUED
```

Now, go ahead and log onto the Cloud ML console to check it's progress. The **Jobs** button will give you an in depth look at errors, training progress, and anything else that you might typically see in your local command line:

The script will output the SavedModel binaries to your cloud storage bucket. If you were able to successfully complete the processes previously, you're on your way to deploying the model! Let's move onto how we can deploy SavedModel as an API.

Deploying for online learning on GCP

When we deploy a TensorFlow SavedModel to the GCP platform, we either need to upload the entire SavedModel directory to a storage location on GCP or train in the cloud as we did previously. Regardless of what method you main use, your TensorFlow model's binaries should be stored in a Google Cloud Storage location.

Your model binaries will be the final that was created after training, and will have the extension .pb.

To start our deployment process, we first need to create a deployed model object. You can create it with the command as follows:

```
gcloud ml-engine models create "deployed_classifier"
```

Next, we'll create an environment variable that will let GCP know where our saved model binaries are:

```
DEPLOYMENT_SOURCE="gs://classifier_bucket123/classifier_model/binaries"
```

All we have to do now is run the command as follows, and our classifier will be deployed! Keep in mind that deployment will take a few minutes to configure:

```
gcloud ml-engine versions create "version1"\
    --model "deployed_classifier" --origin $DEPLOYMENT_SOURCE --runtime-
version 1.9
```

As you see, we've done with a few lines of code what took us an entire section precedingly; platforms as services like AWS SageMaker and Google Cloud ML are extreme time savers in the modeling process.

Now, let's try getting predictions from our model. Before we try asking for a prediction, we'll need to go ahead and setups a few variables. The input data file will be a json file that contains a single line of data. To make it easy, we've included a line from the dataset as `test.json` in the `GitHub` folder:

```
MODEL_NAME="deployed_classifier"
INPUT_DATA_FILE="test.json"
VERSION_NAME="version1"
```

Lastly, go ahead and run the prediction request:

```
gcloud ml-engine predict --model $MODEL_NAME \
                --version $VERSION_NAME \
                --json-instances $INPUT_DATA_FILE
```

Congratulations! Your model is now hosted in the cloud. You should see a returned json object, with probabilities for both of the potential classifications, fraud or not-fraud. While the `gcloud` command previously is great for issuing individual requests, we often want to return requests as part of a web application. In the next segment, we'll run through a simple example of how we can do this with a simple Flask application.

Using an API to Predict

To get started, you'll have to create a Google Cloud service account key so that your application can access the model. Navigate to the link `https://console.cloud.google.com/apis/credentials/serviceaccountkey`, and create a new account. Be sure to download the key as a JSON file. To connect to GCP, you'll need to setup your account credentials as an environment variable that GCP can access. Go ahead and set it's location as an environment variable:

```
GOOGLE_APPLICATION_CREDENTIALS = your_key.json
```

Let's create a script called `predict.py` (you can find the completed script in the `chapter` folder). First, we'll import the Google libraries that will allow our program to connect to the API. `GoogleCredidentials` will discover our access token, while the API client works just as the client we manually created previously; it connects to and authenticates the API:

```
from oauth2client.client import GoogleCredentials
from googleapiclient import discovery
ml = discovery.build('ml','v1')
```

We'll then create a simple script to call the model. Here, we're just hard-coding the the input data. In a real, useful application, we would be receiving that input data from a stream or front-end web interface, but that is outside of the context of this book.

We then tell GCP what our project and model names are, give is a version, and request a response:

```
def predict():
    item = {"x": [-0.23477546, -0.4932691 , 1.23672756, -2.33879318,
    -1.17673345, 0.88573295, -1.96098116, -2.36341211, -2.69477418, 0.36021476,
    1.61549548, 0.44775205, 0.60569248, 0.16959132, -0.07365524, -0.16345899,
    0.56242311, -0.57703178, -1.63563411, 0.36467924, -1.4953583 , -0.08306639,
    0.07461232, -0.34732949, 0.54189984, -0.43329449, 0.08929321, -0.10854652]}
    name = 'projects/{}/models/{}'.format('project-name',
'deployed_classifier')
    name += '/versions/{}'.format('version1')
    response = ml.projects().predict(name=name, body={"instances":
item}).execute()
    return response['predictions']
```

Now, we'll create a file that we'll call `app.py`; this will be the Flask App itself. Let's start with the imports:

```
from flask import Flask, jsonify
from flask_cors import CORS
from predict import predict
```

First, setup the framework of the app. We'll define the Flask App, and setup a CORS handler. **CORS** is a web protocol that allows resources, such as our model hosted on GCP, to be requested by an external domain - our web application:

```
app = Flask(__name__)
CORS(app)
```

For our testing purposes here, we'll just create a single route with a GET request. If you are not familiar with RESTful APIs, GET requests do exactly what they sound like—they *get* a response given a certain input. All this app is doing is calling the predict function that we created previously, and returning the result to the user:

```
@app.route('/predict', methods=['GET'])
def sendPredict():
    response = predict()
    return jsonify(response[0])

if __name__ == '__main__':
    app.run(debug=True)
```

If we were to imagine this in the context of a live web application, this could provide functionality that could check a transaction for fraud upon clicking a button, or some other web action. To run this app, run the following code in your terminal:

```
FLASK_APP=app.py
flask run
```

Your app should now be running on your local machine. From here, you'll be able to request a prediction for our hardcoded example by hitting navigating to localhost/predict . If you're interested in further exploring building web applications of the sort, there are several Packt resources that can help you learn more.

Scaling your applications

Scalability is the capacity for a system to handle greater and greater workloads. When we create a system or program, we want to make sure that it is scalable so that it doesn't crash upon receiving too many requests. Scaling can be done in one of two ways:

- **Scaling up**: Increasing the hardware of your existing workers, such as upgrading from CPUs to GPUs.
- **Scaling out**: Distributing the workload among many workers. Spark is a common framework for doing this.

Scaling up can be as easy as moving your model to a larger cloud instance. In this section, we'll be focus on how to distribute TensorFlow to scale out our applications.

Scaling out with distributed TensorFlow

What if we'd like to scale out our compute resources? We can distribute our TensorFlow processes over multiple workers to make training faster and easier. There are actually three frameworks for distributing TensorFlow: *native distributed TensorFlow*, *TensorFlowOnSpark*, and *Horovod*. In this section, we will be exclusively focusing on native distributed TensorFlow.

In the world of distributed processing, there are two approaches that we can take to distribute the computational load of our model, that is, **model parallelism** and **data parallelism**:

- **Model parallelism**: The distribution of the training layers of a model across various devices.
- **Data parallelism**: The distribution of the entire model across various devices. Copies of the same model are sent to each device, and each of these copies trains on a subset of the training data in each training epoch. The results are then aggregated and a new epoch begins.

Use model parallelism when you have a larger amount of nodes in your computing cluster, and data parallelism when you have a smaller amount of nodes.

With data parallelism, an entity called a **parameter server** controls the process of distribution. The parameter server is typically run on a CPU. This server then distributes the processes to **workers**, known as **TensorFlow servers**. These are typically run on GPUs. One of these workers is the **chief worker**, which manages the initialization, training steps, session, and the saving of the model among the collective grouping of workers, or the **cluster**. Altogether, this architecture looks as follows:

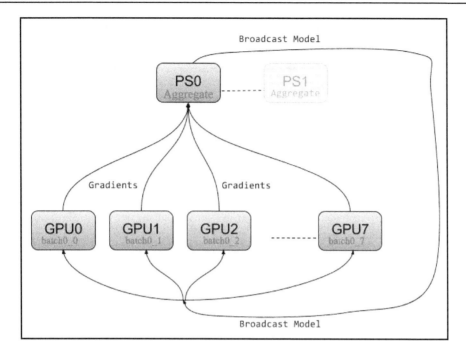

With this architecture, we also have two choices for how we want to handle the actual distribution of our processing:

- **Synchronous distribution**: A task will be distributed to all workers at the same time. Each worker will wait for the other workers to finish their task before moving on to the next task.
- **Asynchronous distribution**: Tasks will be distributed to workers as the workers become available.

Do you remember from our earlier chapters that the main training algorithm for ANNs, stochastic gradient descent, works in iterative update loops? This process is handled differently depending on whether we choose to use a synchronous distribution method or an asynchronous distribution method. With synchronous distribution, our model will wait until all of the individual copies of the model have sent their train results (errors between the actual and predicted model) to the master server before continuing. The new error would be aggregated, and then sent back to each of the workers along with a new batch of data. This has its downfalls in that it is what computer scientists call **blocking**—new operations are blocked by the progress of the previous operations.

With asynchronous distribution, gradients are sent to the workers as soon as they are available to be sent:

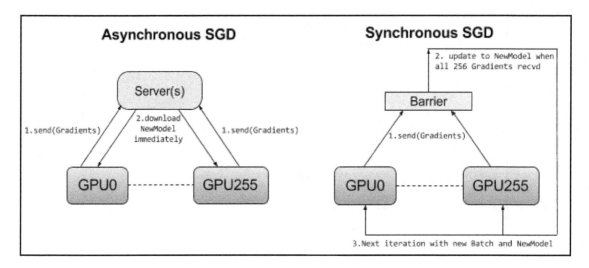

Preparing code for distributed training in TensorFlow takes three steps:

1. Mapping and distributing the model with ClusterSpec and Server
2. Defining the device assignment with tf.device
3. Converting your standard TensorFlow sessions to the Monitored Training Session

Testing and maintaining your applications

With either online or offline learning, we should always institute systems and safety checks that will tell us when our model's predictions, or even its critical deployment architecture, are out of whack. By testing, we are referring to the hard-coded checking of inputs, outputs, and errors to ensure that our model is performing as intended. In standard software testing, for every input, there should be a defined output. This becomes difficult in the field of machine learning, where models will have variable outputs depending on a host of factors - not the great for standard testing procedures, is it? In this section, we'll talk about the process of testing machine learning code, and discuss best practices.

Once deployed, AI applications also have to be maintained. DevOps tools like Jenkins can help ensure that tests pass before new versions of a model are pushed to production. While we certainly aren't expecting you as a machine learning engineer to create development pipelines, we'll review their principals in this section so that you can be familiar with best practices.

Testing deep learning algorithms

The AI community is severely behind on adopting appropriate testing procedures. Some of the most advanced AI companies rely on manual checks instead of automating tests on their algorithms. You've already done a form of a test throughout this book; cross-validating our models with training, testing, and validation sets helps to verify that everything is working as intended. In this section, we'll instead focus on **unit tests**, which seek to test software at the smallest computational level possible. In other words, we want to test the little parts of our algorithms, so we can ensure the larger platform is running smoothly.

Testing our algorithms helps us keep track of **non-breaking bugs**, which have become ubiquitous in open source deep learning code. These bugs might lose gradient, or misreport accuracy, but not actually break our program. For production-level models, this can be extremely dangerous!

1. To write a test, we must import the `unittest` library in Python:

   ```
   import unittest
   ```

   Let's use a small example script; we can test to see if anything has changed by simply using a simple inequality to check for changed values in our variables.

2. In TensorFlow, we can access all of our training variables at once by using the `tf.trainable_variables()` function:

   ```
   ## Run the operation through a TensorFlow session
   with tf.Session() as sess:
       beforeValue = sess.run(tf.trainable_variables())
       multiplication = sess.run(add, feed_dict={input_data: 10})
       afterValue = sess.run(tf.trainable_variables())
       print('The answer is {}'.format(multiplication))
   ```

3. Then, we'll use `assert` to tell us if something has changed or not:

```
for b, a, n in zip(beforeValue, afterValue):
    assert (b != a).any()
```

Some helpful tips for testing your networks are as follows:

1. Write your tests to check the most general use case possible. If we used a specific input, would we receive a specific output in return?
2. Keep tests short and sweet. We don't want to be testing long optimization processes; it's bad form and computationally expensive.
3. Reset the TensorFlow graph between each test. This will ensure that our tests are running correctly.
4. Have an idea of how much error is acceptable from your model. This may be set by business needs if they are willing to accept a less accurate model for one that can be production-ready sooner.

Summary

Building AI applications goes beyond the basics of model construction – it takes deploying your models to a production environment in the cloud where they persist.In this chapter, we've discussed how to take a validated TensorFlow model and deploy it to production in the cloud. We also discussed ways that you can scale these models, and how you can test your applications for resiliency.

When taking a TensorFlow application from development to production, the first step is to create a TensorFlow SavedModel that can be stored in the cloud. From here, there are several services, including AWS Lambda and Google Cloud ML Engine, that can help make your deployment process easily.

Applications can be scaled up or out for more computing power and faster processing. By scaling up, we provide our algorithms with a larger computing resource. By scaling out, we provide our application with more resources at once. Remember, models that are deployed to production should also be tested, and basic tests like unit tests can help prevent your entire application from crashing!

We've now reached the end of the book. As you've worked through the content in the chapters, I hope you have been enlightened to the exciting possibilities that deep learning is creating for the artificial intelligence field. While there is no doubt that research will continue into many of these topics, and that new methods will we be created and used, the fundamental concepts that you've learned throughout these chapters will hold steady, and provide the basis for groundbreaking work going forward. Who knows, the person doing that groundbreaking work could be you!

References

1. Mention Quora
2. Tensorflow client citation

Other Books You May Enjoy

If you enjoyed this book, you may be interested in these other books by Packt:

Artificial Intelligence with Python

Prateek Joshi

ISBN: 978-1-78646-439-2

- Realize different classification and regression techniques
- Understand the concept of clustering and how to use it to automatically segment data
- See how to build an intelligent recommender system
- Understand logic programming and how to use it
- Build automatic speech recognition systems

Artificial Intelligence By Example
Denis Rothman

ISBN: 978-1-78899-054-7

- Use adaptive thinking to solve real-life AI case studies
- Rise beyond being a modern-day factory code worker
- Acquire advanced AI, machine learning, and deep learning designing skills
- Learn about cognitive NLP chatbots, quantum computing, and IoT and blockchain technology
- Understand future AI solutions and adapt quickly to them

Leave a review - let other readers know what you think

Please share your thoughts on this book with others by leaving a review on the site that you bought it from. If you purchased the book from Amazon, please leave us an honest review on this book's Amazon page. This is vital so that other potential readers can see and use your unbiased opinion to make purchasing decisions, we can understand what our customers think about our products, and our authors can see your feedback on the title that they have worked with Packt to create. It will only take a few minutes of your time, but is valuable to other potential customers, our authors, and Packt. Thank you!

Index

Z